Library of
Davidson College

JOURNAL FOR THE STUDY OF THE OLD TESTAMENT SUPPLEMENT SERIES
28

Editors
David J A Clines
Philip R Davies
David M Gunn

Department of Biblical Studies
The University of Sheffield
Sheffield S10 2TN
England

To E.I.J. Rosenthal

my former teacher

in gratitude and affection.

היום קצר והמלאכה מרבה

..... והשכר הרבה

Pirke Aboth II 15

Copyright © 1984 JSOT Press

Published by
JSOT Press
Department of Biblical Studies
The University of Sheffield
Sheffield S10 2TN
England

Printed in Great Britain by Redwood Burn Ltd., Trowbridge

Emmerson, Grace I.
  Hosea.—(Journal for the study of the Old
  Testament supplement series, ISSN 0309-0787;v.28)
  1. Bible. O.T. Hosea-Commentaries
  I. Title   II. Series
  224'.6'06   BS1565.3

  ISBN 0-905774-68-X
  ISBN 0-905774-69-8 Pbk

INTRODUCTION

By its very nature the book of Hosea provides a useful body of material in which to study the interplay of traditions and modes of thought belonging respectively to the northern and southern kingdoms, for whereas its origins lie in the northern kingdom, its transmission belongs for the greater part of its history to Judah.

The northern origin of the prophet whose message forms the nucleus of the book is well substantiated. The evidence is set out in numerous commentaries and other works and need not be repeated here.[1] Few scholars have dissented from the generally accepted view that the northern kingdom was not only the sphere of Hosea's ministry but probably also his homeland and the environment which had shaped his thought.[2] The traditional date assigned to Hosea, which places him broadly within the third quarter of the eighth century B.C., is likewise not open to serious question. Arguments for a post-exilic date,[3] or for a distinction to be made between a proto- and deutero-Hosea[4] have failed to command general approval. The view accepted by the majority of scholars on these two questions is therefore adopted without further discussion as the basis of the present study.

It is clear, however, that although the prophet Hosea is to be located in the northern kingdom, and his message is to be understood primarily in the light of this, we owe the preservation of the material to its transmission in Judah.[5] The entire corpus of literature which comprises the Old Testament, diverse though its origins undoubtedly are, has reached us through the religious life of Judah where the Israelite faith was nurtured and sustained long after the northern kingdom had fallen. The activity of Judean traditionists has clearly left its imprint on the book of Hosea. For immediate evidence of this we need look no further than the title which heads the book

(1:1a). Here Hosea's ministry is dated in a general way by
reference to the reigns of four of Judah's kings, Uzziah, Jotham,
Ahaz and Hezekiah, which together extended from 783 to 687 B.C.[6]
This is followed immediately in 1:1b by a different system of
dating. The chronology is more precise and limited, and, most
significant of all, is given not with reference to Judean kings
but to a northern ruler, Jeroboam II, who was contemporary with
Uzziah alone of the four Judean kings already mentioned. It is
clear from the internal evidence of the book[7] that this second,
more restricted date, which gives a *terminus ad quem* of 746 B.C.,[8]
is applicable only to the early period of Hosea's ministry and
to a limited part of the material now incorporated in the book
which bears his name. The broader date, on the other hand,
encompasses the period of his entire ministry. The juxtaposition
of these two different methods of dating itself suggests that a
process of editing has taken place.[9] In addition, the fact that
the comprehensive chronology given in the title is fixed by
reference to Judean rulers suggests that it is to be attributed
to traditionists in the southern kingdom. Indeed, it is widely
accepted that the overall title given to the book in its final
form is the work of Deuteronomists who were responsible for
editing the prophetic tradition as a whole, for the formula
דבר יהוה אשר היה אל with which the book opens occurs also in
Joel, Micah and Zephaniah, and the date is given in a form
identical to that of Isaiah and Micah.[10] One can, therefore,
affirm confidently at the outset that the material in its final
form has not been left unchanged by the process of its
transmission in Judah. The comment of J. L. Mays that 'the
hand of the Judahistic redactors is evident at several places'[11]
can be taken as representing in general the prevailing opinion
among scholars.[12] The situation is different, however, when we
attempt a more detailed assessment of the nature and extent of
the redactional material, for here we find a variety of
conflicting opinions. To select a few examples by way of
illustration: R. H. Pfeiffer[13] speaks of the large amount of

interpolated material, particularly in ch. 4-14, a view with which E. M. Good in his study of the composition of Hosea[14] expresses profound disagreement. J. L. Mays is able to express confidence that 'very little material that did not originate with Hosea has been added in the formation and use of the book',[15] and H. W. Wolff, similarly, though recognising the presence of secondary material, is convinced none the less that 'for the most part Hosea's own speech is unmistakable'.[16] N. H. Snaith, on the other hand, attributes to a Judean writer a number of passages, including the whole of ch. 3, and considers it important to distinguish between expressions of hope which concern Israel alone, which he regards as authentic expressions of Hosea's thought, and others which include Judah and originated in the southern kingdom.[17] W. F. Stinespring goes still further in this direction and eliminates all expression of hope from Hosea's message in its original form, regarding him as solely a prophet of doom who has been 'turned by the Judean editors into the most forgiving spokesman of divine love'.[18] In this he comes close to the view held by W. R. Harper some decades earlier who included among the material which he regarded as secondary those passages which express hope of restoration, believing them to be 'entirely inconsistent with Hosea's point of view' and directly contradictory to 'the representations which are fundamental in his preaching'.[19] It is not, however, only in this area of future hope that redactional influence has been suspected. R. E. Clements, for example, argues that in the book of Hosea, as elsewhere, prophetic concern with the covenant is Deuteronomic in origin, and that through the influence of Deuteronomic covenant theology the preaching of the prophets was given a deeper dimension.[20] Examples could be multiplied, but sufficient have perhaps been given to illustrate the diversity of opinion which exists among scholars as to the nature and the extent of Judean redactional material in Hosea, and to justify a reappraisal of the question.

It is the purpose of the present study to investigate three important areas where *a priori* there is reason to suspect that

Judean redactional activity may have contributed to the present
form of the material, and to assess whether we still have an
authentic expression of Hosea's thought, or whether alien
elements have been introduced which have given to the message
a significantly new content. The following areas have been
chosen for examination:

i. *expressions of future hope*; for the question of their
compatibility with Hosea's message of judgement, and their
appropriateness in the deteriorating political and religious
situation of his time is inescapable.

ii. *references to the southern kingdom*; for, leaving aside for
the moment any consideration of content, their sheer number is
unquestionably surprising in the message of a northern prophet.

iii. *examples of polemic voiced against the cult practices and
sanctuaries of the northern kingdom*; for the possibility that
it has to some extent at least been motivated by Judean
hostility against a rival cult cannot be ignored. Not only had
Israel's official cult been established in a bitter period of
schism in deliberate opposition to the Jerusalem temple,[21] but
the later hostile influence of Deuteronomistic circles in Judah
must also be taken into account.

In these three areas the nature and extent of Judean
redactional activity will be explored. The fact that the study
has been restricted to these areas alone must not be taken to
imply that the question has been prejudged as it relates to other
areas.[22] Rather it is intended to prepare the way for a more
extended study of the material at a future date.

The final aim of the study will be to consider the
relationship of the Judean redactional elements to the primary
northern core of the material. The question is basically this:
what is the nature of the Judean shaping of the material? Is it
to be understood as a development and extension of Hosea's
message by which the prophet's word has been proclaimed anew to
a separate, though closely related, people, addressing their
need at a different period of history, or has it led to the
introduction of new elements and new emphases of such a kind

INTRODUCTION 5

that the message delivered originally to the people of the
northern kingdom has been overlaid or indeed radically changed?
If the latter proves to be correct, the final Judean form of
the book will be seen to reflect not merely a different
historical situation but a divergent theology.

At this point, however, it must be made clear that the
process of development by which the book came to its final form
is considerably more complex than has been indicated so far.
Between the message of the northern prophet Hosea on the one
hand and Judean redactional activity on the other we must
recognise the probable contribution made by associates of Hosea
to whom it is likely that we owe the initial collection and
preservation of the prophet's words.[23] The existence of a circle
of associates or disciples cannot be substantiated from explicit
evidence in the book,[24] but the fact that the prophet's message
successfully survived the final catastrophe of the northern
kingdom in 721 B.C. and that its future was safeguarded in
Judah is strongly suggestive of this, as also is the
incorporation of the biographical prose narrative of ch. 1.[25]
It is indeed to the work of such disciples that Wolff attributes
the formation of the three large complexes of material (ch. 1-3,
4-11, 12-14) which are still clearly distinguishable within the
book.[26] It is not, however, the purpose of this study to
attempt to distinguish between Hosea and those closely associated
with him who belonged to the same environment and culture and
who shared his theological outlook, and thus to seek for the
ipsissima verba of the prophet,[27] but rather to explore areas in
which distinctively Judean influence can be traced, and thus to
examine specifically the relationship of northern and southern
traditions within the material. I have, therefore, passed over
the earlier stages of transmission which may be assumed to have
taken place in the northern kingdom without attempting to
distinguish them, though I readily acknowledge their existence.
Instead, I have concentrated attention on the process of
transmission which took place in Judean circles. My justifica-
tion for this approach is that in this particular case the

history of the transmission of the material is not one of uninterrupted continuity. The transfer of the tradition of the prophet's words from the northern to the southern kingdom itself constitutes a clearly definable break in the history of its transmission. The subject of the present study is, therefore, not an arbitrarily selected area in a long process of transmission but is justified by the history of the material itself.

The difficulties of an enquiry of this kind are obvious. Too readily we begin with preconceptions of what a northern prophet is likely or unlikely to have said. If the results of the investigation are to be based on substantial evidence drawn from the text, the criteria used to establish what is admissible evidence must be carefully defined at the outset. To attempt to determine the origin of a saying on the basis of lexical usage alone is hazardous since we have too small a sample to determine with any certainty what is characteristic of the prophet; and it is, in any case, clear that a later writer may well have been influenced in this respect by the prophet's own usage. In conjunction with other evidence, however, it may prove to be a useful indication. Similarly, evidence derived from literary structure must be handled with caution since it too may prove ambivalent, for the inference that a saying has been secondarily inserted into its present context is not of itself proof of secondary origin. We are on safer ground where evidence of various kinds coincides. I have, therefore, applied the criterion of incongruity in three areas, in order that the evidence of each may act as a check and control upon the others. The three areas are the historical, where the situation implied in a saying is inconsistent with the period of Hosea's ministry and appears to reflect that of Judah at a later time; the linguistic, where syntactical irregularities suggest the presence of supplementary material; and the theological or conceptual, where the ideas expressed seem to be at variance with the broadly based evidence of the material in general as to Hosea's attitude and thought.

INTRODUCTION

On the basis of evidence in these three areas I have attempted to trace those elements in the material which it is more reasonable to attribute not to the northern prophet himself, nor to a group of his close associates who belonged to the same cultural environment and shared his thoughts and aspirations, but to those Judeans by whom his sayings were transmitted and proclaimed in the southern kingdom during the years which followed. These later redactional elements have a significance of their own as examples of early interpretation and application of the prophetic message.[28] It is they which have given the book its final form, the form in which it came to have a place in the canon of Scripture. It has been increasingly recognised recently that, as R. P. Carroll comments, 'there was always a context of others handling and passing on the tradition. This context was not simply passive but had a creative role to play in the presentation, interpretation and possibly extension of the prophetic traditions'.[29] Yet the attempt to recover by historical-critical study the original meaning of a text is no less important. Both levels of interpretation are fit subjects for theological study, and are significant in their own right. 'The tradition which stemmed from the prophets' original sayings' may not always provide 'the strongest guidelines that we have to what those sayings *really* meant'.[30] We have to reckon with the possibility of a process of reinterpretation. In pursuing the present study I share the conviction of G. M. Landes that 'it is quite conceivable that an important theological meaning deriving primarily from a text's original historical setting may be recoverable only through the exercise of historical-critical as over against canonical analysis, where the present form of the text has either suppressed or overlooked that meaning. Yet the theological import which that text originally scored may speak as vitally and pertinently and powerfully to our present situation as the final canonical understanding'.[31]

There remains one last issue which must be clarified concerning the way in which I have approached the text. In considering the question of primary and redactional material, where is the onus of proof to lie? O. Kaiser holds that 'it is methodologically justified to work with the postulate that it is not the inauthenticity but the authenticity of the sayings ascribed to the prophets that needs to be proved.'[32] I have adopted the opposite principle, accepting the tradition for those parts of the book where no compelling reasons can be urged against their authenticity,[33] on the grounds that the book's distinctive characteristics of both language and thought, readily acknowledged by commentators, support the view that the tradition is reliable, and that we have here, in essence at least, Hosea's own message. I find myself in agreement with Wolff's assessment: 'in view of the book's transmission, we are unable to affirm that its every word belongs to the *verba ipsissima* of the prophet . . . . . For the most part, however, Hosea's own speech is unmistakable'.[34]

An investigation of this kind is, by its very nature, incapable of final proof. It must depend for its credibility on the balance of probabilities. If, however, the conclusions reached serve in any way to illuminate the meaning of the text and to resolve some of its ambiguities, this may in its turn be seen as some measure of self-authentication.

CHAPTER I

SALVATION SAYINGS

In surprising contrast to the judgmental sayings which form the main substance of the book of Hosea, we find a number of sayings which point to hope of salvation. The inclusion of these sayings in a book whose chief preoccupation is with the nation's sin and its consequences cannot but raise the question of their origin and their relationship to the message which Hosea addressed to his northern contemporaries in the last decades of the kingdom's existence. Some commentators have found the content of these salvation sayings so completely at variance with Hosea's radical pronouncements of judgement on Israel that they have considered them to be entirely secondary in origin, regarding Hosea solely as a prophet of doom.[1] In general, however, this extreme position has not been adopted by modern scholars, for increasingly there has been a recognition that a prophet of doom may also be a prophet of salvation, though the relationship of the two roles has been understood in various ways.[2] As regards Hosea, however, the history of the book's transmission suggests the possibility that some at least of the expressions of hope may have been formulated in Judah after the fall of the northern kingdom, a view which at first sight seems to be supported by the fact that three of these sayings relate to Judah. In contrast to most of the expressions of hope which concern solely the northern kingdom (2:16-17, 18-25; 11:8-11; 14:5-9), 1:7 applies to Judah alone; 2:1-3 concerns the reunion of Judah and Israel; 3:5 envisages the renewal of northern allegiance to the Davidic king. Although most of the salvation sayings occur in chs. 1-3, each of the other main tradition complexes (chs. 4-11; 12-14) concludes with

a salvation prophecy.³ To whatever extent we attribute the
present arrangement of the material to editorial activity, we
are faced with the question of the origin of the sayings, for
it must be acknowledged at the outset that even those sayings
whose present position is redactional may have formed part of
the original northern core of the material. Others may have
arisen in Judean circles. Some indeed may have had a more
complex history, originating in Hosea's message to the northern
kingdom, but later reshaped and reinterpreted under Judean
influence to meet the needs of a new situation. These three
possibilities must be taken into account throughout.

The question of origin must first be raised in general
terms. Only then can we safely proceed to a detailed examination
of the sayings individually. The fundamental question is this:
are promises of salvation and the expectation of restoration
theologically consistent in principle with Hosea's pronouncements
of judgement against the nation? The judgmental sayings are
frequently couched in uncompromising terms. The message of ch.1
reaches its dramatic climax in the symbolic name לא עמי.⁴ The
nation's obstinate persistence in apostasy, its refusal to
return to Yahweh, allows no ground for future hope. Moreover,
Hosea represents Yahweh not only as one who punishes and
disciplines his wayward people but as one who destroys them.
In such passages a note of finality sounds:

> Shall I ransom them from the power of Sheol?
> Shall I redeem them from Death?
> O Death, where⁵ are your plagues?
> O Sheol, where is your destruction?
> Compassion is hid from my eyes.⁶ (13:14)

With this may be compared the finality of the pronouncement in
9:15:

> Because of the wickedness of their deeds
> I will drive them out of my house.
> I will love them no more.

SALIVATION SAYINGS 11

This sense of the ultimacy of the judgement which the prophet proclaims is emphasised by the inclusion in it of the coming generation on whom the nation's future depends:

> Give them, O Lord -
>   what wilt thou give?
> Give them a miscarrying womb
>   and dry breasts . . . . .
> Ephraim is stricken,
>   their root is dried up,
>   they shall bear no fruit.
> Even though they bring forth,
>   I will slay their beloved children   (9:14, 16).

Is it likely that the prophet who uttered words of judgement such as these could envisage also some kind of future hope?

Various answers have been given to this question:

i. Hosea's message warns of a judgement so total and inescapable as to preclude any possibility of hope for the future.

ii. The judgmental sayings belong to a different period of the prophet's ministry from the expectations of hope. In their immediate context within his ministry they did not, therefore, stand in tension and present a paradox. It is only in the final collection of the material that this is so. At this point, however, scholarly opinion differs as to their mutual relationship. Some have suggested that the salvation sayings belong to the early period of Hosea's ministry, and were influenced by his optimism about Israel's future, an optimism which could not survive the onslaught of the nation's obduracy. Others have drawn from the same evidence the opposite conclusion, arguing that expressions of hope belong to Hosea's later more mature ministry when an increasing awareness of the power and persistence of the divine love convinced him that God's final word to Israel could only be a word of salvation.

iii. The salvation sayings in essence at least (for the details must be considered later) form an integral part of Hosea's message, and only in the light of these expressions of hope with their theological implications can the judgmental sayings be properly understood. They come not from development and change in the prophet's outlook in one direction or another but are a consistent element in his preaching throughout.

We turn now to consider which of these views can be substantiated from the text. The rather extreme position expressed in the first alternative which allows no room in Hosea's message for any expression of hope may seem logically acceptable. But human logic is not the limit of the prophet's thought. He is concerned with that dimension in which the divine will and purpose operate.[7] It is not sufficient, of course, to make a general statement of this kind without adducing evidence to support it. Such evidence is forthcoming from those salvation sayings which cannot be detached from their present setting as independent units but form an integral part of a larger context. Two of the expressions of hope fall into this category; the one in 2:16-17, the other in 3:5. There has been considerable discussion on the question of the presence of secondary elements in the latter. I shall return to this matter later.[8] The point I wish to establish here is that the very context in which this saying appears requires that it should be understood as an integral part of its context, namely 3:1-5. Indeed v. 5 is to be seen as the key to interpreting the whole. Only a failure to understand the passage can allow us to categorise the whole of v. 5, as distinct from elements within it which I shall consider later, as 'certainly . . . a redactional addition', as R. E. Clements does on the grounds that 'Hosea's action towards the woman of Hosea 3 . . . is primarily a sign of divine discipline and judgement, as Hosea 3:3-4 makes plain'.[9] I do not, of course, wish to deny that there are elements in v. 5 which seem questionable in the message of a northern prophet, and which must be given detailed consideration later; but to regard the whole of this expression of hope for future restoration as a secondary addition to the material leads to a distortion of Hosea's message and arises from a failure to take sufficient account of the context.

The passage begins with Yahweh's command to the prophet, 'Go again,[10] love a woman . . .'. The content of this initial command אהב ־ אשה requires that the discipline imposed on the woman in v. 3 cannot express the prophet's ultimate relationship with her, even though the narrative does not itself include an account of the restoration of the intimate personal relationship. The limiting expression 'many days' also carries this implication. The essence of the command to the prophet is not to punish but to love, and it is in the context of the fulfilling of this command that discipline and severity find a place. We must not be misled by the fact that no mention is made of the woman's eventual restoration, and that therefore the salvation saying of v. 5 has no parallel in the human relationships described, for the purpose of the narrative is not primarily autobiographical.[11] The one overriding aim is to proclaim Yahweh's word to Israel by means of a symbolic act performed by the prophet. In his personal life he is to act out, and thus to proclaim, Yahweh's word to the nation. Thus the central concern of the passage is not to give an insight into the prophet's domestic life, fascinating though from our modern perspective we might find it. It is to affirm the reality of Yahweh's love, not only in the unspoilt days of Israel's early life,[12] but for faithless Israel in the present time described in the circumstantial clause, 'though they turn to other gods . . .'.[13] If on the other hand, as Clements argues, the meaning of the passage is expressed in the discipline and punishment of vv. 3-4, then Yahweh's command to the prophet אהב ־ אשה seems to have remained strangely unfulfilled, and the proclamation of the divine love through the symbolic action appears bitterly ironic.[14] The whole context requires that the deprivation and discipline imposed on the nation (v. 4) should be temporary, to be followed by restoration (v. 5). The discipline is evidence of Yahweh's love which refuses to relinquish Israel to the consequences of her own rebellion. Though for Israel judgement is a harsh reality, it is only an

element in Yahweh's ultimate purpose of salvation. As Wolff
aptly comments on the passage: 'Only in the end does God's act
as portrayed become completely understandable as "love"'.[15] To
summarize, the nature of the command in v. 1, if it is indeed to
be meaningful, requires as its corollary a salvation saying such
as we have in v. 5. It is true that certain elements within
that saying raise questions as to their provenance and will be
considered later,[16] but the expectation of future hope
represented here is, in one form or another, integral to the
passage and indeed its climax.

The second passage which I wish to adduce as evidence that
future hope is an intrinsic element in Hosea's thought is 2:16-17.
Here too, as in the case of 3:5, I shall consider the saying in
detail at a later stage. I wish only to establish here the
general point that the expression of hope is integrally connected
with the judgmental sayings which precede it. The unity of
2:4-17 is widely recognised by commentators on the grounds of
its stylistic and thematic coherence.[17] The form of divine
speech is used consistently throughout the allegory of vv. 4-17
where Yahweh is depicted as the wronged husband and Israel as
the unfaithful wife. The passage is carefully structured.
Three times the word לכן is used to introduce the action of
Yahweh in response to the nation's sin (vv. 8, 11, 16). Wolff,
after a detailed study of the form of 2:4-17, concludes that
'in v. 16, "therefore" (לכן) should not be interpreted as a
"connecting particle" which . . . connects a new speech unit
secondarily. Rather, לכן in v. 16, as in vv. 8 and 11, belongs
to the internal structure of the kerygmatic unit'.[18] It is true
that there is an unexpected change from the threat of punishment
in vv. 8 and 11 to an expression of future restoration in v. 16
which might appear to militate against the unity of the passage.
Various approaches to the question of their relationship are
discussed below,[19] and it is not necessary to deny the unity of
the passage on these grounds. It is significant that here also,
as in 3:1-5, the passage requires for its completion an
expression of future hope. Implicit throughout is a movement

towards restoration. The rift in the marriage relationship is
not to be regarded as final and irretrievable, for the court
scene portrayed in the allegory is not a divorce hearing but an
attempt at reconciliation. The statement, 'she is not my wife,
and I am not her husband', is not intended as a formula for
divorce, a point sometimes misunderstood.[20] It is indeed the
basis of what follows, expressing at one and the same time both
the estrangement of husband and wife and the motivation for the
husband Yahweh's action. It stands as the reminder of a
relationship which is still *de jure* but no longer *de facto*, for
were the former no longer true there would be no basis for
Yahweh's concern and for his action. The statement therefore
describes not the finality of divorce but a broken relationship
which needs to be restored.

A third passage which provides evidence that Hosea's
judgmental sayings, radical though they are, do not exclude
the possibility of Yahweh's intervention in salvation is ch. 1
with its symbolic names by which judgement is proclaimed against
the nation. Once again hope is latent in the word of judgement.
The allusion to Jezreel in a judgmental context is fraught with
overtones of violence and disaster,[21] but its etymological
meaning is inescapably a word of hope.[22] Similarly, it is not
without significance that the second and third symbolic names
are negative formulations. As such, לא רחמה and לא עמי are
constant reminders of a relationship now broken. They do not
permit the hearer to forget that Israel was once רחמה and עמי.
Symbolic names formulated as positive expressions of hatred and
rejection would have conveyed as powerful a word of judgement.[23]
There would not have been implicit within them a reminder of
salvation. Thus לא עמי is for Israel the ultimate word of
judgement. It is, however, to be understood in relation to the
parallel formulation לא אשתי in 2.4. As I have argued above,
these words which describe the ultimate breach of the marriage
relationship express at the same time the motivation of
Yahweh's action towards his unfaithful wife. It is for this
reason that even in the proclamation of judgement God continues

to address the nation as 'my people'.[24] It is justifiable not on logical but on theological grounds.

In short, the evidence adduced above justifies our believing that expressions of hope are an integral part of Hosea's message, and that the judgmental sayings are to be interpreted accordingly. Viewed in the context of the divine love, the nature of Israel's punishment is itself transformed. It is not vindictive retribution, but has a necessary place within Yahweh's overall saving action by reason of the fact that he cannot condone sin. Salvation sayings can be said, therefore, at the outset to occupy a significant place within Hosea's message. They are not incompatible with his pronouncements of judgement, but provide the framework within which they are to be understood. They do not detract from the seriousness of the divine judgement, but point beyond it to a new action of God. Hence it is true, as Wolff comments, that 'especially those prophets who place decisive importance on God's love . . . are the most radical in their description of divine wrath'.[25]

We can now turn to the second view set out above,[26] that sayings of judgement and salvation belong to two different periods of the prophet's ministry. The idea that development and change can be traced in Hosea's message takes two forms, as we have seen: that an early period of optimism gave way to an increasing sense of despair; or conversely, that in his mature ministry an increasing conviction of Yahweh's love overcame his despondence at Israel's failure to respond. The answer is implicit already in the discussion above. Theologically, the expression of future hope is not incompatible with the pronouncement of judgement. The two must be held in tension if love is not to degenerate into sentimentality, and if the nature of God is not to be diminished. Hence there is no necessity to locate them in different periods of the prophet's life unless there is compelling evidence to the contrary. The fact that conflicting conclusions have been reached betrays both the uncertain nature of this undertaking and the danger of attempting to treat the material biographically. This is the

temptation to which Lindblom[27] succumbs in attempting to draw
from the prophet's own experience the key to his message. He
argues that Hosea's personal experience of failure in his
attempt to reclaim his unfaithful wife served finally to
convince him that the unfaithful nation was likewise beyond hope
of restoration. It is clearly fundamental to such argument that
the details of the prophet's life must be reconstructed. The
lack of any reference to children in ch. 3, and the restraints
imposed there on the woman in respect to normal marital relations,
lead Lindblom to the conclusion that this chapter must belong
chronologically before ch. 1, where he believes the period of
restraint has ended; hence the birth of children. He argues
further that the names of the second and third child indicate
illegitimacy, as also does the omission of לו after ותלד in
vv. 6 and 8.[28] According to this reconstruction of the prophet's
experience, ch. 1 is to be understood as the account of Gomer's
persistence in adultery after the attempt at reconciliation in
ch. 3, which finally convinced the prophet that, for those who
persist in unfaithfulness, restoration ultimately becomes
impossible. What was true of Gomer was true also of the nation;
for the unrepentant northern kingdom there remains only
annihilation.

There are, however, two serious objections to this view.
First, it rests on an unjustifiable attempt to reconstruct the
circumstances of the prophet's personal life. It is a
misunderstanding of the nature of the material to regard it
as evidence of this kind. It is arguable that there are
authentic glimpses of Hosea's domestic affairs in chs. 1 and
3, but they are limited.[29] They are not the focus of attention,
for the narrative is not concerned primarily with the prophet's
life and circumstances, but is the account of symbolic actions
(four in ch. 1 and one in ch. 3) performed by Hosea as the means
of proclaiming Yahweh's word to the nation. I have noted already
in discussing ch. 3[30] how far the prophet is from being the
centre of attention there, so that, as far as his own experience
is concerned, the end of the story is left untold. The purpose

of the account is theological not biographical. It is concerned with Yahweh's word to the nation.[31] Consequently, an attempted rearrangement of the material in order to present a consistent account of the prophet's life cannot be regarded as a valid basis for interpreting his message. The reconstruction is not only hazardous;[32] it is a misuse of the material.

The second objection to Lindblom's view is that it rests on the mistaken assumption that Hosea's personal tragedy was the means by which he came to an insight into the nature of Yahweh's relationship to Israel. Neither ch. 1 nor ch. 3 is to be understood as a 'call' narrative. When Yahweh addresses Hosea and enjoins upon him the symbolic actions of ch. 1, he is already Yahweh's prophet and his appointed spokesman to the nation. The purpose of the narrative, therefore, is to recount not the means of revelation, God's speaking to the prophet,[33] but the means of proclamation, God's speaking through the prophet (בהושע). When the divine command comes to him in ch. 3, the symbolic action is required of him on the basis of Yahweh's love for Israel (v. 1). Whatever the relationship of chs. 1 and 3 to each other, they are not the means by which the prophet came to know of Yahweh's judgement or his love. They are the proclamation of that judgement and that love in dramatic fashion to the nation. Had the narratives been concerned with the means of revelation to the prophet, greater attention must have been paid to details of the prophet's experience. Yet the reverse is true. The result of the prophet's attempt at reconciliation with the unfaithful woman is not recounted, a sure indication that the centre of interest lies elsewhere than in the matter of the success or failure of the prophet's personal relationships.

In short, an attempt such as Lindblom's to reconstruct details of the prophet's life rests on a failure properly to appreciate the nature of the material. It is prophetic proclamation not biography. Lindblom's conclusion is suspect, for Hosea's marriage to Gomer expresses symbolically the initial message addressed through him to the nation (תחלת דבר ־ יהוה בהושע) v. 2), and the details of the account indicate that the narrative covers a period of only a few years.[34] It appears, then, that the ultimate word of judgement לא ־ עמי, which signifies the breaking of the relationship between God and the nation, belongs to the early period of the prophet's ministry. Lindblom's thesis of a progression in Hosea's thought from optimism to despair not only rests on a very tentative reconstruction but is in fact contrary to the evidence of the material.

We must now briefly consider the suggestion that development in the prophet's thought leads in the opposite direction, from despair to a growing conviction of the power of the divine love. The content of ch. 3 has sometimes been used as evidence of a change of emphasis of this kind in the message given by the prophet.[35] Yet once again the conclusion to which the material itself points is otherwise. Arguments have already been adduced for the view that the expression of future hope in 2:16-17 is an integral part of the context in which it stands.[36] The background to the preceding verses, in particular vv. 7, 10, 11, is a prosperous economic situation with undisturbed celebration of joyful and indeed lavish religious festivals (vv. 13, 15), which suggests that it belongs to the stable reign of Jeroboam II before the years of mounting anarchy which brought the northern kingdom's history to a close. It is difficult, therefore, to exclude from the early period of Hosea's ministry all reference to future hope and to attribute this insight only to the period of his maturity as a prophet.[37] Although, in contrast to Lindblom's reconstruction of the details of the prophet's life, it is generally agreed that the events of ch. 3 belong to a later period than those of ch. 1,[38] the content of the former is no more amenable than that of the latter as the basis for tracing the development of the prophet's thought. I have already stressed above that both chapters alike are concerned not with the means of revelation to the prophet but with the means of proclamation of God's message to the nation. It was not Hosea's own patient love for one who failed to respond which led him to understand the love of Yahweh for his people. Rather it is clear from 3:1 that he is commanded to undertake a symbolic action in the light of the awareness which was already his of the persistence of the divine love in the face of the nation's faithlessness. The passage cannot, therefore, be used in any attempt to reconstruct a biography of the prophet. It does provide evidence, whatever the date to which it is assigned, that judgement and salvation are the two poles of Hosea's message for, as has been noted already,[39] only in the light of v. 5 is the proclamation of divine love through the prophet's symbolic action understood. Judgement and salvation stand in tension as essential ingredients in God's relationship with his people. Both judgmental sayings (ch. 1) and hope of restoration (2:16-17) belong to the early period of Hosea's ministry. The evidence of ch. 3 suggests that the same is true also of his later period.

In the light of this conclusion that expressions of hope have a significant place with judgmental sayings in the northern core of the material, we move now to a consideration of the salvation sayings individually in order to assess the relationship of primary and redactional material within them. Those that refer to Judah (1:7; 2:1-3) and to the Davidic king (3:5) will be considered more appropriately with other references to the southern kingdom. I shall, therefore, postpone discussion of them to the next chapter. I intend to consider here those sayings which tell of future hope for Israel, for it is an unwarranted assumption to suppose that these sayings can be expected to have escaped redactional influence. After the fall of the northern kingdom Judah remained as sole bearer of the name Israel in its sacral sense of the people of God.[40] It is, therefore, reasonable to suppose that sayings which originally concerned the northern kingdom should, in the period after its fall, have seemed applicable to the people of Judah. We must consequently allow for the possibility of reinterpretation in these sayings also.

2:16-17

This passage has already been shown to be integrally connected both by form and content to the preceding words of judgement (vv. 4-15). Yet, although its position is not editorial, the question arises whether it has been supplemented in any way by secondary material. The consensus of scholarly opinion attributes it to Hosea.[41] Using the criteria laid down as the basis of this study[42] we find nothing to suggest that secondary material is present here. Nothing in its structure or content suggests other than a northern origin. The traditions which are drawn on here are those with which Hosea is familiar. As in 12:9 and 13:4, Israel's relationship with Yahweh is regarded as beginning with the deliverance from Egypt. The wilderness period is characterised by faithful devotion, as it is also in 13:5. But Hosea's attitude is not that of the Rechabites. A nomadic existence is not the ideal. The cultivated land is Yahweh's gift to Israel, Yahweh's land (9:3), and it is the same attitude which is reflected in 2:17. The wilderness experience is not Yahweh's purpose ultimately for Israel. It is but the prelude to the renewal of prosperity in the cultivated land.[43] There are, moreover, no syntactical difficulties to suggest the presence of supplementary material. Nor are there any linguistic features to challenge this opinion and lay it open to suspicion. As has been already noted above,[44] a decision about the origin of a saying cannot rest on the evidence of lexical usage alone since in this book we have too small a sample to determine what is or is not characteristic of the prophet, and in any case a redactor may have been influenced in his lexical choice by imitating the prophet's own usage; nevertheless we may draw on such linguistic features as supporting evidence. The expression ודברתי על לבה is the language of courtship,[45] and it would be arbitrary to deny its use by the very prophet who has been so bold and so innovative as to portray Yahweh's relationship to Israel as marriage. It is true that מפתיה has an unusual meaning here in that it signifies

Yahweh's wooing of his people, in contrast to its more familiar
reference to seduction and enticement.[46] It is arguable,
however, that this is more easily accounted for as the prophet's
creative use of language, again boldly and deliberately chosen in
the light of the fact that Israel is described as easily seduced
(פותה ; 7:11), than as the work of a redactor. Is it not the
prophet's way of affirming that Yahweh is able to turn this
foolish characteristic of Israel's, this naive readiness to
yield, to good account by 'enticing' her in the wilderness?
Hence, there seems no valid objection to the widely held view
which attributes these verses to Hosea, and consequently it is
justifiable to take this saying as the basis on which to begin
an assessment of the elements which constitute Hosea's hope for
the future. Yahweh's saving action is twofold. Deprivation
precedes restoration. By Yahweh's own deliberate action Israel
will suffer the loss of the blessings of the cultivated land in
the pursuit of which she had forgotten Yahweh and devoted herself
to Baal (2:15; 9:10; 13:6). But the purpose of this deprivation
is a saving purpose. It is that she may know Yahweh as the
sovereign Lord of nature.[47] Only then, when the broken relationship has been renewed, will he restore to Israel, in testimony
of this, his gift of the fertile, settled land. There is no
condoning of sin, no weak and sentimental love relationship which
ignores unfaithfulness; there is on Yahweh's part no 'cheap
grace'.[48]

From the passage under consideration (2:4-17), with its
integral connection between judgement and salvation, a
significant feature of Hosea's theology emerges. Yahweh's
saving action is not envisaged as dependent upon Israel's prior
response in penitence. The fact that vv. 15 and 16 are
juxtaposed in such stark contrast to each other is highly
significant. After the description of Israel's unfaithfulness
with its solemn climax, forceful in its brevity, ואתי שכחה,
there follows by divine not human logic the surprising sequel,
'Therefore, behold I will allure her, . . . and speak tenderly
to her'. It is this which will elicit Israel's response (v. 17).

The nation's response is not the prerequisite of Yahweh's saving
action, but issues from it, the result of his gracious act on
her behalf. The initiative in the renewal of the broken
relationship lies not with Israel's repentance but with Yahweh's
persistent love. The prophet's hope rests not on the nation's
efforts at reform but solely on Yahweh's grace. This point has
unfortunately sometimes been obscured by a rearrangement of the
passage. The apparent lack of a logical connection between
vv. 9 and 10 and the abrupt transition from v. 15 to v. 16 has
suggested that some dislocation of the text has taken place, and
that the problem is to be resolved by the transfer of vv. 8-9
to follow v. 15.[49] Yahweh's gracious act in v. 16 then follows
the woman's admission that life with her husband was preferable
to her present state, and her expressed intention to return. But
this response cannot in any sense be regarded as repentance. It
is motivated entirely by self-interest, with no awareness of the
essential incompatibility of Yahweh and Baal. It serves only
to highlight the blindness and poverty of Israel's response to
God, and can hardly be regarded as the motivation for his saving
action. Be that as it may, arguments against the rearrangement
are convincing. Particularly relevant is the essay by D.J.A.
Clines in which the formal structure, the conceptual structure
and the narrative structure of the passage are considered.[50]
He argues that the logic and significance of the triple לכן is
destroyed by rearrangement of the verses, affirming that the
sequence of thought is as follows:

i. because Israel has played the harlot (v. 7) *therefore*
Yahweh will bar her way to future harlotry (v. 8a)

ii. because Israel does not recognise Yahweh as the giver of
her gifts (v. 10) *therefore* he will take back his gifts (v. 11a)

iii. because Israel has forgotten Yahweh (v. 15b) *therefore* he
will cause her to remember him (v. 16).

In short, in the first judgement speech Israel is debarred from
what she believes to be the source of her well-being; in the
second it is the well-being itself of which she is deprived; in

the third, without any merit on her part, her well-being is restored by Yahweh its true source. Clines is justified in concluding that 'this developing movement is destroyed if we adopt the rearrangement of vv. 7-8 to follow v. 15. The "therefore" (לכן) of v. 8a does not follow naturally upon "me she has forgotten" of v. 15b, nor is the barring of her way to her lovers a natural sequel to the deprivations of vv. 11-14'.[51]

The present arrangement of 2:4-17 is, therefore, to be retained, and its theological significance to be observed as a fundamental emphasis in Hosea's thought. It is for this reason that the prophet's emphasis on Israel's inability to repent and to continue in loyalty to God does not exclude his hope of future restoration. His conviction that 'their deeds do not permit them to return to their God, for the spirit of harlotry is within them' (5:4) does not preclude redemption, for this depends solely on the divine initiative. The point is well made by Clines:'vv. 16-17 are entirely unexpected - and illogical, given the nexus of sin and punishment, or even the impossibility of un-living the past. Yahweh's answer to Israel's ignoring him will be to turn the clock back and let her begin her history with him all over again.

We have here more than an ironic or novel use of traditional language of the judgement speech (*Gerichtsrede*). It is a theologically creative and profound move that in effect negates the validity or effectiveness of punishment as a response to sin'.[52]

On the basis of this insight into Hosea's theology of redemption we can move to an examination of the salvation sayings which follow in 2:18-25, where the fragmentary nature of the sayings, and the generally agreed view that their context and arrangement is redactional,[53] make the question of their provenance altogether more difficult to determine.

The absence of stylistic and thematic coherence suggests that we have here a loose collection of fragmentary sayings. Vv. 18, 21 and 22 can be described as assurances of salvation addressed directly to Israel in the second person; vv. 20 and 25 are proclamations of salvation in which the nation is referred to in the third person.[54] In their present arrangement the sayings fall into three groups, each section being marked by the formula 'in that day' (vv. 18-19, 20-22, 23-25). Variations of style and theme suggest, however, that this arrangement is itself redactional. The nation is referred to in v. 18 in the second singular feminine, but in v. 19 in the third singular feminine; in v. 20 in the third plural, but in vv. 21-22 in the second singular feminine; in vv. 24-25 the symbolic names of ch. 1 reappear, but Jezreel is strangely resumed by a third feminine suffix. Similarly, the coherence of theme which marked vv. 4-17 is no longer present. From concern with the name Baal we move to the covenant of peace (v. 20), to the theme of betrothal (v. 21), to the cycle of nature and the land's fertility (vv. 23-24), and finally to a reinterpretation of the symbolic names (v. 25). It is clear, then, that the present context of a saying cannot be allowed to influence the decision which is reached concerning its provenance. Each must be assessed on its own merits.

The sayings fall into two groups according to their central theme. Vv. 18,[55] 21-22 and 25 tell of the restoration of Israel's relationship to Yahweh. Vv. 20, 23 and 24, on the other hand, speak of future hope in terms of peace and prosperity in the land. I shall begin with the former.

2.18.

Arguments for attributing this saying to the northern prophet are generally accepted.[56] The marriage motif not only has parallels elsewhere in the book,[57] but, more significantly, is best explained as arising from his creative use of motifs associated with the fertility cult of Canaan against which his polemic is directed.[58] Moreover, the pejorative connotation of בעל and its deliberate contrast with איש reflect the historical situation of Hosea and his protest against paganised forms of religion in the 8th century B.C. This negative connotation is not intrinsic to the word בעל when applied to the marriage

relationship. It is clear from 2 Samuel 11:26 that בעל as well
as איש can express a relationship based on affection. In this
context the words are used not merely in juxtaposition but as
synonyms. Indeed the term associated here with the grieving
wife's emotion is not איש but בעל.[59] The word בעל is used also
in Proverbs 31:11 where the tenor of the entire passage precludes
a derogatory attitude towards the wife there described.
Similarly it is to be noted that when in Isaiah 54:5 the prophet
reminds the nation that Yahweh is בעליך the context is one of
compassion (v. 7) and love (v. 8). For these reasons I cannot
agree with Wolff[60] that the primary meaning of Hosea 2:18 lies
in the contrast between the deep personal relationship with a
wife expressed by איש and the position of the husband as lord
and owner of the wife expressed by בעל, and that the allusion to
the god Baal is only a secondary implication of the saying. The
prophet is not concerned with the superiority of the personal
relationship expressed by איש as against that expressed by בעל,
but explicitly with Israel's syncretistic worship in which her
failure to understand the nature of Yahweh and to appreciate
what he requires of her allows her to confuse him with Baal, and
to worship him under the guise of a fertility god. For it is
clear from 8:2 that this, in essence, was the nature of Israel's
apostasy, not an open disregard of Yahweh in favour of Baal, but
an insidious confusion of two different views of the deity.[61]
Indicted by the prophet for breaking God's covenant, they plead
in defence their relationship with Yahweh: 'My God, we Israel
know thee'.[62] They regard themselves as worshippers of Yahweh,
but the prophet confronts them with the obligation to choose where
they thought none existed. It is, in essence, the story of
Elijah on Mount Carmel over again.[63]

In short, the content of v. 18 has clear affinities with
Hosea's historical situation and with the protest against
syncretism which his circumstances evoked. The language of the
saying is explicable as the prophet's response to the traditional
motifs of the fertility cult of Canaan. There are no grounds
for rejecting it as an authentic expression of Hosea's hope for

Israel's restoration.

2:21-22

Israel's restoration to Yahweh is here described as betrothal. The language is bold, but not more so than the language of courtship in v. 16, and of marriage in v. 18, both of which, as we have seen, are to be explained as the prophet's creative use of terminology which had its origins in Canaanite religion. This figurative use of the verb ארש has no parallel elsewhere in the Old Testament. There is, therefore, no evidence to suggest that it is to be attributed to a later writer, as a secondary development from Hosea's use of the marriage motif, rather than to the creativity of the prophet himself. In theological content the saying is comparable with v. 18 in that it is concerned with Israel's recognition of Yahweh's true nature and of his demands upon her. The emphasis laid here on the moral aspect of Yahweh's relationship to Israel is germane to Hosea's thought.[64] The concluding words of v. 22, וידעת את ־ יהוה, though echoing a recurrent theme in the book,[65] are not in themselves sufficient evidence to allow us to determine the origin of the saying. As I indicated above,[66] it is self-evident that a later writer may have been influenced in his lexical choice by the prophet's characteristic usage. Yet they have a significance in the relationship in which they stand to what precedes. Israel's knowledge of Yahweh[67] is seen not as the prerequisite to her restoration but as the result of Yahweh's action on her behalf. A new relationship will be established on the basis of Yahweh's own attributes,[68] not by Israel's efforts and her uncertain loyalty.[69] Its permanence will thus be guaranteed. It can be categorised as לעולם.

It is clear, then, that in both language and thought this saying is consistent with material which we have already had reason to attribute to Hosea and not to Judean influence. There are no elements here which suggest that it is of secondary origin.[70]

2:25

Unlike the verses discussed above, where there is general agreement that they are to be attributed to Hosea, the origin of this saying has been called into question. O. Eissfeldt has argued that in comparison with 1:4 the name Jezreel 'is used in a quite different sense, as a designation for Israel, and this change of meaning can hardly be attributed to Hosea himself'.[71]

Reinterpreting the symbolic names of ch. 1, the saying proclaims a reversal of the judgement. Yet it is clearly a fragmentary saying for it draws on the etymology of the name Jezreel, even though the name itself does not appear. The connection with v. 24 is a purely external one, an example of the linking together of originally separate sayings by means of a catchword, in this instance the name Jezreel, which is found frequently in the prophetic books. The two sayings differ in content, the first being concerned with the renewal of the earth's fertility, the second with the resettlement of the people in the land and their reinstatement as the people of God. It is not only justifiable to consider v. 25 in isolation from v. 24 but indeed imperative, for in attempting to determine the provenance of a fragmentary saying we cannot be guided by considerations arising out of its present context.[72]

What evidence, then, can we draw on in attempting to determine whether it originated in the northern kingdom or in later Judean circles? First, stylistically it can be said to have parallels elsewhere in the book in sayings where there is no reason to query their northern origin. There is a play on the etymology of the names Israel and Jacob in 12:4, and three striking instances of paronomasia with reference to the name Ephraim: אפרים ‎- פרא (8:9) and אפרים ‎- פרי (9:16; 14:8).[73] If the suggestion made above[74] is correct that the symbolic names of ch. 1, even while they proclaim judgement on the nation, are deliberately formulated in such a way that they are at the same time implicit reminders of the possibility of salvation, there is *a priori* no reason to reject v. 25 as an authentic expression of Hosea's future hope. Second, historically the saying is consonant with the circumstances of Hosea's ministry. Its emphasis on restoration to the land and reinstatement as the people of God is appropriate to the situation in 733 B.C. when the hostile incursions of Tiglath-pileser III resulted in deportation of the population from the valley of Jezreel.[75] Indeed, it may be this particular historical circumstance which has contributed to the different sense in which the name Jezreel is used here as a designation of the nation, in contrast to 1:4 where it denotes a geographical area, a difference which in Eissfeldt's view, as we have seen, calls into question its Hosean origin. But the significance of this difference of usage ought not to be exaggerated, for in the light of the historical situation of 733 B.C. outlined above it is possible to see how the prophet's thought could move easily from the devastated area to its threatened inhabitants who, in their turn, possibly through the assonance of the name Jezreel with Israel, become in his thought representative as *pars pro toto* of the nation as it faces disaster. The shift in usage is not of so significant a kind as to necessitate postulating a difference of origin. Third, it is reasonable on literary critical grounds also to attribute the saying of 2:25 to Hosea. It is noticeable that Jer. 31:27 is reminiscent of this verse, for there, too, the verb זרע is used with Yahweh as subject and the nation as object to describe God's saving action. A comparison of the two passages suggests that the form of the saying in Hos. 2.25 is primary, and is therefore unlikely to have come from Judean redactors. It is true, of course, that where literary relationship is suspected it is hazardous to try to establish in which direction dependence lies. In this particular instance, however, the marked contrast between the terse expression of Hosea and the more developed form in Jeremiah creates the impression that the latter has been influenced by the former. The use of the metaphor of sowing to express God's saving action is not common in the Old Testament,[76] but is most readily explained as having arisen out of the prophet's creative reversal of the symbolic judgmental name Jezreel.

To summarize: there are strong grounds for attributing the
saying of 2:25 to Hosea and not to later Judean redactors.
Though the use of the name Jezreel (by implication) here differs
in important respects from that in 1:4, the change is explicable
in the light of particular historical circumstances and as a
development from the judgmental use of the word. It is
significant that here, too, we have that distinctive emphasis
on Yahweh's initiative which has begun to emerge in the passages
which have been considered up to this point as characteristic of
Hosea's theology of restoration. Israel's confession 'Thou art
my God' is not the prelude to Yahweh's acceptance of her and the
restoration of his love, but the response of an already accepted
and restored people to his initiative: 'I will sow . . . I will
have pity . . . I will say . . .' and he shall say, 'Thou art my
God'.

We turn now to the sayings in vv. 20 and 23-24 where Israel's
future is portrayed in terms of peace and security in the land.

2:20

Israel's future is described here in terms of a covenant
with the world of nature. Yahweh himself is not one of the
parties to the covenant, but the covenant mediator.[77] The
recognition that men's ultimate security must necessarily
involve a relationship of peaceful co-existence with the animal
world finds expression several times in the Old Testament, notably
in Is. 11:6ff., Ezek. 34:25, Lev. 26:6 and Job 5:23. Of these
the three last mentioned have most resemblance to the passage
under discussion in Hos. 2:20. They are set out below for
purposes of comparison.

Ezek. 34:25

וכרתי להם ברית שלום והשבתי חיה ־ רעה מן הארץ וישבו במדבר לבטח
Here the opening words are identical but the covenant is called
ברית שלום. Thereafter the sayings differ in the terms used,
though both conclude with the word לבטח.

SALVATION SAYINGS

Lev. 26:6

ונתתי שלום בארץ ושכבתם ואין מחריד והשבתי חיה רעה מן ־ הארץ וחרב
לא תעבר בארצכם

Here the chief resemblance to the Hosea passage is the fact that
it portrays not only peaceful co-existence with the animal world
but the cessation of hostilities among men.

Job 5:23

כי עם ־ אבני השדה בריתך
וחית השדה השלמה ־ לך

Here too, in spite of points of resemblance to Hos. 2:20, there
are noteworthy differences. Although in both the expression
חית השדה is used in contrast to חיה רעה in Ezek. 34:25 and Lev.
26:6, the point can hardly be pressed since it is a common
expression and can scarcely be called distinctive.

Nevertheless, the general resemblance of content invites the
question whether the saying in Hos. 2:20 may perhaps represent a
later elaboration of that hope for the future which we have seen
to be a significant aspect of Hosea's original message. Is it
to be attributed to later Judean influence? No conclusions can
be drawn from the lexical evidence. The expression כרת ברית
recurs in 10:4 and 12:2 where the reference is to political
treaties; חית השדה and עוף השמים in 4:3, though the judgmental
saying there cannot be said to be the counterpart of the
salvation saying in 2:20, for the threat envisaged is not from
the hostility of nature but from its devastation; the combination
of קשת with the verb שבר can be paralleled in 1:5; the association
of קשת and חרב with מלחמה in 1:7. Only the last of these is in
any way distinctive, and since 1:7 is itself of questionable
origin the matter must be left open. As has already been noted,
lexical evidence is of little value when only a small sample of
material is available for consideration, and it can never be
more than an uncertain guide as to what is primary and what is
secondary, since a redactor may well be influenced, perhaps
unconsciously, by the lexical choices of the original author.

Nevertheless, there are several factors which suggest, though they cannot decisively prove, that the saying is attributable to Hosea. In several passages the judgement depicted is the counterpart to this expression of hope. The cultivated land will be devastated by the incursions of wild animals (חית השדה, 2:14), and the threat of hostile powers is mentioned frequently (7:16; 10:14; 11:6; 14:1). The circumstances of Hosea's ministry, in particular the Assyrian attack of 733 B.C. and subsequent devastation of the land, provide the background against which such an expression of hope might appropriately be formulated.

The main argument, however, for attributing the formulation of hope in 2:20 to Hosea himself rather than to a later Judean redactor is the fact that it contrasts in a significant way with the idea of the new covenant which appears in Jer. 31:31-34. The saying in Hosea lacks the theological content of the latter and shows no evidence of having been influenced by it. This fact, together with the argument above on historical grounds, strongly suggests that it belongs to the primary northern stratum of the material. It is true that the message of Hosea lacks the universal perspective of Is. 11:6ff. The saying of 2:20 need not, however, be understood in terms of cosmic peace, for ארץ in Hosea refers not to the world but to the land of Israel. Given this more limited reference, the saying is compatible with the circumstances and the concerns of Hosea.

We find, then, no reason to dissent from the view of commentators[78] who regard this saying as an authentic expression of Hosea's future hope. It has come down to us as an isolated saying which speaks only of Yahweh's action, not of Israel's response, and therefore provides no evidence of the way in which Hosea understands the relationship between them. It does, however, strongly emphasise the initiative of Yahweh in the establishing of peace and security for his people.

SALVATION SAYINGS   33

2:23-24

The form of this saying sets it apart from the surrounding
verses. Its content suggests that it was formulated in response
to a situation of famine, or at any rate the threat of such, but
this background is too indeterminate to allow us to draw
conclusions as to its origin. A significant element is the use
of the name Jezreel which clearly refers here, not to a
geographical location, but to a starving people for whom the
processes of nature must be set in motion. As was noted above
in the discussion of v. 25, this use is not incompatible with
Hosea's use of the name as a proclamation of judgement. Indeed
its transfer from a place name to a designation of the nation
can be understood in the light of historical circumstances in
Hosea's lifetime,[79] assisted not only by the assonance of Jezreel
with Israel but by its association in the prophet's thought with
the other symbolic names לא רחמה and לא עמי which are both of
immediate relevance to the nation. It should not, therefore,
seem surprising that Jezreel too has taken on a similar
connotation.

As to its form, it is an 'oracle of assurance' such as we
find in liturgical contexts.[80] In the listing of the participants
in the cycle of nature the influence of wisdom interests can be
seen.[81] The influence of both cult and wisdom is widespread among
the prophets[82] and is, therefore, inconclusive as evidence. Must
the question of its provenance, therefore, remain open, or is it
possible to go further in seeking to establish its probable
origin? There is perhaps in one respect reason to attribute it
to Hosea rather than to a later redactor. The emphatic
repetition of the verb אענה is entirely consonant with Hosea's
chief preoccupation, namely the affirmation that Yahweh alone,
not Baal, is the giver of fertility and the one who at will
dispenses the gifts of nature. The needs of the starving people
will be met by the land's resources, but all is set in motion
by the sovereign Yahweh himself.

In short, dogmatism as to the origin of the saying in question is impossible. Suffice it to say that it contains nothing which renders it incompatible with the circumstances of Hosea's ministry, and much that is compatible with his primary concern in his opposition to the Baal cult. When we ask how this saying relates to Hosea's view of the relationship between Yahweh's saving action and Israel's response in penitence which has emerged up to this point we are faced with an ambiguity. As an oracle of assurance expressing confidence that Yahweh will hear and respond to Israel's cry for help it seems to imply the primacy of that plea, even though here the plea itself is not recorded. I should like to suggest, however, that, in view of Hosea's concern with the claims of Yahweh *versus* Baal as the giver of fertility, it is to be understood not as Yahweh's answer to Israel's initiative as a suppliant beseeching his help, but rather as his gracious response in the context of her frenzied plea to Baal. The following can be cited in illustration:

> They do not cry to me from the heart,
>   but they wail upon their beds;
> for grain and wine they gash themselves,
>   they rebel against me (7:14);
>
> You have played the harlot, forsaking your God.
>   You have loved a harlot's hire
>   upon all threshing floors (9:1).[83]

It is in this context that Yahweh both punishes and saves: punishes because Israel's sin is not to be condoned but to be taken seriously: saves because Israel cannot save herself, and if Yahweh's love is ultimately to triumph it must be by his initiative. It is in this context of Israel's plea to Baal that Yahweh responds (אענה). Understood in this way the saying is virtually an Old Testament equivalent of Romans 5:10: 'While we were enemies we were reconciled to God . . . . ' Yahweh graciously responds even to his still apostate people.

SALVATION SAYINGS   35

    To review the discussion so far: detailed examination of
the disparate and fragmentary sayings of which 2:18-25 is
comprised suggests that the sayings individually show no evidence
of later Judean influence. They are consistent with the
circumstances of Hosea's ministry in the northern kingdom, a
view commonly accepted by commentators.[84] Their concern is with
the restoration of the personal relationship existing between
God and his people (vv. 18, 21-22) and with the blessings of the
settled land (vv. 20, 23-24). In v. 25 the two themes are
brought together. Thus in content they resemble the salvation
saying of 2:16-17 which we took as an appropriate starting
point for the investigation since it stands within a context to
which it is integrally related, and was therefore more productive
of evidence as to its origins and to its setting within Hosea's
message. The distinctive theological emphasis of 2:16-17 that
Yahweh's saving action is not dependent upon, but rather the
prelude to, Israel's repentance, recurs within this collection
in those sayings which make reference both to Yahweh's action and
to Israel's response (vv. 21-22, 25). For the rest, v. 18
mentions only Israel's response, and v. 20 only Yahweh's action,
though it strongly emphasises Yahweh's initiative in establishing
peace and security for his people. V. 25 was patent of two
different interpretations. In form an 'oracle of assurance', it
implied Yahweh's answer came in response to the nation's prior
plea. Did it therefore represent a different theology of
repentance from that outlined above? The whole tenor of the
book suggests the contrary. Nowhere are the people depicted as
seeking in Yahweh the source of fertility. It is from Baal that
they seek the fruits of the earth (2:6, 10, 14; 7:14; 9:1). But
it is Yahweh who responds. The response is, therefore, the
divine initiative of grace.

    So far we have spoken only of the content of the individual
sayings. Their arrangement must, however, also be considered.
Since they are clearly fragmentary and their original context is
now lost, their collecting and arranging is to be attributed to
editorial activity. But the result of this is of significance

since it sets each saying within a new context which in its turn
influences the meaning of the saying. The first question which
must be considered is whether the editing which has taken place
is to be attributed to Judean circles, or whether it is the
work of close associates of the prophet, northerners like
himself, which I readily acknowledge but which lies outside the
scope of this study.[85] If it proves to be the former we must
then consider whether it diverges in any significant respect
from the message proclaimed by Hosea.

One significant feature of this sayings collection in
2:18-25 is the occurrence three times of the formula 'in that
day'. The formula occurs only here and in the similarly
fragmentary and originally independent oracle of 1:5,[86] and
nowhere else in the book. This fact suggests that its
introduction belongs to the process of editing of chs. 1-3.
Is the editing northern or Judean? H.W. Wolff thinks it is
northern, identifying the editor responsible for the present
arrangement of 2:18-25 with the author of the biographical
section in ch. 1 whom he rightly considers to be a close
associate of the prophet in the northern kingdom.[87] J.L. Mays
similarly believes that the collecting of the sayings in 2:18-25
is to be located in the northern kingdom, suggesting that it may
be the work of Hosea himself.[88] If this view is correct, the
passage provides evidence of the transmission of the prophet's
words in the northern kingdom but has no relevance to the
question of Judean redactional influence which is the subject
of the present study. I would suggest, however, that although
it is reasonable to regard the author of the material preserved
in ch. 1 as an associate of the prophet who was aware of details
of his life and parentage of which we have no other information,[89]
the suggestion that he is to be identified with the editor of chs.
1-3 in general, and of 2:18-25 in particular, is unlikely. The
probability has already been noted that the saying in 1:5 owes
its present position to the same editorial activity which was
responsible for the arrangement of 2:18-25, since the formula
'in that day' occurs in these sayings alone. It is beyond

dispute, however, that 1:5 breaks the highly schematic arrangement evident in ch. 1.[90] It differs not only from the preceding verse where the significance of the symbolic name Jezreel is explained, but upsets the balanced structure of the passage by overweighting the interpretation of the first symbolic name in comparison with the second and third which follow in vv. 6 and 9. It is likely that 1:5 owes its present position to the catchword Jezreel which occurs in both v. 4 and v. 5, but this can hardly be attributed to the composer of the biographical narrative since it destroys the deliberate climactic structure of the passage. One must conclude, therefore, that it belongs to a different stage of editing. The frequent occurrence of the formula 'in that day' in the book of Isaiah[91] suggests Judean influence.[92] It is reasonable to conclude that what is true of the present arrangement of 1:5 is true also of 2:18-25.

On the basis that the present arrangement of these verses is due to Judean editing of the material, we move now to the question whether, in their new context, they are at variance in any significant way with what has so far emerged as characteristic of Hosea's message. The fragmentary sayings of 2:18-25 serve, in their present position, to fill out the expectation of future restoration presented in 2:16-17. There is, however, a significant shift in emphasis. The present context of v. 20 suggests that the restoration of peace and security is consequent to Israel's repudiation of Baal worship. Similarly the present position of v. 23 implies that Yahweh's response to Israel is subsequent to her recognition and knowledge of Yahweh described in v. 22. Thus the implication of these verses, that Yahweh's saving action and the demonstration of his love are his response to a changed attitude on Israel's part, contrasts with what we have seen to be the distinctive emphasis of the sayings themselves. Hosea understands salvation as an act of divine grace, unmerited by his people, the result solely of Yahweh's initiative. If sin is not to be condoned, there must be penitence on the nation's part, the transformation of her rebellion into loyal devotion, but this is the result of Yahweh's saving action, not the prelude to it. In contrast, the theological implication of the present arrangement of vv. 18-25 is that Yahweh's saving action is elicited by the nation's prior response.

There is, moreover, another respect in which these verses imply an emphasis different from that which we have detected in Hosea's message. It was clear from the integral connection between judgmental and salvation sayings in 2:4-17 that not God's judgement but his saving action created the new relationship; the woman's response issued from his gracious act. Within the collection of sayings in 2:18-25 there occurs one judgmental saying similar in content to the judgmental sayings in 2:4-17. V. 19 speaks of Yahweh's action in separating Israel from the Baals whom she worships.[93] It is clearly a fragmentary saying, differing from the previous verse both by its use of the plural בעלים and by its reference to Israel in the third person, in contrast to the direct address of v. 18. Undoubtedly it owes its present position to the fact that it shares with v. 18 a concern with Baal worship, though it differs markedly in its concern with apostasy whereas v. 18 is concerned with syncretism. The one is concerned with those who are openly worshippers of the Baals; the other with those who claim to worship Yahweh but have failed to recognise the nature of the allegiance he requires.[94] The juxtaposition of vv. 18 and 19 carries the implication that Israel's new awareness of Yahweh, that he is to be called איש not בעל, is associated with the fact that he has acted in judgement to break the relationship between the nation and the gods whom she sought to worship. This action corresponds to that in 2:8 whereby Yahweh obstructed her path so that she could not find her lovers, and in 2:13f. where he brings to an end her festive worship addressed to the Baals. Yet it was not these acts of judgement which elicited from the nation the required response. It was, so Hosea proclaims,

Yahweh's renewed wooing of his beloved and his words of
affection (v. 16). The RSV has rightly interpreted the meaning
of vv. 18 and 19 in their present relation to each other: '.....
you will call me, 'My husband', and no longer will you call me,
'My Baal'. For I will remove the names of the Baals from her
mouth .....' The introduction of the conjunction 'for', rightly
interpreting the implication of the juxtaposition of the sayings,
I believe, makes it clear that Israel's change of heart in no
longer confusing Yahweh with Baal is the outcome of Yahweh's
judgmental action. The theology expressed here in the
arrangement of the material is not consistent with the emphasis
which was seen to belong to Hosea's message in its original
context, that it is Yahweh's saving action which brings the
nation to repentance.

In short, a consideration of the salvation saying in ch. 2
leads to the conclusion that there is no evidence of redactional
influence on the language or content of the individual sayings;
it is in the collection and arrangement of fragmentary sayings
that this is seen. Vv. 16-17 are integrally related to their
present context and are, therefore, invaluable as evidence of
the relationship of judgement and salvation as Hosea understands
it. It is clear from these verses that the nation's response to
Yahweh which characterises her new relationship with him is not
the result of his judgement, nor is it the prerequisite to his
saving action. It is the outcome, the result of his grace, for
it is his saving action, not his judgement, which proves to be
creative. In contrast, the theological assumption which
underlies the present arrangement of the fragmentary sayings in
2:18-25 is that the nation's penitence must precede Yahweh's
salvation. The initiative rests, therefore, with the nation.
It is probable, as I have argued above, that this arrangement
is the work of Judean editors. This new and distinct theological
emphasis stems not from alteration or supplementation of the
material, but simply from the new context in which the sayings
have been set by their association with each other. Two
distinct theologies of repentance thus begin to emerge, the one

exemplified in 2:4-17 which is demonstrably Hosean, the other implicit in the contextualisation of the fragmentary sayings of 2:18-25 which is probably of Judean origin.

We move now to a consideration of the two remaining salvation oracles with which the complexes of ch. 4-11 and 12-14 conclude.

11:8-11

That these verses have an integral connection with the indictment which precedes them is indicated by their opening words:

> How can I give you up, O Ephraim!
> How can I hand you over, O Israel!

This lament presupposes both the foregoing portrayal of Israel's persistence in sin and the affirmation of Yahweh's love as it is expressed in vv. 1, 3 and 4, which was the foundation of his relationship with his people. Verse 9 also, I believe, presupposes a reference to Yahweh's love such as is found in the previous verses: לא אשוב לשחת אפרים. The meaning of אשוב here has been variously understood.[95] We must note, however, that in addition to indicating the repetition of an action שוב can be used to signify a change in the course of an action. An example of this use is to be found in Josh. 24:20, where the context makes the meaning clear. If the people forsake Yahweh he will turn, they are warned, 'and do you harm' (ושב והרע לכם). That a change in the course of an action is meant here, not the repetition of an action, is clear from the concluding words of the statement: אחרי אשר ־ היטיב לכם. Such, I believe, is also the meaning of שוב in Hos. 11:9: 'I will not turn back (i.e. from my love) to destroy Ephraim'.[96] When the saying is understood in this way it becomes clear that an intrinsic connection exists between 11:1-7 and 8-9, for the content of the latter presupposes the former. The context of vv. 8-9 is not, then, to be regarded as secondary. The fact that consistency of style is not maintained throughout, in that the nation is

SALVATION SAYINGS   41

referred to obliquely in vv. 1-7 whereas it is addressed
directly in vv. 8-9, does not tell against the unity of 11:1-9.
Indeed, as Wolff has demonstrated,[97] the inconsistency is to be
explained on form critical grounds, for the speech is structured
according to legal procedure. When the transition is made from
the accusation to the 'proposal to reach a settlement'
(*Schlichtungsvorschlag*) the addressee naturally changes; the
accusation is addressed to the court, but the proposal to reach
a settlement is addressed directly to the defendant. In v. 11
we again have an oblique reference to the nation describing the
consequence for Israel of Yahweh's compassion. With v. 10,
however, the structure of the passage is interrupted. In place
of the divine speech which has been maintained consistently
throughout we now have prophetic speech in which Yahweh is
referred to in the third person. Its connection with v. 11 by
the catchword יחרדו is a purely external one. In content and
form of expression it has little in common with v. 11, and the
depiction of Yahweh as a lion in v. 10 and of Israel as birds
in v. 11 serves only to emphasise the difference. It is
reasonable to conclude that its present position is secondary.
Is the same true also of the origin of the saying itself? The
evidence points in this direction. The vague, general reference
to the west (מים) is in marked contrast to the specific reference
elsewhere in the book to the great powers Assyria and Egypt[98] of
whose changing fortunes Israel was continually conscious in the
8th century during the years of Hosea's ministry. There is
reason, therefore, to suspect that the saying of v. 10 is
secondary not only in position but in its provenance. To this
question I shall return.

To summarize: vv. 8-9 are bound both by form and by content
to vv. 1-7 whose Hosean origin is not disputed. The whole tenor
of these verses suggests that they belong to the last tragic
years of the northern kingdom.[99] We can conclude that, in
general, vv. 8-9, with their unique portrayal of the struggle
within the heart of God between his justice and his love,

unparalleled as it is elsewhere in the Old Testament, are to be attributed to Hosea. When we turn to consider them in detail a query arises concerning v. 9b, for the expression 'the Holy One' as a designation of God is rare in Hosea, its only other occurrence being possibly in 12:1 where it is used in the plural, though whether with reference to Yahweh or to other deities is uncertain.[100] It is, however, of frequent occurrence in Isaiah, where God's holiness is also, significantly, related not primarily to judgement but to salvation.[101] We must consider, then, whether v. 9b is perhaps an example of later Judean supplementation under the influence of the Isaiah tradition. This seems unlikely, not only on the grounds that the distinctive expression in Isaiah is 'the Holy One of Israel', but also because the profound statement in vv. 8b-9a of God's intention to save his people, undeserving though they are, requires an explanation; and it is this which v. 9b provides: that only the divine nature as wholly other than man can account for the triumph of his love over Israel's sin. We conclude, then, that vv. 8-9 owe their origin to Hosea himself.

The same is true also of v. 11. Not only is the figurative language whereby Israel is compared to צפור and יונה reminiscent of 7:11-12 for whose Hosean authorship there are strong arguments,[102] but the salvation saying appears to have been formulated as a direct reversal of the situation there described:

> Ephraim is like a dove (יונה),
>   silly and without sense,
>   calling to Egypt, going to Assyria (7:11).

But when Yahweh acts in order to redeem the situation,

> they shall come trembling like birds (צפור)
>   from Egypt,
> and like doves (יונה) from the land of Assyria (11:11).

Moreover, the concern of v. 11 with resettlement in the land is a prominent theme in the message of Hosea.[103] In form, v. 11 is

to be compared with 2:17b, of whose Hosean origin there is
little doubt. In both of these sayings Israel is the subject
of the statement which depicts the situation arising from the
saving intervention of Yahweh.[104]

These salvation sayings show the same emphasis as that
which characterised 2:16-17. The rhetorical questions of v. 8
are indicative of the extent to which the prophet despairs of a
future based on Israel's will for reform. Yet hope of salvation
rests not on Israel's response but solely on the persistence of
the divine love. Israel's past was grounded solely on that
love (v. 1f.); so will her future be. The nation in her guilt
may be compared to Admah and Zeboiim, cities annihilated in the
divine judgement,[105] but by her relationship to Yahweh she
stands apart. Their fate cannot be hers. Into Israel's history
a new factor has entered; she exists in a relationship grounded
in Yahweh's love, a relationship in which her existence as a
nation took its beginning. Thus hope for Israel lies not in the
remote possibility of her repentance, but in the certainty of
Yahweh's compassion. His anger is a reality, for sin cannot be
condoned, but in his nature as God, wholly other than man, he
resolves not to carry it into effect (v. 9). Here supremely is
the prophet's statement of Yahweh's sovereign freedom as the
transcendent Holy One, holiness which, significantly, is made
evident not in judgement but in salvation.[106] There is in the
Old Testament no more penetrating statement than this of the
limitless nature of the divine love.[107]

We now return to consider v. 10. Reasons have already
been noted for believing it to be secondary not only in its
present position but also in origin. It remains for us to
consider whether it is to be attributed to Judean influence.
This is suggested by the use of the verb שאג to describe the
summons of Yahweh; not only is this verb absent elsewhere in
the book of Hosea, but it occurs in this sense in Amos 1:2;
Jer. 25:30; Joel 4:16. Each of these passages is a hymnic
formulation associated with Jerusalem or with its heavenly

counterpart. The similarity between them is probably due not to
literary dependence of one on another but to the fact that all
have drawn on a traditional motif of the Jerusalem temple cult,
that Yahweh's dwelling is in Zion. The opening words of Amos 1.2
יהוה מציון ישאג ומירושלם יתן קולו are in general considered to
belong not to Amos' message to the northern kingdom, for their
style and theme are those of the hymn not the prophetic saying,[108]
but to later editing of the material to form a solemn introduction
to the prophetic message. The fact that they resemble Is. 2:3 =
Mic. 4:2, passages which are central to the Zion traditions, in
any case emphasises the southern roots of the tradition.[109] The
occurrence of the identical formulation in Joel 4:16 supports the
view that there are cultic connections, for it is widely
recognised that this material is based on liturgical forms, if
not itself actually liturgical.[110] The evidence points,
therefore, to the association of שאג to denote the summons of
Yahweh with Jerusalem not northern tradition. It should be noted
also that Hos. 11:10 appears to have been influenced by Amos 3:8
and assimilated to it. The saying in Hosea seems unduly
repetitive, and the phrase כאריה ישאג has the appearance of an
explanatory gloss intended to clarify the meaning of שאג. In
Amos 1:2, as also in Jer. 25:30 and Joel 4:16, the verb 'roar'
is not specifically associated with the lion. Indeed in Job
37:3f. שאג is explicitly associated with thunder as the voice
of Yahweh:

תחת־כל־השמים ישרהו ואורו על־כנפות הארץ : אחריו ישאג־קול ירעם בקול גאונו

There are, however, two passages in Amos where שאג occurs in
connection with אריה as in Hos. 11:10. The first of these is
Amos 3:4 where the words occur in a list of cause and effect
sayings drawn from nature: הישאג אריה ביער וטרף אין לו
More significant for our purposes here, however, is the second
which, as has already been noted, occurs in Amos 3:8. Here the
full allusive force of שאג is present. The lion's roar no
longer describes a purely natural phenomenon but is understood
allegorically, and is associated deliberately with Yahweh's

utterance. The explanatory gloss in Hos. 11:10 seems to have
arisen by assimilation to this, and thus once again betrays
Judean influence. As supporting evidence it should also be
noted that, in contrast, in Hosea שחל is used of the lion,[111]
and its application to Yahweh carries a different connotation.
It concerns not his solemn summons to his people, as in the
Jerusalem cultic tradition, but depicts his consuming wrath.

Finally, the vague reference to the return of exiles מים,
which contrasts with the otherwise specific geographical
references in the Hosea material to Egypt and Assyria, has
parallels in Isaiah,[112] again suggesting a Judean provenance.

It appears, then, that not only does v. 10 interrupt the
salvation saying of 11:8-11, but it stands in close relation
to material associated with Jerusalem. It seems reasonable,
therefore, to attribute the saying to Judean influence. Its
purpose is to extend future hope to Judah's exiles and refugees
of a later time in places other than Egypt and Assyria which
were the main focus of attention in the 8th century B.C. But
how does it relate theologically to Hosea's message? The
portrayal of the majestic summons of Yahweh in salvation has
no parallel here, though the power of his word through the
prophets, albeit in judgement, is stressed in 6:5: חצבתי בנביאים
הרגתים באמרי־פי. The basic emphasis of this secondary material,
however, is in line with Hosea's fundamental conviction that the
process of salvation is initiated by Yahweh himself, and that
the positive response of the people is consequent upon this,
not prior to it. In view of the limited nature of the saying,
however, no deduction can safely be made concerning a theology
of repentance. We can say only that in this instance the
secondary material has served not to alter but simply to widen
the scope of Hosea's salvation saying. In short, although its
language differs from Hosea's and belongs instead to the
traditions of Jerusalem temple worship, within the limits of
its theological content it does not diverge from the message
of the northern prophet.

14:5-9

This salvation oracle is preceded by one of the rare summons to repentance which occurs in the book of Hosea.[113] The question of its relationship to Hosea's theology of repentance will therefore be of prime importance. But we must first consider the question of the origin of the salvation saying itself.

The first issue concerns the unity of vv. 5-9, a matter which is commonly allowed to pass unquestioned.[114] Closer examination suggests that two originally distinct salvation sayings consisting of vv. 5-8 and v. 9 respectively have been juxtaposed because of the similarity of the imagery which they employ, drawn from the world of nature. In content, however, and in the way in which the figurative language is applied, they show significant differences. In vv. 5-8 restored Israel is portrayed as a flourishing tree nourished by Yahweh as the dew. In v. 9, on the other hand, it is Yahweh who is compared to a fruit-bearing tree, imagery unique in the Old Testament. Thus despite superficial points of contact the imagery of the two sayings is distinct. The failure to distinguish between them has, in its turn, contributed to further confusion through a misunderstanding of the meaning of בצלו in v. 8. As the third person suffix indicates, the reference is to Israel, not to Yahweh, for it is Israel which is consistently portrayed in vv. 5-8 under the image of various trees.[115] The commonly accepted emendation to בצלי[116] is therefore not only unnecessary but incorrect. Restored Israel is represented as a luxuriant tree under whose protection[117] agricultural life will prosper once more. The words ישבו ישבי בצלו יחיו דגן are to be translated: those who dwell in its shade will again grow corn.[118]

Consequently, I shall consider vv. 5-8 separately from v. 9. As regards the origin of vv. 5-8, there is no reason to suspect that they belong to the secondary material. Imagery of this kind drawn from an appreciation of luxuriant plant life is not unfamiliar in the Old Testament,[119] and was undoubtedly stimulated by the interest in the world of nature apparent in

SALVATION SAYINGS   47

the Wisdom literature. It is, however, particularly appropriate
to the circumstances of Hosea with his concern to claim for
Yahweh, not Baal, sovereignty over nature. The evidence of the
language used serves to corroborate this. (A caveat was entered
above[120] concerning the use of linguistic evidence alone. As
supporting evidence, however, it is of value.) The use of רפא
to describe Yahweh's saving action has parallels in 7:1 and 11:3;
אהב is used of Yahweh's attitude to Israel in 3:1; the idea of
God's wrath (אף) occurs also in 8:5 and 11:9; שוב with the
meaning 'turn away' rather than 'return' is paralleled in 11:9.
There is, indeed, no form of expression here which prompts doubt
in attributing the saying to Hosea, as do the majority of
commentators.[121] Its contents can be said to balance the
judgmental sayings of 2:5b and 13:15, and are an explicit
reversal of the deprivation there depicted.

We must now consider the context of the saying. How does
it relate to the summons to repentance in 14:2? In liturgical
worship confession of penitence would normally elicit an oracle
of assurance such as we find evidence of in the Psalms;[122] this
is the form of vv. 5-8. It has seemed natural, therefore, to
understand these verses as the divine decree proclaimed in
response to the preceding penitential song. Thus J. Mauchline,
for example, describes them as 'the Lord's response to Israel's
penitent cry'.[123] From this he draws the theological inference
that 'Israel had to make the first move; the first step in
redemption had to be their return to the Lord from whom they
had strayed so seriously. But when they manifested their
willingness to return, the Lord was ready to receive and save
them'.[124] J.H. Eaton in his recent work expresses a similar
view: 'the prophet issues a summons to repentance before turning
again to God to voice the people's prayer and hope ...... Hosea
is then able to give Yahweh's rejoinder, a word of acceptance'.[125]
This is undoubtedly implicit in the present contextualisation of
the passage, but the possibility must be considered whether here
too, as in 2:18-25, the arrangement of the material is
redactional.[126]

The language of vv. 5-8 has no points of contact with vv. 2-4.
The significance of this is emphasised when comparison is made
with 6:1-6 which likewise consists of penitential song (vv. 1-3)
followed by Yahweh's response (vv. 4-6). There, although Yahweh's
response is not the expected 'oracle of assurance' but a lament
over the inadequacy of the nation's knowledge and commitment
(v. 6), the imagery is consistent throughout. The song of
penitence draws on terminology from the world of nature such as
גשם and מלקוש. In the response of Yahweh also it is the world
of nature which provides the imagery, and comparison is drawn
with ענן־בקר and טל. The absence of any such consistency in
the imagery of 14:2-4 and 5-8 suggests that, in spite of its
present context, the salvation saying is not integrally related
to the summons to penitence, but rather owes its position to
editorial arrangement.[127] Hence, implications of its context
are a guide, not to the theology of Hosea himself, but to that
of traditionists to whom we are indebted for its preservation.
It is they who have understood the expression of Yahweh's grace
as his 'response to Israel's penitent cry', a cry which must
elicit his saving action. When vv. 5-8 are considered apart from
their present context the emphasis is seen to lie differently.
Whether or not they belonged originally within a context which
spoke of the nation's repentance it is impossible now to
determine; but there is no doubt that the very nature of the
lexical choices within these verses is such that it serves to
focus attention on Yahweh's gracious initiative in salvation.
The use of the word נדבה in v. 5 conveys the spontaneity and
generosity of God's love for Israel, the totally unmerited
divine grace. God's love does not correspond to Israel's
deserts but to the nature of God. Similarly, without over
pressing the matter, it may be said that the use of the verb
רפא with משובתם as object has the effect of emphasising the
generosity of God towards his people in their need.[128] Yahweh
will not merely disregard the nation's sin. He will heal Israel,
curing that sickness which disposes her to evil. Thus the

SALVATION SAYINGS

implication of v. 5 comes close to the utter abandon of
inexplicable love portrayed in 11:8. Israel's salvation will
be effected solely because Yahweh takes the initiative of love;
the nation's entire blessing and prosperity arises out of
Yahweh's forgiveness. The statement in v. 5, כי שב אפי ממנו,
gives the basis of the new order, namely God's action, not
primarily Israel's repentance. The only non-modal suffix
conjugation form present (שב) stands in significant contrast
to the modal forms of the other nine verbs in the passage which
express the speaker's thoughts about the future. Thus the
grammatical technique serves to reinforce the theological
emphasis implicit in the lexical items chosen.[129] In short,
the primary emphasis in vv. 5-8 lies not on the necessity for
the nation to repent in order to elicit Yahweh's response, but
on his sovereign freedom to act in salvation consistently with
his own nature to effect a total reversal of an existing
situation. This emphasis is entirely consistent with Hosea's
theology as it has already emerged from the foregoing study of
the salvation sayings.

We turn finally to consider 14:9. Reasons were given
above[130] for the view that v. 9 has been linked secondarily
with vv. 5-8 because of their common use of imagery drawn
from nature. We must consider, then, whether any evidence is
available to help in determining the provenance of v. 9. The
comparison of Yahweh with a fruit-bearing tree has no parallel
elsewhere in the Old Testament. In all probability it derives
from Canaanite religion where the sacred tree as a symbol of
fertility is one of the most familiar motifs in Canaanite art.[131]
It appears that we have an example here of the use of elements
from Canaanite fertility religion in the interests of Yahwism.
The terminology of the fertility cult is adopted for the
purposes of polemic against it. It can be stated without fear
of contradiction that this is a familiar device of Hosea himself,
boldly used by the prophet, and seen most notably perhaps in his
adaptation of the marriage motif.[132] There is strong reason,

therefore, to locate the form of expression in v. 9 within the
setting of Hosea's message. For the prophet this familiar motif
becomes the means by which he voices his conviction that Yahweh
is the sole source of fertility. This adaptation of the
terminology of the fertility cult for the purposes of polemic
against it appears strongly also in v. 9a. Its language is bold
in the extreme as Yahweh lays claim to the powers which Israel
attributed to other deities in its paganised cult. In the
affirmation אני עניתי ואשורנו, 'I myself have answered and will
watch over him',[133] a deliberate play on words can be detected.
Yahweh is for Israel both Anath (ענת) and Asherah (אשרה).[134]
Since Hosea's practice of using motifs drawn from Canaanite
religion for the purposes of polemic against it has already been
noted, and can readily be illustrated, there is strong reason for
attributing this saying to Hosea himself. It is consonant with
the historical circumstances of his ministry and with the main
thrust of his message. It may indeed be that the original form
of the allusion to the Canaanite deities was even more bold and
that the present form of the text with its indirect allusion by
means of a play on words is an example of later alteration in
the interests of avoiding an unseemly expression. I raise this
only as a suggestion since it is impossible to answer the question
with any certainty. It is worth noting, however, that the
context supports the reference to deities. The expression in
question follows immediately on a reference to idols (עצבים),
and is itself followed by a reference to ברוש רענן, surely a
significant expression in view of the fact that Asherah appears
to have been represented by a wooden image or possibly a tree.[135]
In any event, the content of the saying with its emphasis on
Yahweh as sovereign over the powers of nature is entirely
compatible with Hosea's thought, and the form of expression can
be seen to arise directly from the circumstances of his ministry
which drove him into conflict with the fertility cult.

It remains now to consider what relationship, if any,
exists between the salvation saying of v. 9 and the summons to

penitence in vv. 2-4. In contrast to vv. 5-8 it is evident that
v. 9 contains one of the motifs of the penitential liturgy,
namely the renunciation of false gods (v. 4), for v. 9 asserts
uncompromisingly that there is no place for any other deity
alongside Yahweh. Yet we must set against this the fact that
the question addressed to Ephraim in v. 9 carries the implication
in its pleading tones that the nation continues to associate
Yahweh with idols, failing to understand his nature and his
demands. For this reason it is unlikely that the salvation
saying of v. 9 is to be regarded as Yahweh's response to
Israel's penitence, even if there were evidence that the people
did, in fact, respond to the prophetic summons. Yahweh's
response implied in the verb עניתי is not necessarily a response
to the nation's penitence but to its need. In any case, as has
already been noted,[136] the use of this verb is probably due to a
play on the name ענה. In short, the present position of this
saying, as of vv. 5-8, appears to be editorial.

We conclude, then, that the content of the sayings in
vv. 5-8 and in v. 9 suggests that they originated with Hosea in
his particular circumstances in the northern kingdom. Their
present position, however, in juxtaposition with the summons to
repentance in vv. 2-4, is editorial, and there is no integral
link between them. The language in which both of the salvation
sayings are couched lays emphasis on Yahweh's initiative in
salvation and the spontaneity of his gracious action. The
present arrangement of the material, however, carries a
different implication; the connection of the salvation sayings
with the call to penitence in vv. 2-4 suggests that Yahweh's
saving action is elicited by Israel's repentance. Thus we have
here once again an example of theological reinterpretation which
has introduced an element alien to Hosea's theology. It has
already become clear that this new emphasis, which lays stress
on the nation's repentance as the prerequisite to Yahweh's
saving action, is Judean in origin.[137] I do not wish to imply,
of course, that the prophet's concern for a penitent and

transformed nation is any less real than that of Judean
traditionists. It is in the *relationship* of repentance to
salvation that he differs. For Hosea, repentance cannot precede
the gracious action of God, for it can itself emanate only from
the divine initiative in salvation.[138]

The conclusion to which an examination of the salvation
sayings as regards both content and contextualisation has led,
that there are two distinct theologies of repentance discernible
within the material, the one originating with Hosea himself, the
other attributable to editorial activity during the process of
transmission, serves to resolve a tension which appears within
the book of Hosea. There are, indeed, two significant and
diverse strands. The first of these is an attitude of despair
at the nation's inability to repent and return to God:

> Their deeds do not permit them to return to their God.
> For the spirit of harlotry is within them,
>   and they know not the Lord (5:4).

Despite all their cultic activities, their diligence in carrying
out the sacrificial rituals, their search for God is ineffective:

> With their flocks and herds they shall go to seek the Lord,
>   but they will not find him; he has withdrawn from them
>   (5:6).

This note of despair, that the nation's best efforts are
unavailing in healing the breach between Israel and her God,
is a recurrent one,[139] and there is no reason to doubt that it
is an authentic expression of Hosea's thought. Indeed, the
language of the two passages cited above has elements which
corroborate this view, for the phrase רוח זנונים occurs only
in Hosea[140] and nowhere else in the Old Testament, as also does
the verb חלץ used in an intransitive sense, which is perhaps an
example of northern dialect.[141] Yet alongside this despair of
the nation's ability to repent and turn to God are the
expressions of future hope which, as we have already
established, are integral to Hosea's message and consistently

SALVATION SAYINGS   53

form part of it. It is clear, therefore, that the prophet's
expectation of the nation's restoration to Yahweh is based on
some other foundation than the penitence of the people.

The second strand which appears in the book stands in
tension with the prophet's expressed despair at the nation's
inability to repent. The clearest expression of this divergent
viewpoint occurs in 5:15 which states explicitly that God will
not take the initiative in restoring the broken relationship
until such time as Israel first responds in penitence:

> I will return again to my place,
>   until they acknowledge their guilt[142] and seek my face,
>   and in their distress they seek me.

If the hypothesis formulated above, that Hosea stresses the
initiative of God, and that the emphasis on the primacy of the
nation's repentance comes from Judean redactors, is correct, we
should expect to find that the saying in 5:15 has arisen from
Judean influence. A close consideration of the evidence does
indeed point in this direction. Whereas in 5:4, 6 significant
expressions occurred which had no parallel elsewhere in the Old
Testament, we find the reverse to be true in 5:15. Thus the use
of מקום to indicate Yahweh's heavenly dwelling place has no
parallel elsewhere in Hosea but occurs a significant number of
times in material of Judean provenance. It occurs as here with
a personal pronoun but no further qualification in Mic. 1:3 and
Is. 26:21. We may also compare the use of the expression
מקום שבתך in 1 Kings 8:30 = 2 Chron. 6:21, material which is
Judean in origin. It may be objected that the use of מקומי in
Hos. 5:15 is not parallel to the passages referred to above but
is due to the continuation of the simile of v. 14 into v. 15
and applies to the lion's lair. This is, I believe, an incorrect
understanding of the passage; there is no inherent connection
between vv. 14 and 15, but merely the external link by the
catchword אלך. The simile of v. 14 is not continued into v. 15.
Whereas in the former Yahweh is depicted as a lion which carries
off its helpless prey, in the latter he is described as

withdrawing from his sinful people. I have discussed this matter in detail elsewhere[143] and the arguments need not be repeated here. Suffice it to say that the simile of v. 14 does not account for the use of מקומי in v. 15, which is to be understood as referring directly to Yahweh's heavenly dwelling. In short, the tension between the explicit statement of 5:15 that the nation's repentance is the *sine qua non* of Yahweh's saving action and the unequivocal assertion elsewhere in the book of Hosea that such is the nation's apostasy that it is impotent to take the first step towards reconciliation is to be accounted for on the grounds that the former is not part of the primary northern stratum of the material but is due to redactional influence. This is, in fact, the only point at which such an assertion is made explicitly. Elsewhere, as we have noted,[144] it has been implicit in the arrangement of the material.

The existence in the book of Hosea of two distinct theologies of repentance, the one emphasising Yahweh's gracious unmerited initiative in salvation, the other regarding the nation's repentance as the prerequisite to restoration, is illustrated by the difference in the conclusions reached by commentators. On the one hand, for example, J.L. Mays[145] and J. Mauchline[146] note the emphasis laid on the need for Israel to take the first step towards the restoration of the broken relationship by due repentance. A rather different conclusion is reached by M.J. Buss. He remarks that the announcements of the saving process in 2:16 and 3:1 do not presuppose the nation's penitence, but concludes that on balance Hosea 'places greater demand on human turning than does the Christian, for salvation is a promise rather than a reality to be believed'.[147] Finally we have the view represented by G. Fohrer's comment, that in Hosea's despair of the nation's repentance coupled with his conviction of the saving power of God the prophet ultimately took 'a crucial step toward belief in redemption' through his insight that 'God's gracious mercy does not become effective only after the repentance and return that man must accomplish;

it is instead the active principle, which human decision and action must follow and respond to'.[148] As a further example of this viewpoint I should like to quote the conclusion reached by G. Farr in his study of Hosea, that 'the undeserved, forgiving love of God for no better reason than the impulse of its own nature pardons and restores'.[149] It is this view, I believe, which represents the distinctive emphasis of Hosea in contrast to that which belongs to the Judean redaction of the material.

CHAPTER II

JUDAH AND THE DAVIDIC MONARCHY

Although Hosea's ministry seems, on the evidence available to us, to have been confined to the northern kingdom,[1] the record of that activity in its canonical form incorporates a considerable number of references to the southern kingdom. It is not so much the inclusion of sayings concerned with Judah which is surprising, but rather the frequency of them, for we find here no less than fifteen direct references to Judah by name[2] and one mention of the Davidic king.[3] The surprising number of these references is emphasised when the book of Hosea is compared with that of Amos which contains in all only four references to Judah[4] and one to the Davidic king,[5] although Amos himself was a native of the southern kingdom.[6] It is imperative, therefore, to investigate further the question whether, or at any rate to what extent, the interest in the southern kingdom which characterises the present form of the book of Hosea is due not to the northern prophet himself but to the process of transmission by which it has reached its final form. Few if any would now subscribe to the view taken by Marti,[7] among others early in this century, that none of the Judah references belongs to the primary stratum of the material; but none the less scholarly views have differed widely on this question. Harper[8] attributed most of them to the work of a later editor in the southern kingdom, although he acknowledged the possibility that an interest in Judah may already have had a place in Hosea's message. In contrast we may cite G.A. Danell[9] who holds that in all probability all the occurrences cf the name Judah are original. Note must also be taken here of the views of Engnell[10] whose strongly positive attitude towards tradition leads him to conclude that it is wrong in principle to attempt to distinguish between primary and secondary elements in a text. The word of the prophet has been handed down by traditionists, but the two now form an indissoluble unity, for the prophet himself is to be understood not only as the original source of the sayings which have been transmitted, but also as the constitutive influence on the circle of disciples who transmitted them. Consequently, the different strata are not distinguishable from one another, and the text in its final form is to be understood as giving due expression to the prophet's message. The pro-Judean and pro-Davidic attitude which appears in the book[11] is therefore a true reflection of Hosea's own thought. Engnell thus comes to the conclusion that Hosea was either Judean himself or at any rate shared a Judean attitude of mind, and that any northern linguistic features which are evident are due not to the northern origins of the prophet himself but to the fact that his words were transmitted in north Israelite circles.[12] However, the view which is generally accepted by commentators today is a mediating one between the two extremes, namely that although in certain circumstances some reference to Judah may reasonably be thought to have formed part of Hosea's message,[13] it is to redactional influence that other instances are to be attributed. When presented in general terms such as these this seems to offer a balanced approach to the question at issue; but when the attempt is made to relate it to specific passages we encounter the dangers of dogmatic preconceptions.[14]

Before we proceed to assess the extent of redactional influence in this area we must first take note of an explanation of a different kind which has been proposed to account for the high frequency of references to Judah in the Hosea tradition. H.L. Ginsberg[15] suggests that they are to be accounted for as textual errors, and that they arise from the use of the letter *yod* as an abbreviation for the name Israel, which was subsequently misunderstood and resulted, in six passages,[16]

in the reading יהודה. If Ginsberg's theory is correct, the
resultant references to Judah have no theological or exegetical
significance but are purely fortuitous, an accident of textual
transmission. The suggestion is interesting, but I believe it
to be suspect in that it provides a deceptively simple way of
solving not merely one but a number of problems. It offers no
convincing reason why such misunderstanding should have
occurred, and, still more seriously, it gives no adequate reason
why, if it did occur, it should have produced such varied
results, giving rise not only to mistaken references to Judah,
but also to Jehu (1:4) and to Yahweh (8:1) in place of Israel.[17]
Indeed, the awkward question remains unanswered why the
misinterpretation should have occurred so spasmodically that
the name Israel still remains intact in many passages. The
theory is of interest but the danger is that it can be utilised
too readily to resolve a variety of problematic readings, and
too little scientific control on it is possible for it to
provide a convincing solution.

On balance, therefore, it seems reasonable to conclude
that the view is to be preferred which allows for the
possibility of redactional influence exerted on the material
in the southern kingdom which has either overlaid or supplemented
the primary material with reference to Judah. Since we know
that the transmission of the prophet's words took place in
Judah,[18] the possibility must be considered that some at least
of the references to the southern kingdom are to be attributed
to these traditionists and not to the prophet himself. There
is, however, no need to abandon the possibility, or rather even
the probability, that Hosea himself may on occasion have turned
his attention to the neighbouring kingdom which, despite any
differences exhibited by its political[19] and religious
institutions, was closely associated with his own by the ties
of history and religious tradition. Despite periods of
hostility and even of outright conflict, we must not allow
ourselves to lose sight of the fact that 'in the view of the
prophets . . . . . the people Israel has a unity which

supersedes its political divisions'.[20] The close relationship
which existed between the two kingdoms must not be overlooked.
Yet, having duly recognised this fact, to allow that some of
the references to Judah may come from a period later than
Hosea's is not merely to take account of the processes of
history: it is to affirm the conviction that the divine word
spoken through the prophet, though rooted originally in one
particular historical context, was not restricted to that one
situation. In the process of transmission the prophet's words
were freed from their anchorage in the past, as a message now
over to a nation which had since disappeared from the stage of
history, and continued to exist as a living and relevant word
addressed to Judah as the sole surviving people of God.[21] The
material which is attributed to redactional activity of this
kind may appropriately be described as secondary, but it is
secondary only in a chronological sense and not with regard to
its intrinsic value. It is significant both for exegetical and
for theological reasons: the former because in these passages
we have an early example of reinterpretation of the prophetic
word, and its reapplication to a new situation, the latter
because it testifies to the conviction that the proclamation of
the word of God by a prophet, although related originally to a
particular moment in history, has a relevance beyond its primary
setting, and that the content of the message is not exhausted
when the circumstances to which it was first addressed have
changed.

Stated thus in general terms such a view would command
broad agreement. To attempt to distinguish in detail, however,
between primary and secondary material is a formidable task,
and one which is easily distorted by unacknowledged presuppositions. It is at this level that there is scope for a wide
divergence of opinion. The criteria used to determine the
question must be carefully established in order to avoid on
the one hand an uncritical conservatism and on the other an
undue scepticism in approaching the material. It is clear that,

as I noted earlier,[22] a fundamental principle of methodology is involved which must inevitably affect, to some extent, the conclusions reached eventually. Are the sayings which, in the canonical form of the text, are attributed to the prophet to be accepted as such unless proved otherwise, or, conversely, is the balance to be tilted in favour of the presumption that they are redactional unless there is overwhelming evidence to the contrary? I have made it clear already that it is my intention to adopt the former position, not in the interests of conservatism, but on the objective grounds that the book's distinctive characteristics of both language and thought, characteristics frequently acknowledged by commentators, make it the most acceptable procedure since they strengthen the arguments for the reliability of the tradition that we have in essence the proclamation of Hosea. I have already made reference to Wolff's comment that 'in view of the book's transmission, we are unable to affirm that its every word belongs to the *verba ipsissima* of the prophet. . . . . For the most part, however, Hosea's own speech is unmistakable'.[23] Rudolph's discussion[24] of the distinctive features of Hosea's language implies a similar viewpoint.

I propose to follow the pattern of the previous chapter, examining each of the relevant passages in turn, and drawing on the evidence of both literary and situational context in formulating my conclusions. I believe the latter, that is to say the historical background of a saying, wherever it can be deduced, to be extremely valuable in serving as a control on inferences which may be drawn on literary grounds. Literary criticism may indicate the presence of supplementary material which has not been fully integrated into its context; the present *arrangement* of such material can then rightly be regarded as secondary and redactional, but we ought not to conclude forthwith that such is necessarily true of its *origins*. The distinction between the provenance of the material itself and its present context must not be overlooked. The criterion

JUDAH AND THE DAVIDIC MONARCHY

of the content of a saying is a more difficult one to apply.
It is an unwarranted assumption that as a northerner Hosea's
attitude to the southern kingdom is likely to have been either
openly hostile or at least highly critical. Whether a saying
belongs to the primary stratum of the material or has arisen
from later Judean influence cannot in the first instance be
determined on the basis of the attitude which it evinces towards
Judah. It is at least a possibility which we must take into
account that, in view of the increasing religious corruption
and political instability in the northern kingdom, and the lack
of response evoked there by his message, the prophet's hopes may
have turned towards Judah as the place where the ancient
traditions of Yahwism might yet be preserved.[25] Likewise the
assumption that sayings which express a favourable attitude to
Judah are likely to have arisen in Judean circles is also open
to serious question. One is justified in assuming that the
Judean redactors were concerned not merely to preserve the
memory of Hosea's message but to keep alive its challenge and,
if possible, to safeguard Judah from disaster similar to that
which had overtaken Israel. The question of the provenance of
a saying is, therefore, far more complex than would appear from
the two simple alternatives posited by Harper with reference, in
this particular instance, especially to 12.1b. He asks the
question: 'have the words of 1b a *good* sense, and are they then
from a later hand (for no motive can be conceived for Hosea's
inserting here a eulogy of Judah); or have they a *bad* sense,
and are they then really from Hosea's own hand'?[26] This is an
over-simplistic approach to the question. In general, however,
the complexity of the question has been recognised by scholars,
to such an extent that some have postulated evidence for not one
but two Judean redactions distinct from each other, being
different in kind and differently motivated. The one exempts
Judah from Hosea's strictures against Israel, the other
reapplies their warning to Judah.[27] I shall return to this
point at a later stage; I have mentioned it here only in
illustration of the difficulties encountered in attempting to

employ the criterion of content in judging the question of
provenance of the material. Nevertheless, I believe that the
criterion of content may usefully be applied, as long as due
caution is exercised, at a later stage in the investigation
in certain problematic instances when the general lines of
Hosea's attitude to Judah have begun to emerge, for the
cumulative evidence of other relevant passages ought not to
be entirely discounted. The evidence of content, however, must
never be treated as a primary indication of origin, but only as
corroborative.

I have already discussed the first reference to Judah,
which occurs in the title of the book.[28] It is clearly
secondary and belongs to the final editing. On this point
scholars are agreed, and I shall not discuss it further. The
remaining passages which refer to Judah or the Davidic king fall
into several categories. There are among them judgmental
sayings (5:5, 10, 12, 13, 14; 6:4; 8:14; 12:3), salvation
sayings (1:7; 2:1-3; 3:5), a warning about the nation's present
(4:15) and a reminder of Yahweh's purpose in the past (10:11).
The two remaining references to Judah (6:11; 12:1) are so
problematic that they cannot be included in any of the foregoing
categories until their meaning has been clarified. I shall
therefore leave them aside until conclusions about Hosea's
attitude to Judah have begun to emerge on the evidence of other
sayings. To include these obscure passages at an earlier stage
of the enquiry would be to risk prejudicing the results of the
study by admitting ambiguous evidence.

I shall consider first the judgmental sayings. Here, as
in the previous chapter, the question of methodology is
fundamental. I have already excluded as an inadmissible
criterion whether the sayings express a pro- or anti- Judean
attitude. It is, therefore, necessary to establish first
whether there is in any of these sayings any clear evidence of
redactional influence from which we may begin by a process of
induction to assess the relationship of the primary to the

secondary material. Such evidence does, in fact, occur in 12:3, and accordingly I propose to begin with a consideration of this passage.

12:3

The present form of the text is clearly not original. Two names appear in v. 3:

The Lord has an indictment against Judah,
and will punish Jacob according to his ways . . . . .

Then come the etymologies of two names in v. 4. By a chiastic arrangement that of Jacob comes first: בבטן עקב את־אחיו. Surprisingly, however, the second is not the etymology of Judah as might have been expected, but that of Israel: ובאונו שרה את־אלהים. It is difficult to avoid the conclusion that it was these two names Israel and Jacob which stood originally in v. 3 and that Judah has been substituted for Israel. A. Gelston[29] concludes from the presence of the conjunction before לפקד that the original text was longer than the present form and that both Israel and Judah were included in the indictment. The argument is far from convincing, and the evidence is patent of different evaluation. Wolff,[30] for example, regards the conjunction as a secondary addition which itself came into the text at the time of the substitution of the name Judah for Israel. Thus the explanation given to account for the presence of the conjunction is influenced by the decision already taken on other grounds concerning the original form of the saying. It is, of course, possible that the conjunction is intended purely for emphasis, a usage which can be paralleled in Amos 8:4: שמעו־זאת השאפים אביון ולשבית ענוי־ארץ and in Psalm 104:21: הכפירים שאגים ולבקש מאל אכלם. The evidence of the two etymologies is, in my opinion, decisive. The isolated reference to Judah is obtrusive in the context of vv. 3-5 which draw on the ancient traditions concerning the patriarch Jacob/Israel associated with Bethel. Moreover, if the latter part of the saying is to be meaningful, the party to be punished must correspond to the one accused in

v. 3a.³¹ In the context of Hosea's ministry in the northern kingdom, if indictment and threat of punishment are to apply to the same community, the name Israel must form a parallel to Jacob. The present form of the text with its reference to Judah destroys this correspondence. In the new situation, however, which was created by the fall of the northern kingdom, the name Jacob referred to Judah which alone remained as heir to the ancient traditions of God's people, a usage familiar elsewhere in the Old Testament.³² Understood in this way in its later Judean context the necessary correspondence still exists in the present form of the text between the party accused in v. 3a and the one to be punished in v. 3b. By the substitution of the name Judah for Israel the prophetic word of judgement has been applied to a new situation. Hosea's accusation of his own contemporaries in northern Israel has become an explicit indictment of the southern kingdom. If, as Ginsberg has suggested,³³ the reference to Judah has arisen accidentally by scribal error, it has in fact produced not a misunderstanding but a correct interpretation adapted to fresh circumstances. This sounds altogether too fortuitous, and it is a more satisfactory approach to attribute the change to deliberate editorial activity motivated by the serious purpose of challenging Judah to renew her allegiance to Yahweh. It may be objected that the substitution of one name for another is a radical change, and that the name Israel itself which stood originally in the text could have been reinterpreted with reference to Judah, as has clearly been done elsewhere in the Old Testament.³⁴ However, the problem of satisfactorily accounting for the substitution of one name for the other, rather than the reinterpretation of the existing name, does not obscure the clear evidence that in this particular instance substitution has in fact taken place. It may be that the present form of Hos. 12:3 has been influenced by Dt. 33:7 where the blessing of Moses relating to Judah includes the words ידיו רב לו. M. Gertner³⁵ has indeed argued that an allusion to this passage is intended, though clearly the meaning of the two is hardly comparable.

JUDAH AND THE DAVIDIC MONARCHY

In short, although it is difficult to account adequately for the substitution of the name Judah for Israel, when the latter itself was patent of reinterpretation, the evidence of the etymologies in v. 4 can be seen to confirm this substitution. Here, judgmental saying addressed originally to the northern kingdom has been reapplied to Judah. It is at this point that the content of the indictment must be noted. The judgement pronounced is comprehensive in scope: Yahweh will punish the nation 'according to his ways, and requite him according to his deeds'. Thus, in the form in which the saying has been transmitted in Judah, it is Judah's entire way of life which falls under Yahweh's judgement. We must conclude that, in this instance, the threat of judgement on the nation, comprehensive as it is in range, is the work not of Hosea but of Judean redactors. It remains, then, to determine whether comprehensive judgement against Judah comparable to this example has a place in the primary northern stratum of the material or whether it is entirely due to the influence of Judean redactors.

5:5

We turn now to 5:5 where Judah is associated with Israel/ Ephraim in its guilt: כשל גם יהודה עמם. It is widely agreed by commentators that the inclusion of Judah here is redactional,[36] though somewhat surprisingly W.R. Harper,[37] who attributed only two of the Judah references to Hosea, accepted this as original. He comments that there is nothing here which demands an origin later than Hosea's time, observing, 'An occasional side glance at Judah, a people so intimately connected with his own, must not be denied to the prophet'.[38] Although this is undoubtedly true in general, it is questionable whether it applies in this particular instance. Several considerations indicate that the reference to Judah is a secondary expansion of the text. The loose connection of the clause under discussion with the preceding lines,[39] the occurrence of the perfect כשל[40] in a sequence of imperfects (יכשלו v. 5; ילכו and ימצאו v. 6), together with the fact that this solitary reference to Judah is obtrusive in a context otherwise solely concerned with the northern kingdom in which the names Israel[41] and Ephraim occur several times in parallelism, all create the impression that these words are not integral to the passage.

Furthermore, a careful examination of the precise meaning of the opening words of v. 5, וענה גאון־ישראל בפניו[42] confirms that they referred originally only to the northern kingdom and were not applicable to Judah. The expression גאון־ישראל is difficult to interpret precisely. It has sometimes been compared to the expressions גאון יעקב (Amos 8:7), נצח ישראל (1 Sam. 15:29), and like them has been understood as an appellation of Yahweh.[43] Others have taken it in a pejorative sense as referring to the nation's arrogance. Thus J.L. Mays explains it as 'the undisturbed confidence which Israel places in the cultic activity mentioned in the next verse'.[44] It is worth noting, however, that there are several instances in the Old Testament where the word גאון seems to carry a more specific connotation. Amos 6:8 is an example. Here גאון יעקב undoubtedly has a pejorative meaning, and G.A. Danell[45] seems correct in his view that reference is intended to Israel's principal sanctuary Bethel, the epitome of her pride, for otherwise the word עיר is left without an antecedent. Similar instances can be adduced in Is. 13:19 where גאון refers specifically to Babylon, and Zech. 9:6 where it is used of the Philistine cities. In view of the cultic activity described in Hos. 5:6, it is reasonable to suggest that in the previous verse גאון is intended to convey not merely the abstract meaning 'arrogance' but also the expression of that pride specifically in Israel's major sanctuary Bethel. It is here above all that they stumble in their guilt, here that in the cult they seek Yahweh and fail to find him since he has withdrawn his presence from them. If this argument is correct and the expression refers primarily to the Bethel sanctuary, it follows that Judah was not originally involved and that its inclusion is secondary. Thus we appear to have here a deliberate extension of the range of the prophet's word to include Judah also. In its new context גאון־ישראל has

acquired fresh meaning relevant to the southern kingdom.
R.E. Clements[46] has argued convincingly that in Psalm 47:5
גאון יעקב, standing as it does in parallel to נחלתנו, is best
understood as a designation of the Jerusalem temple. This, I
suggest, is probably the meaning of גאון־ישראל in the present
Judean form of the saying whose concern is no longer with
Bethel but with Jerusalem. The name Israel is used now not in
its political sense with reference to the northern kingdom but
in its sacral sense of the people of God.[47] In short, in the
present form of the saying it is Jerusalem which comes under
judgement. Despite their elaborate sacrificial rituals (v. 6)
God's people fail to encounter him in their worship; he has
withdrawn from them. Once again it is to be noted that this
stern criticism of Judah's religious life and worship has
emanated not from Hosea but from Judean redactors.

To summarise the conclusions reached thus far: the evidence
suggests that neither the reference to Judah in 12:3 nor that in
5:5 originally formed a part of Hosea's message. They are the
work of Judean redactors who were concerned about the corruption
in Judah's religious life and sought to confront the nation with
a powerful prophetic word, which had already been reinforced by
the catastrophe which had overtaken the northern kingdom. In
12:3 the message is reapplied to Judah by the substitution of
that name in place of Israel. In 5:5 the message is given new
thrust by the addition of a reference to Judah. In both
instances the reapplication of the message is assisted by the
fact that the names of both Jacob and Israel were used in a
sacral sense to denote the people of God, of whom Judah remained
as sole representative after 721 B.C. In 12:3 there is a
comprehensive indictment of Judah's whole way of life; in 5:5
criticism is directed against the Jerusalem cult in its failure
to provide a true means of encounter with Yahweh.

Most of the judgmental sayings which include a reference to
Judah occur within the section 5:8 - 6:6. Following the
important study undertaken by A. Alt,[48] this sequence has been

widely recognised as a unit[49] having a common setting in the
events associated with the Syro-Ephraimite war of 733 B.C. It
is particularly during this period when the fortunes of the two
kingdoms were so closely involved with each other, and the
political activity of each impinged in a serious fashion upon
the other, that we might expect to find Hosea's attention
extended to include Judah, especially in connection with its
relations with Israel. Nevertheless, to admit this in principle
does not forthwith justify the assumption that every saying
within this section which concerns Judah belongs in its present
form to the primary stratum of the material. It is possible
that in some instances at least the material has been supplemented
or in some way reinterpreted. Here, too, each of the sayings must
be considered separately.

5:10-14

Within the section the first reference to Judah occurs in
5:10, a saying which includes both accusation and pronouncement
of judgement against the military leaders (שרים) of Judah. Their
guilt is compared to that of 'those who remove the boundary',
that is to say, those who encroach unjustly on territory which
is their neighbours'. The ancient law invoked here is a
domestic one; it concerns the mutual relationship of those who
together comprise the people of God.[50] The implication of the
accusation thus emphasises the essential unity of Israel and
Judah. The content of the saying is appropriate to the period
of the Syro-Ephraimite war when, as a result of the intervention
of Tiglath-pileser against Syria and Ephraim, the troops[51] of
Ahaz were able to advance northward,[52] and could be accused of
encroaching on Israel's territory. There is no problem,
therefore, about locating this saying within the context of
Hosea's ministry.[53] Moreover, the reference to 'the tribes of
Israel', the only occurrence of the expression in a pre-exilic
prophet, seems particularly appropriate to a setting in the
northern kingdom with its strong associations with pre-
monarchical traditions.[54] Hence, it is not surprising that a

strong body of opinion among commentators is inclined to
attribute this saying to Hosea himself. In light of this, the
nature and scope of the criticism of Judah must be noted. It
is not, as in 12:3, a comprehensive indictment of Judah's
entire way of life, nor, as in 5:5, criticism of her cultic
worship. The accusation is specific and limited; it concerns
Judah's hostile attitude towards the northern kingdom. The
prophet speaks from an 'all Israel' perspective (בשבטי ישראל)
and condemns the disintegration of the people of God.

    The association of Judah with Ephraim in the pronouncement
of judgement of v. 12 also has an appropriate setting in the
period of the Syro-Ephraimite war. Both north and south shared
in the guilt of their internecine hostility with its disastrous
consequences, Ephraim in conspiring with Syria[55] against Judah
(v. 11), and Judah by its military opportunism already condemned
in v. 10. More than political coexistence is at stake as far
as the prophet is concerned. Their very existence as the
people of one God demanded recognition of their mutual
interdependence.

    The parallelism of Ephraim and Judah continues through
vv. 13-14. Here, too, the meaning is elucidated when it is seen
in the context of the Syro-Ephraimite war and its aftermath.
Both kingdoms suffered at this time through their mutual
hostility, while much of Ephraim's territory was subjugated by
Tiglath-pileser. Judah, by its appeal to Assyria for help, may
be said to have moved voluntarily towards vassalage.[56]
Commentators in general agree that this passage belongs to the
period of Hosea's ministry.[57] Indeed, the reference to Judah
is so appropriate to the circumstances of the period and its
particular concerns that it may be questioned whether the
parallelism between Ephraim and Judah did not originally extend
into v. 13b, reading וישלח יהודה.[58] Whether this surmise is
correct or not, it is the prophet's own contemporaries in the
north who are directly addressed in the concluding words: 'but
he is not able to cure you or heal your wound'. It is the

people of the north who form his immediate audience, and it is perhaps for this reason that the parallelism between Ephraim and Judah has been deliberately dropped in the latter part of v. 13. It is clear, however, that the point open to dispute is the extent of the reference to Judah and not the fact that it is included as an object of the prophet's denunciation.

In short, the reason for the inclusion of Judah with Ephraim in both guilt and punishment in vv. 10, 12, 13, 14 is to be explained by the particular circumstances of the Syro-Ephraimite war. It is the recognition of this historical context which has contributed largely to the change in the general consensus of scholarly opinion so that the view taken by Harper,[59] for example, that Israel should be substituted for Judah throughout the passage, no longer prevails. Moreover, as far as syntax is concerned, nothing in the structure of the verses in question suggests that the references to Judah are a secondary expansion of the prophet's message, nor are there grounds for suspecting that the name Judah has been substituted for Israel. Indeed the MT carries conviction as authentic in that the parallelism between Ephraim and Judah is not rigidly maintained but, as is entirely appropriate to the circumstances of Hosea's ministry, with v. 13b attention is once more focussed primarily on the northern kingdom. Yet Hosea regards both nations alike as implicated in the guilt and the judgement, for his concern throughout is with the disruption of the unity which should have characterised the one people of the one God. In the rupture of that relationship both north and south have, for their own ends, resorted to Assyria for assistance at various times, an alliance repugnant to the prophet.[60] We conclude, then, that the references to Judah in 5:10-14 belong to the primary stratum of the material.

6:4

The widely accepted view that 5:8 - 6:6 form a literary unit, which is reflected in the arrangement of the material in the standard commentaries,[61] has led to the corresponding

JUDAH AND THE DAVIDIC MONARCHY

assumption that the reference to Judah which follows in 6:4 also belongs to the primary northern material. Too little critical attention seems to have been paid to this question, since clearly the conclusions drawn from the examination of 5:10-14 can only be valid for 6:4 if it has an integral connection with that passage. I do not wish to deny that in the present form of the text 5:8 - 6:6 form a connected sequence, but it must be recognised that this connection may be editorial, and that the units which together now form the sequence may not themselves have an inner coherence such as Mays,[62] for example, suggests. It is this question which I now wish to pursue, for it is perhaps significant that Mays follows his statement that 'the collectors assembled this larger composition of related material because they knew or recognised its coherence' by the comment, 'under just what specific circumstances each saying was spoken and with what interval between them cannot be known'. He thus allows, in effect, for a considerable variation in situational context. As the text stands, the song of penitence in 6:1-3 is clearly intended as a response to the threat of Yahweh's withdrawal in 5:15. The LXX, by supplying in its use of λέγοντες at the end of 5:15 an explicit connection with the penitential song which follows, not only serves to emphasise the link between them but implies that the expression of penitence is acceptable to Yahweh. Whether this is the intention of the MT also is not clear. Indeed, the response of Yahweh in 6:4 makes it doubtful. More probably the song is to be regarded as the superficial penitence of a complacent nation.[63] Wolff comments that the words sound like a kind of self-appeasement (Selbstbeschwichtigung), especially since Yahweh is not directly addressed.[64] Either way, however, the penitential song of 6:1-3 is closely connected with 5:15, whether as the response required by Yahweh, or as the inadequate response offered by the people. Yet the question must be raised whether this necessarily implies that it has an integral, as opposed to a redactional, connection with 5:8-14. The conclusion to which I came in the previous chapter, that two distinct theologies

of repentance can be traced in the material, the one coming from
Hosea himself, the other arising from later Judean influence, led
me to the view that 5:15 belongs not to the primary material but
to the influence of redactors,[65] a conclusion supported by the
language used. In this case 5:15 can have no intrinsic
connection with 5:8-14. An examination of the material
corroborates this view. The link between 5:15 and the preceding
verses is a purely external one provided by the catchword אלך.
The simile which appears in v. 14 does not continue into v. 15.
In v. 14 Yahweh is depicted as a lion which carries off its
helpless prey. There is no escape from his judgement. But the
judgement of v. 15 is described in quite different terms as the
withdrawal of Yahweh from his sinful people. Wolff[66] seems
scarcely justified in his view that the figure of v. 14 extends
into v. 15 and that מקומי is intended as a reference to the
lion's lair. Even if such a meaning for מקום can be supported
elsewhere, though I consider this to be doubtful,[67] the marked
difference in the nature of the judgement expressed in the two
verses argues against it. It is worth noting that although
J.L. Mays is convinced that 5:15 has originated with Hosea he
recognises that it stands apart both from the verses which
precede it and from those which follow.[68] He notes rightly
that the theriomorphism in v. 14 is dropped and that the
connection lies, as I have argued, in the catchword אלך.
Nonetheless he considers v. 15 to be an indispensable transition
to the penitential song, and comments that 'what the announcement
of Yahweh's withdrawal does in effect is to interpret Yahweh's
wrath in such a way that the experience of punishment becomes
an invitation to penitence'. Yahweh is thus portrayed as 'the
God who waits for the response of His people'.[69] However, it
is this very emphasis on repentance as the necessary prelude to
salvation which I have argued is not characteristic of Hosea's
message but belongs to its later interpretation. For Hosea it
is the expression of Yahweh's love not of his anger which can
achieve the restoration of his people.[70] To summarize: v. 15 is

to be understood as a redactional expansion which provides a smooth transition from 5:8-14 to 6:1-6. The two passages therefore, have no intrinsic connection with each other. The conclusions drawn from the historical setting of 5:8-14 in the Syro-Ephraimite war and its aftermath, which accounts for the inclusion of Judah with Ephraim in the prophet's message, do not apply automatically to 6:1-6. Indeed, we find when we turn to 6:4, where also Judah is included with Ephraim, that the question at issue is a very different one. It is no longer the mutual relationship of the two kingdoms which is the focus of attention, a fact rightly emphasised by Wolff[71] in his comment that in this context 'the relationship between Ephraim and Judah plays no role' (die Beziehungen von Ephraim und Judah zueinander keine Rolle spielen).[72] Instead, the saying is concerned with the loyal devotion (חסד) which ought to exist between the nation and their God. It is clear, then, that the conclusions reached concerning 5:8-14 on the basis of their particular concern with the interrelationship of the two kingdoms cannot be determinative in assessing the likely provenance of the reference to Judah in 6:4. This reference must be considered independently.

The song of penitence in 6:1-3 draws largely on the language of fertility religion.[73] It should probably 'be understood entirely in terms of the popular piety which had been influenced by the Canaanization of the Yahweh cult'.[74] Since Hosea himself boldly employs motifs from Canaanite religion as the vehicle of his message, Mays is perhaps justified in describing the song as having a 'double character; its language is determined in part by its relation to Hosea's preaching, but its significance and intention depends (sic) on the cultic environment of Israel's Canaanized worship'.[75] It is followed by Yahweh's response in 6:4-6 which is itself closely connected with the following passage in vv. 7-10 for, as Wolff observes,[76] והמה never introduces a new prophetic saying. In this passage (vv. 7-10) interest is focussed solely on the northern kingdom

and no accusation is directed against Judah. The suspicion thus
arises that the reference to Judah in v. 4 is not appropriate
to the context, which is corroborated by the fact that
references to Judah which appear to belong to the primary
stratum of the material are indirect references, unlike the
example under discussion here. The only other passages which
can be described as directly addressed to Judah are 4:15 where
a third person reference to Judah is followed by a series of
imperatives which (in the present form of the text) seem to be
addressed directly to Judah, and 6:11, both of which I have
concluded are redactional.[77] On balance it seems plausible to
conclude that in 6:4, as in 12:3, the name Judah has been
substituted for Israel, which originally stood in parallel with
Ephraim. Whether this is the result of scribal error or an
editorial change of deliberate and serious intention it is
impossible to say with certainty. In view of the fact that
redactional influence on the text has already become evident
beyond any reasonable doubt, the latter alternative seems the
more likely. If we are correct in concluding that this
reference to Judah, in which its entire relationship of
commitment to Yahweh expressed in the word חסד is called into
question, belongs to the secondary stratum of the material, it is
significant that here once more comprehensive criticism of the
southern kingdom is not to be attributed to Hosea himself.

8:14

There remains one further judgmental saying in which Judah
is included with the northern kingdom. In 8:14 both structure
and content of the verse indicate that its original context
was different from that in which it now stands. Not only is it
set apart from the preceding verses by its use of imperfect
consecutives, but its concern also differs. Moreover, the
background of prosperity implicit in its reference to extensive
building works is hardly compatible with the distress portrayed
in the rest of the chapter which, as I have argued elsewhere,[78]
should be regarded as a unit rather than as the product of a

process of compilation. Yet, as I have emphasised,[79] the view
that the contextualisation of a saying is redactional does not
necessarily imply that the origin of the saying should be
regarded as secondary. Wolff[80] holds that the content of
v. 14a is probably attributable to Hosea himself, a possibility
which Mays[81] also admits though with considerably less conviction.
Certainly the language here is reminiscent of Hosea's use of שכח
(2:15; 4:6; 13:6) to describe Israel's sin as forgetfulness of
Yahweh and his requirements, and of his use of הרבה (8:11; 10:1)
in attacking the proliferation of sacrifices which he deplores.
Although this in itself is clearly insufficient evidence on
which to base arguments for attributing the saying to Hosea,[82]
there is, on balance, nothing which prohibits such an
attribution. Consequently, I find myself in agreement with
Wolff on this point. It must be admitted that the resemblance
between the latter part of v. 14 and the judgmental sayings in
Amos chs. 1 and 2, especially that of 2:5, raises the question
whether a connection exists with the Judean redaction of the
book of Amos,[83] implying that Hos. 8:14b is also redactional.
But the resemblance is equally explicable as the use by Hosea
of a stereotyped formula already in existence.[84] Certainly,
v. 14a needs to be linked with a pronouncement of judgement
such as that provided by v. 14b. We come then to the point at
issue. The present position of the saying is undoubtedly
editorial. Nevertheless, is there any reason to regard the
saying as secondary in origin? Since the saying is now
detached from its original context, the question of its
origin must be determined largely on the grounds of its
compatibility with the circumstances of Hosea's ministry.
First, however, a question of exegesis must be resolved. Why
are these building works condemned? Is its motivation to be
found in the prophet's mistrust of city life,[85] or is criticism
directed against the nation's dependence on material protection
for its security?[86] It is difficult to find substantial
evidence in support of the former suggestion. The references

to the destruction of fortresses (10:14; 11:6) which Wolff[87] adduces in this connection indicate not so much the prophet's dislike of city life as the extent of the disaster which he envisages. The evidence of 10:13 can be offered in support of the second alternative, but there the sin in question is specified: 'you have trusted in your chariots[88] and in the multitude of your warriors'. This is not closely parallel to 8:14 where no specific accusation is made, and we must ask whether some particular historical situation lies behind the judgmental saying of 8:14 which would make the association of Israel's palaces[89] with Judah's fortified cities especially meaningful. It is arguable that something more serious than over-grandiose building operations must have provoked the stricture that Israel had forgotten its Maker. If, however, the situation to which this saying relates is that of mutual hostility between Israel and Judah, such as we found presupposed by 5:8-14, there is both reason for the association of Israel's palaces with Judah's fortified cities,[90] and an explanation why the sin in question is regarded with such gravity. The palaces built by Israel for her kings are the result of schism from Judah and the establishing of an independent monarchy. Likewise Judah's fortified cities are necessitated by her hostility against Israel. If this interpretation of 8:14 is correct, the criticism levelled here against the two kingdoms is more than social comment on the extravagance of the time. It arises from a theological conviction that the disruption of the unity between the kingdoms is in itself sin against Yahweh for which he will call his people to account.[91] Each occasion of mutual hostility on the part of Israel and Judah is evidence of their forgetfulness of the one Lord to whom they owe allegiance. Understood in this way the saying fits the circumstances of Hosea's ministry; to this we may add the conclusion reached above that nothing in the forms of expression of the saying militates against its attribution to Hosea. In accordance with the stance which I have adopted of accepting the tradition for those sayings where no compelling reason can be urged against it,[92] I conclude that it has a place in the primary stratum of the material and is not to be regarded as redactional. Here again it is significant that although the prophet's criticism of Judah in 8:14 is severe, it is not of a comprehensive kind but relates specifically to the rupture of Judah's relationship with Israel.

In short, an examination of the judgmental sayings in which Judah is associated with Israel suggests that they fall into two categories. Those which emanate from Hosea direct criticism against Judah in one specific area, namely its hostility towards Israel, since disunity between north and south is a denial of their commitment to the one Lord. In contrast, the references to Judah which appear to owe their origin to Judean redactors are distinguished by an altogether more comprehensive criticism of Judah's life and worship. It is clear, therefore, that Hosea's attitude towards Judah cannot be described as essentially negative, nor his attitude towards his own nation as nationalistic; nor are the Judean redactors biassed in favour of Judah. Rather it is from the latter that far-reaching criticism comes as they strive to preserve the authentic faith in the midst of increasing apathy and corrupt practice.

4:15

From the judgmental sayings I turn now to the one example of a warning to the nation concerning its cult practice. In 4:15 Israel is addressed directly and Judah is included in the third person. The odd grammatical structure of v. 15a suggests that not only the name Judah but the entire clause in which it occurs, אל־יאשם יהודה is a supplementary expansion of the primary form of the saying. The verse opens with direct address to Israel: אם־זנה אתה ישראל. This is continued in the three prohibitions with which the verse concludes:

ואל תבאו הגלגל ואל תעלו בית און ואל תשבעו חי יהוה:

Between them, however, there occurs a third person reference to

Judah. It is surprising in view of its structure that this
passage is one of only two which Harper considers are
attributable to Hosea himself,[93] and he adduces evidence which
he believes indicates that Judeans did in fact worship at the
Gilgal sanctuary together with those of the northern kingdom;[94]
however, the evidence is less than convincing. J.L. Mays is
also prepared to attribute to Hosea the admonition to Judah,
though he feels it necessary to comment, in dissenting from
Harper's position, 'Whether Judeans were inclined to visit
Gilgal and Bethel is beside the point'[95] - a statement which
hardly strengthens his argument. It is disappointing to find
that neither he nor Harper before him has paid adequate
attention to the sentence structure which is remarkable since
Israel, the nation directly addressed, is named in the opening
subordinate clause introduced by אם, while the main verb which
follows (אל־יאשמו) makes reference indirectly to those who do
not constitute the prophet's immediate audience. The impression
that the reference to Judah is a supplementary expansion of a
saying addressed originally to the northern kingdom is
strengthened by the fact that, *pace* Harper, the Old Testament
does not provide evidence that after the dissolution of the
united kingdom Judeans went to northern sanctuaries to worship.
It is not without significance that the similar prohibition in
Amos 5:5 is addressed solely to the northern kingdom. One
might also add that the saying of 4:15 occurs in a context
which is otherwise concerned exclusively with the northern
kingdom; but this is scarcely a sound argument. It must be
recognised that there is no integral connection between v. 15
and the preceding description of Israel's degenerate religious
practices, and the present relationship in which they stand may
be due to their common theme of 'harlotry', a theme which runs
through vv. 12-14.

Before leaving this passage other possibilities of
interpretation should be noted. Van Selms[96] has offered the
suggestion that the word אל in v. 15 is not the common

negative particle but an example of northern dialect having the
meaning 'surely', a usage which may be compared with that which
occurs in Ugaritic.[97] The resultant meaning however, does not
seem particularly apt:

> If thou, Israel, play the harlot,
>   surely Judah offends.

It is worth noting that אל occurs twice elsewhere in Hosea in
its common Hebrew sense as a negative introducing a prohibition
(4:4; 9:1). As emphasising particles we find כי several times
(6:9; 8:6; 9:12; 10:3) and אך (4:4; 12:9, 12). Yet, in
whatever way the word אל is understood, the reference to Judah
seems to be a rather weak aside, and its main result is to divert
attention from those who are primarily addressed in the saying.

Another possibility is offered by the LXX rendering of the
verse in which the sentence division differs from that of the
MT and the reference to Judah is more fully integrated into the
prohibition:

καὶ ὁ λαὸς οὐ συνίων συνεπλέκετο μετὰ πόρνης. Σὺ δέ, Ισραηλ,
μὴ ἀγνόει, καὶ Ιουδα, μὴ εἰσπορεύεσθε κτλ.

On balance, however, it appears unlikely that this represents
the original form of the saying from which the more difficult
MT has come.[98] The concluding words of v. 14 in the Hebrew
text, with their alliterative quality, ועם לא־יבין ילבט have
the appearance of a traditional proverbial saying used here to
drive home the intended warning. In contrast the LXX, 'the
people without[99] understanding was entangled[100] with a harlot',
is simply a rather verbose and generalised repetition of what
has preceded. One can only conjecture the reasons which
resulted in the divergence of meaning, but once אם came to be
understood as עם, perhaps through the occurrence of עם twice in
the preceding verse, a different sentence division was
inevitable. But whatever the processes by which the LXX text
came to diverge from the MT,[101] it seems more likely that the
more difficult MT is to be preferred.

On balance, then, I conclude that the reference to Judah in 4:15 is secondary, and has expanded a saying addressed originally to the northern kingdom. The change from singular pronoun אתה to plural verb forms תשבעו ..... תעלו ..... תבאו cannot be taken as firm evidence to the contrary, for the stylistic variation from singular to plural can be paralleled elsewhere.[102] If my view is correct, we have here an example of a later reshaping of the prophet's message so that the example of Israel's apostasy might be held up as a warning to Judah at a time when there still seemed to be opportunity for repentance.

We come now to consider whether in its present form in which Judah is addressed the purport of the saying remains consistent with the prophet's original intention, or whether it now contains some new element or emphasis. The saying in its present form, with its warning to the people of Judah to keep themselves free from the guilt incurred by Israel, is an appropriate expression of the fierce opposition to Bethel and other northern sanctuaries which manifested itself in the Josianic reform.[103] To try to reach back to the original form of the saying in its northern context is more problematic. If the view is correct, that not only the name Judah but the clause which contains it is a secondary addition, and that its loose connection with the sentence as a whole is evidence of this, it is arguable that by setting aside the words in question (אל־יאשם יהודה) we are left with what is in essence the primary form of the saying, addressed consistently to Israel:

> If you, Israel, play the harlot,
> do not enter[104] into Gilgal,
> nor go up to Bethaven,
> nor swear, 'As Yahweh lives'.

In short, Hosea's words are to be understood, not as an absolute prohibition of worship at Bethel and Gilgal, but as the prohibition of worship there as long as Israel remains guilty of 'harlotry'. Such worship is unfitting at the ancient

sanctuaries hallowed by Israel's past tradition of encounter with
God. It belongs rather to the hill-top shrines and shady trees
where the rites of the fertility cult are practised (4:13). Thus
it is not the sanctuaries at Gilgal and Bethel *per se* which are
condemned,[105] but the nation by whose apostasy the sanctuaries
are defiled. This understanding of the passage in question
offers an adequate explanation for the inclusion of the third
prohibition concerning the swearing of the Yahwistic oath. The
prophet does not condemn the oath itself, but its use by
apostate Israel. The inclusion of this prohibition had seemed
to call for an explanation: on what grounds might the prophet
take exception to this oath formula? The difficulty was felt
already in the Targum, which found it necessary to clarify the
meaning by adding לשקר, 'and swear not falsely'.[106] Modern
commentators also have felt the need to elucidate the reason
behind the objection to what seems from the Old Testament
itself to be an acceptable oath. As an example we may cite
J.L. Mays: 'Hosea even goes so far as to prohibit the traditional
oath taken on the life of Yahweh (Judg. 8:19; Ruth 3:13;
1 Sam. 14:39, etc.). In the mythological poetry about Baal
from Ugarit, the cry

> "Alive is the powerful Baal
> Existent the Prince, the Lord of Earth"!

is the greeting which interprets the return of the land's
fertility in spring. The formula calling upon the "life of
Yahweh" may have been used in a similar fashion in the fertility
cult and given cause for Hosea's prohibition'.[107] Clearly Mays
is driven to propose a hypothetical explanation of the reason
why Hosea should regard the oath taken in Yahweh's name as
objectionable. He goes on, significantly, to note - without
further comment - that 'Jeremiah reckons the oath-formula
legitimate when it is sworn in truth (Jer. 4:2; 5:2)'.[108] This
is certainly true elsewhere in the Old Testament, as the
references given above by Mays indicate. It is true also of
Hosea if the view for which I have argued above is correct, for

then it is not the oath itself to which the prophet objects, but the use of the sacred oath by adulterous Israel, a nation who 'have left their God to play the harlot' (v. 12).[109] Two further points must be taken into account if the suggestion I have proposed is to be credible. First, the objection may be raised that the designation of Bethel as Bethaven in 4:15 implies that the sanctuary itself is obnoxious to the prophet, that it is 'a house of wickedness'. However, it must be recognised that the vocalisation of בֵּית־אָוֶן which gives to the name a perjorative meaning may itself be secondary in origin.[110] The original form may have been בית־און whether in the sense of 'house of wealth', a meaning און has in 12:9, or 'house of lament',[111] a meaning it has in 9:4. Secondly, the question must be raised whether the apparently similar saying in Amos 5:5, where the shrines at Bethel and Gilgal are clearly condemned, does not argue against the view of Hos. 4:15 which I have proposed above. But in the Amos passage it is made explicit that to worship at these sanctuaries is not compatible with seeking Yahweh; we must beware of allowing a superficial similarity between two sayings to disguise an essential difference of emphasis. Neither the situation nor the attitude of Hosea and Amos are the same. It is entirely reasonable in the light of his greater involvement in the life of the northern kingdom that Hosea should evince greater respect and sympathy towards the ancient shrines of his own country, hallowed by past tradition but now defiled by the rituals practised there by his contemporaries, than Amos did with his southern antecedents. One may note in passing that Amos perhaps shows himself less virulent towards the southern sanctuary of Beersheba than towards the northern sanctuaries of Bethel and Gilgal, for although Beersheba is associated with these in the prohibition of Amos 5:5, it is not included in the doom which is pronounced - assuming, of course, that the Beersheba reference is original.

To summarize: the structure of 4:15 is itself such as to suggest that the original form of the saying has been supplemented by the addition of a warning to Judah (אל-יאשם יהודה) to avoid the apostasy of which the northern kingdom had been guilty. In its original form the saying was addressed only to Hosea's own contemporaries in the north. The secondary expansion of the saying to include an indirect reference to Judah detracts from the direct thrust of the words, and, in the hostile attitude it expresses to the major sanctuaries of the northern kingdom, shows an affinity with the motivation of the Josianic purge of those sanctuaries in the interests of the centralisation of sacrificial worship in Jerusalem, or at least with the Deuteronomistic account of the purge.[112] The fact that the apparently similar sentiment expressed in Amos 5:5 which explicitly prohibits worship at Bethel and Gilgal is now seen to be related, not to the primary northern form of the saying but to the secondary Judean expansion of it, is significant. Hostility to the northern sanctuaries themselves emanates from Judean circles. The northern prophet holds them in higher esteem, although the criticism which he makes of the religious life of his contemporaries is nonetheless severe and unremitting. The warning to Judah which has been added by redactors is in accordance with the implications of the theology of repentance which we saw in the previous chapter was also attributable to them, namely that hope of reform from within the nation still existed. Hosea, in contrast, recognises that for his own people this is no longer available as a way forward to a renewed relationship with God.

10.11

From concern with the nation's present activity in 4:15 we turn now to a reminder of Yahweh's purpose for them in the past, described in 10:11, a purpose which had remained sadly unfulfilled during their history:

I will harness Ephraim;
Judah shall plough;
Jacob shall harrow.[113]

Scholars differ in their assessment as to whether the reference here to Judah belongs to the primary northern core of the material. Mowinckel[114] regards it without hesitation as a secondary addition, describing it as a 'clumsily placed written gloss', on the grounds that the parallelism of the verse requires that Ephraim and Jacob should balance each other as identical entities leaving no room for a third party. Mays,[115] too, attributes it to the work of a redactor on the grounds that the name Judah does not fit into the sequence, though he differs from Mowinckel in regarding it not simply as an addition but as a substitution for the name Israel. Wolff,[116] on the other hand, finds no difficulty in the idea that the prophet is here concerned with the entire nation.

In attempting to reach a conclusion on a point which has given rise to such a diversity of opinion among scholars the first requirement must be to define the limits of the unit to which v. 11 belongs. The imagery of ploughing and reaping binds together vv. 11-13a,[117] while a new subject begins in vv. 13b-15. Seen in context v. 12 is not, as it appears at first sight, an exhortation addressed to the prophet's contemporaries, but refers instead to Yahweh's commission to his people in the past which they have failed to fulfil. Indeed, the nation's history is described in v. 13a; it is a history of failure.

Such is the context, with its past orientation, in which the origin of the reference to Judah in v. 11 must be considered. Wolff admits that its presence is surprising here, though he argues for its originality on the grounds that structurally the threefold reference in v. 11 to Ephraim, Judah and Jacob corresponds to the threefold exhortation of v. 12 and to the threefold description of the nation's sin in v. 13a, and that we have evidence elsewhere for Hosea's concern extending beyond the northern kingdom to 'all Israel'. Accordingly, Wolff understands v. 11 to refer first to the separate kingdoms of Ephraim and Judah, then to the whole nation as Jacob. I do not wish to dispute that this is the meaning of the text in its present form, but the question remains to be answered whether this form is original. There is without doubt an 'all Israel' perspective to Hosea's thought,[118] but Wolff's argument from structure does not necessarily entail the corollary that the name Judah is itself part of the original saying, only that it does not represent simply an addition to the text. Mowinckel is surely correct in his view that the sense of the passage requires that the names should refer to the same entity. The one who is harnessed is the one who is to plough and harrow in preparation for God's harvest. The one on whose neck the yoke is laid[119] is described specifically as Ephraim. It is Ephraim who is the trained heifer, just as the bride who comes out of Egypt[120] and the son who is called out of Egypt[121] are the northern kingdom as far as Hosea's message is concerned, even though these traditions had come to form part of Judah's heritage as truly as Israel's. Whether we follow Wolff and understand vv. 13b-15 as explanatory of vv. 11-13a and connected with vv. 9-10 by the common theme of war, or dissociate them as Mays does, the opening words of v. 11 make clear that Ephraim is here the focus of attention. It is they, the prophet's audience, who are referred to in v. 11, and addressed in v. 12, with a reminder of the task to which they had been called by God.[122] We have noted already in our discussion of 12:3[123] that the name Jacob there referred in its original context to the northern kingdom[124] and was later reinterpreted as referring to Judah. This seems to be true also of 10:11, whether we regard Judah as a substitution for the name Israel or simply as an addition. Hosea is here concerned with the history of failure of his own people. Under redactional influence the scope of the message has been widened to include the entire people of Yahweh, reaffirming the belief that Ephraim and Judah together constitute the true people of God. This same conviction underlies the 'all Israel' perspective of Deuteronomy, the Deuteronomistic history, and comes to clear expression also in Ezekiel's hopes for the future (37:15-23). Once again it

is significant that the comprehensive criticism which we find in
v. 13a is levelled against Judah not by Hosea himself but by
redactors who have substituted or added its name here. This
conclusion is in line with the results already reached from the
examination of other relevant passages.

6:11

Before turning to consider the salvation sayings in which
Judah is included I wish to review the saying in 6:11 which,
because of the uncertainty of its meaning, I have so far
refrained from including in any of the categories of sayings.
The ambiguity lies in the meaning of the word קציר. Does this
betoken salvation for Judah, or judgement? If the sentence
division of the MT is retained the meaning is as follows:

> Also for you, Judah, a harvest is appointed[125]
> when I restore the fortunes of my people.

It is, however, the practice of most recent English versions[126]
to redivide the sentence and to connect v. 11b with 7:1.[127] The
words addressed to Judah in v. 11a then stand apart from the
following verses. In view of their loose connection by the
particle with what precedes,[128] many commentators,[129] rightly I
believe, consider them to be redactional comment. Undoubtedly
they interrupt the sequence of thought which extends from
6:10 - 7:2. But in what sense is קציר to be understood? Its
association with the expression שוב־שבות might be taken to
indicate that קציר also is to be understood as an expression of
blessing. Yet the fact that it is connected by גם and not by an
adversative particle to the preceding catalogue of Israel's
wickedness and its implied consequences makes it clear that
קציר has here a judgmental sense, a meaning which the
metaphorical use of the word has elsewhere in the Old Testament.[130]
V. 11a is best understood, then, as redactional comment intended
to give warning to Judah in the light of the disastrous history
of the northern kingdom.[131] The present difficult sentence
division of the MT which links קציר, an expression of judgement,

so closely with בשובי שבות, which signifies salvation, may have arisen as a result of the addition of the redactional comment, since the existing parallelism of the passage in which בשובי שבות עמי[132] was parallel to כרפאי לישראל was thereby disturbed. A different and chiastic parallelism arose as a result, giving rise to the existing form of the text:

גם־יהודה שת קציר לך
בשובי שבות עמי: כרפאי לישראל......

Whether the saying in v. 11a may have originated with Hosea, and if so in what sense, it is impossible now to determine, for the saying is too truncated to allow of a firm decision on this point. But there can be little doubt that its present position, and the meaning which it derives from its present context, is redactional. The warning presupposes an attitude of complacency among the people of Judah of the kind reflected also in Jer. 5:12ff.:

> They have spoken falsely of the Lord,
>   and have said, 'He will do nothing;
> no evil will come upon us,
>   nor shall we see sword or famine.'[133]

Once again significant for the present study is that the comprehensive judgement pronounced on Judah originates not from Hosea but from Judean redactors who were under no illusions as to the seriousness of their nation's sin.

We turn next to the group of salvation sayings which make reference to Judah. Arguments were set out in the previous chapter for maintaining that expressions of future hope, far from being incompatible with Hosea's message of judgement, were an essential element in his proclamation. So far, however, only salvation sayings relating solely to the northern kingdom have been discussed. There remain three passages to be considered in which Judah, too, is included in the future hope. The three passages differ considerably from each other in content: in 1:7 Judah alone is to be the recipient of the promised

salvation; the hope to which expression is given in 2:2 is no
less than the restoration of unity between Israel and Judah
under common leadership; in 3:5 the future envisaged includes
the return of Israel to its former allegiance to the Davidic
king. As far as 1:7 is concerned, it is generally agreed by
scholars that we have redactional material of Judean origin.[134]
The assurance with which this conclusion is accepted is
reflected in the NEB treatment of the material, where 1:7 is
removed from its place in the text and relegated to a footnote!
3:5 also, at least in its reference to the Davidic king, is widely
regarded as Judean in origin.[135] In contrast, a number of
scholars accept 2:2 as belonging to the northern core of the
material.[136] Despite their common concern with Judah, the
important differences in the content of the sayings require
that the question of their origins must be examined with
reference to each individually. The difficult nature of this
undertaking is evident, and in the interests of impartiality
I have endeavoured, in evaluating the evidence, to avoid as
far as is possible the extremes of both conservatism and
scepticism with regard to their Hosean origins, while giving
due weight to the fact that for some cause or other they have
found a place within the tradition of Hosea's sayings. This
is a datum from which to begin the investigation. To it we must
add the conclusion reached thus far that Hosea himself was
not anti-Judean in outlook.

1:7

As far as 1:7 is concerned, it is superficially plausible
to adopt the view that we have here the comment of a Judean
redactor, and that the hope expressed has no place in Hosea's
thought. Further consideration, however, reveals certain
problems inherent in this view. How does this statement of
confidence in Judah's future relate to the redactional activity
of which we have so far found evidence? We have seen that the
redactors, far from regarding the situation in Judah with
optimism, were striving for the very survival of the people of

JUDAH AND THE DAVIDIC MONARCHY 89

God, and to this end reinterpreted for Judah Hosea's words of
accusation and judgement. In so doing they widened the range of
the criticism which he had directed against Judah and which
related specifically to its disunity with the northern kingdom,
so that it included Judah's entire way of life and its cultic
activity.

The complexity of the question may be illustrated by the
example of the widely differing conclusions reached by two of the
commentators on this passage. G.A. Danell[137] attributes 1:7 to
Hosea, believing that during the early part of the prophet's
ministry, which he finds reflected in chs. 1-3, Hosea's hopes
were set on Judah. Disillusionment then followed, Danell argues,
and consequently Judah was included with Israel in the
denunciations of chs. 4-14. Wolff,[138] on the other hand,
considers 1:7 to be evidence of an early Judean redaction which
supplemented Hosea's message with a Judean salvation eschatology,
a redaction which was wholly distinct from that which later
applied Hosea's judgmental sayings to Judah. However, he does
not entirely divorce the verse in essence from Hosea's own
ministry, but suggests that a connection is to be seen with the
latest phase of Hosea's activity when he looked with hope towards
certain circles in Judah. Evidence for this Wolff finds in 12:1b,
an extremely problematic verse discussed at length below.[139] It
is significant that Wolff finds at least some connection between
the hope expressed in 1:7 and Hosea's own attitude towards Judah.

It cannot be denied that the saying of 1:7 is unique in its
expectation of salvation for Judah alone, a word of salvation
set in contrast to a judgmental saying concerning Israel. There
can be no question at all that the position of 1:7 is secondary.
It interrupts the sequence of the passage, and both in form and
in content is inappropriate to its context. The arrangement of
vv. 2-9 is highly schematic.[140] Four times Yahweh commands that
a symbolic action should be performed; each time the command is
followed by an explanation of it which is introduced by כי.
Increasing brevity of expression leads the passage to its

dramatic climax:

v. 2	ויאמר יהוה אל־הושע
v. 4	ויאמר יהוה אליו
v. 6	ויאמר לו
v. 9	ויאמר

The form of 1:7 is clearly intrusive here. Of this there can be no doubt. Its content is also inappropriate on two counts: first that it is a salvation saying in a context otherwise solely concerned with the pronouncement of judgement, and second that it is an isolated and unintegrated reference to Judah in a context otherwise solely concerned with the northern kingdom. Why then has it been introduced here? It is easy to rush to the conclusion that it is the comment of a chauvinistic Judean who wishes to contrast the favoured place which Judah holds in the purposes of Yahweh with the disastrous fate of Israel. We have seen, however, that this is not consistent with the attitude of the redactors and their serious desire to challenge their own nation to new commitment, of which we have found evidence elsewhere. The transmission and reapplication of the prophetic word were not intended to bolster the confidence of a nation already prone to be complacent.[141] Its purpose was no less serious, and no less worthy, than that of Hosea's message to the northern kingdom. If we accept this premise, then it is reasonable to believe that the incorporation of 1:7 into its present context serves a serious purpose, namely that of defining more exactly the meaning of 'house of Israel' against which the judgement of v. 6 is pronounced. The inclusion here of v. 7 indicates that 'Israel' is to be understood in its limited political sense as a designation of the northern kingdom after the schism, and not in its sacral sense of the people of God. It is, therefore, a serious affirmation of faith that despite the severity of God's judgement there is ground for future hope. God's saving purpose will persist and not be thwarted, but the scene of his saving action will be Judah. That the present setting of the saying is the work of Judean redactors and not of an associate of the prophet in the northern kingdom can be deduced, not from the content of the saying, that it displays a pro-Judean attitude, which is an uncertain criterion as I have emphasised throughout, but from the fact that it is intrusive in the context of the biographical material which in all probability originated in the north among the followers of Hosea.[142] It is highly unlikely that the carefully structured material with its dramatic climax should have been disrupted by the insertion of an intrusive saying by those who were its authors.

Thus far, however, we have considered only the present unsatisfactory position of the saying. We have yet to determine the question of its origin. Two points must be taken into account: does its content require that it should be dated later than the period during which Hosea ministered, and does it conflict with what we have now established to be Hosea's attitude to Judah? To take first the question of date: the view is sometimes expressed that the origin of the sentiment of 1:7 is to be traced to the deliverance of Jerusalem from the armies of Sennacherib in 701 B.C.[143] This is questionable.[144] It presupposes that the saying is not genuinely predictive but is a *vaticinium ex eventu*. Yet, as R.P. Carroll has rightly emphasised in his recent work,[145] we must allow for a predictive element in prophecy even though, as he wisely comments, 'we have no controls by which we could guarantee that any predictive oracle was given before the events to which it referred'. The events of 701 are not the only, nor even the most likely, motivation for the saying in 1:7. It expresses the ancient concept of Holy War whereby deliverance is won by Yahweh's power alone without recourse to human strength.[146] There is no need to regard it as later than Hosea's time. It may, of course, be argued that much of the biblical thinking about war is probably Deuteronomistic in origin. Nevertheless there can be little doubt that an ancient concept underlies it.[147] The second point to be taken into account, which concerns Hosea's attitude to Judah, presents the greater difficulty. Is it conceivable not only that Hosea might have held, but that he would have expressed, a sentiment

of this kind? Evidence from the language used can only be
inconclusive, for if the saying is of secondary origin it may
be a deliberate echo of v. 6. This is the view taken by Wolff[148]
who describes it as an easily recognisable gloss in that it takes
up the key words of v. 6. The evidence of the language used is
ambivalent. The verb הושיע cannot be said to be characteristic
of Hosea for it occurs otherwise only in 14:4; on the other hand
it occurs frequently in the Deuteronomistic literature.[149] On
the other side, however, we may note the rare use of the
preposition ב to express the personal agent.[150] This is not
unknown elsewhere in the Old Testament[151] but, in view of its
general infrequency, the number of occurrences in Hosea is
noteworthy.[152] The sequence of בקשת,בקרב and במלחמה, and the
concrete connotation of 'weapons of war', rather than the
abstract 'warfare', which the latter derives from its context,[153]
occur only in Hosea, and that in 2:20, a passage plausibly
attributed to Hosea himself, as I have argued above.[154] We may
also note that the slight awkwardness of style in that 'the Lord
their God' is referred to in the third person immediately after a
first person verb 'I will save them' has parallels elsewhere in
Hosea. In the context of divine speech the Lord is referred to
in the third person in several passages,[155] though admittedly in
none is there such stark juxtaposition of first and third persons
as there is here. The attribution of the saying to a redactor
does not, of course, ease the difficulty in any way. In any event,
the evidence of the language is not such as to allow conclusions
to be built upon it.

As for the content of 1:7, the conviction that Yahweh's
power is sufficient to deliver his people without the aid of
military resources is consistent with Hosea's thought. The
penitential liturgy (14:2-4) to which the prophet summons Israel
includes a specific repudiation of military aid.[156] In more than
one instance the inadequacy of human might is contrasted with the
power of Yahweh (5:13f.; 7:11f.). Yahweh alone is mighty and
irresistible.

In short, although the language and thought of 1:7 cannot in any way be said to provide proof positive that the saying originated with Hosea, it is clear that there is no need to suppose that they preclude the possibility. The heart of the problem, however, lies in the application of this sentiment to Judah. Is this compatible with what can be known of the prophet's attitude to the southern kingdom? The results of our enquiry so far have shown that Hosea at times includes Judah in his denunciation, but that his criticism relates specifically to the hostile relationships existing between the two kingdoms. It is the later Judean redactors who bring to bear on their nation the full weight of Hosea's judgmental sayings. This fact itself suggests the possibility that as political anarchy and religious apostasy increased in the last years of the northern kingdom Hosea's hopes for the future of God's people may have turned to the southern kingdom.[157] He had seen a breakdown in the transmission of the traditions which he cherished in the established cult of the northern kingdom.[158] Instruction of the people in the law of Yahweh had ceased for the priests themselves were forgetful of that law (4:6). Hosea saw this to be nothing less than the destruction of the people and divine rejection of the priests. Even in the future generation he sees no prospect, but utters the divine word of judgement: 'I also will forget your children'. No sanctuary remains where the traditions of Yahwism can be faithfully preserved and transmitted.[159] Yet there was still one place to which Hosea might look for continuity with the past traditions of his people. Small wonder if his hopes rested there even though it lay beyond the confines of the northern kingdom. In the worship of the Jerusalem temple, despite elements alien to the tradition in which Hosea stood, the traditions of ancient, pre-monarchic Israel had a place, and were celebrated in its festal worship.[160] W. Beyerlin, in discussing the Sinaitic traditions, remarks: 'In the festival worship of the Jerusalem Temple there existed parallel cultic practices to the tradition of Moses' proclamation of the commandments in Ex. 19:7f., 24:3, 7'.[161] This is particularly significant when we consider it against Hosea's criticism of his own people in 8:12: 'Were I to write for him my laws by ten thousands, they would be regarded as a strange thing'.

In short, arguments can be adduced for the view that Hosea's hopes for the continuity of the authentic traditions of Yahwism were compelled, by the deterioration of religious life in the northern kingdom and the consequent break in the means of transmission of those traditions, to centre on the southern kingdom, a people closely allied to his own, whose religious and political institutions were exempt, as far as Hosea was concerned, from the strictures which he addressed to his own people. Whether this belongs to the early period of his ministry, as Danell suggests,[162] or to the latter part as Wolff believes,[163] is difficult to determine. His severe strictures on Israel, that

> there is no faithfulness or kindness,
> and no knowledge of God in the land,

and his indictment of the priesthood for failure to fulfil their obligations occur in ch. 4 which is probably to be dated in Hosea's early period.[164] Similar accusations continue throughout the book, reaching their climax in the condemnation of Samaria's rebellion in 14:1 which probably belongs to the period immediately preceding the final catastrophe.[165] Moreover, at no point have we found any broader criticism of Judah on the part of Hosea, such as Danell's view would require. The wide-ranging criticism we have seen to belong to later redactors. It seems likely, then, that Judah consistently had a positive place in Hosea's thought. We established at the beginning of this study[166] that a movement either from despair to hope or from hope to despair is not discernible in Hosea's attitude to his own nation. But doom is not Yahweh's final word to Israel. Beyond the disaster Hosea sees a new saving action by which Israel herself will be transformed. It may be that his hopes were centred on Judah in the interim period as the preserver of the continuity of the

people of God, a viewpoint which history itself validated. In
short, once the preconception that Hosea as a northerner is
likely to have had an anti-Judean stance is abandoned, the
possibility must be recognised that the saying of 1:7 gives
expression to an aspect of his thought, although undoubtedly
its present position is secondary.

2:2

The second passage for consideration is 2:2. Here a future
is envisaged in which Israel stands alongside Judah as partner
in a reunited nation. Several commentators agree in attributing
this saying, in essence at least, to Hosea.[167] It forms a unit
with 2:1 with perfect consecutive verbs used throughout. It
stands apart, however, from its present context. That 2:1 is
clearly marked off from 1:9 and begins a new unit needs no
argument. Wolff summarizes the position thus: 'a series of
perfect consecutives in 2:1f. sets off this new unit from its
previous context; as a prophetic saying about the future it
stands in contrast to the rigidly styled report concerning the
prophet's family in 1:2-9 with its imperfect consecutives'.[168]
It is, moreover, only loosely connected with v. 3 by means of
the external link provided by the association of the symbolic
names which now bear, not as at first a message of doom, but
a word of hope. That the link is an external one, not
integral to the material, is evident from the fact that the
final words of v. 2 conclude the announcement of salvation and
bring it to a dramatic close. The marked difference of form of
v. 3, a command addressed directly to an unspecified audience,
indicates its separate origin. The unit which we must consider
consists of 2:1-2.

The impersonal style of v. 1, particularly the repeated
passive form יאמר, contrasts with the usual form of the
salvation sayings where divine speech in the first person
emphasises Yahweh's action in salvation.[169] This has naturally
led to doubts about attributing it to Hosea. The problem,
however, is more apparent than real for, as Wolff points out,

'after the announcement of God's action, there is frequently a
transition to a description of Israel's attitude changed by
God's action'.[170] He suggests that vv. 1-2 provide the sequel
to 2:25. Whether this is so or not, it is the detachment of
the saying from its original context which has caused undue
emphasis to be laid on its supposed unusual form. Here the
insights of form criticism are valuable, as Wolff has demonstrated,
and it is evident that objections to Hosea's authorship on
stylistic grounds are not convincing. The passives ימד and יספר
are stereotyped forms deriving from the patriarchal narratives,
and the unexpected impersonal passive יאמר is possibly due to
assimilation to these.

In content v. 1 shows no inconsistencies with Hosea's
situation in the northern kingdom in the 8th century. Indeed,
the portrayal of future hope in terms of increase of population
is particularly appropriate to the period after the Assyrian
invasion of 733 B.C. when Israel's population was decimated,[171]
and to Hosea's conflict with the Baal cult and its promise of
fertility. It is, moreover, to be seen as the counterpart to the
judgmental sayings which include the rising generation, the seed
of future hope, in the proclamation of doom (9:12, 16; 14:1).
It is not without significance that the form in which the promise
is cast is that which agrees with the Jacob tradition in
particular,[172] a tradition which is rarely drawn on by other
prophets but is alluded to in two instances in Hosea (12:4f., 13),
possibly through Hosea's association with Bethel to which this
tradition belonged. Joined with the promise of increased progeny
is the hope of restoration to Yahweh. Those who were named לא
עמי לא will be called בני אל חי. Wolff[173] sees in this change of
terminology evidence of Hosea's creativity in contrast to more
exact imitation which might be expected from a later hand. The
expression בני אל חי is unique in the Old Testament. The
designation of Yahweh as אל חי is itself uncommon,[174] but there
is nothing to require that it should be dated later than Hosea's
period. It may have been prompted by his conflict with the
fertility cult of Canaan in his conviction that Yahweh alone is

the source of life. Above all the words with which v. 2
concludes have unmistakably a north Israelite character:
גדול יום יזרעאל. The loss of the plain of Jezreel to the
Assyrians in 733 B.C. was of serious consequence to Israel.[175]
Moreover, Jezreel had been the scene of Jehu's abortive attempt
to unite the northern and southern kingdoms under his control.[176]
This military terminology belonging to the concept of holy war[177]
may well have epitomised the nationalistic pretensions of Jehu.
There is no reason not to attribute it to the northern prophet
Hosea. That Jezreel held an important place in his thought is
seen from its occurrence as one of the symbolic words of
judgement in ch. 1. It was on account of the bloodshed at
Jezreel that the end of Israel's kingship was threatened (1:4).
Israel's history past and present provided Hosea with many
instances of social injustice and religious corruption, but the
bloodshed specifically associated with Jehu which took place at
Jezreel not only removed the reigning king of Israel but brought
death to the legitimate occupant of David's throne.[178] For
reasons which I shall discuss later this event seemed to Hosea
the ultimate cause of the disaster which was to befall Israel's
reigning dynasty, and beyond that to threaten the very existence
of the institution of kingship in the land.

The terminology used in v. 2 to express the restoration of
unity between Israel and Judah is also suggestive of a northern
origin for the saying. The neutral term ראש to designate the
appointed leader is unlikely to come from Judean circles. It
echoes the terminology used of pre-monarchic leaders (Num. 14:4;
Jud. 11:8) and is associated with the tribes of Israel (1 Sam.
15:17).[179] The contrast between the expression ראש used here and
the royal terminology of Ezek. 37:22: ומלך אחד יהיה לכלם למלך
strengthens the likelihood that the former comes from Hosea and
has not been shaped by Judean influence.[180] Lastly we must
consider the difficult expression ועלו מן הארץ. It is unjustified
to assume that the reference here is to return from exile and
that this expectation must, therefore, post-date the ministry
of Hosea.[181] The singular הארץ is inappropriate to this meaning,

and some commentators have been inclined to emend it to the plural.[182] But throughout the material associated with Hosea's name the singular is used to denote the land given by Yahweh to his people (2:21; 4:3; 9:3). The expression has been variously understood,[183] but the context suggests that the key to its meaning lies in the etymology of Jezreel, 'God sows'. The verb עלה is used of crops sprouting in 10:8, and this gives an appropriate meaning here: 'they shall sprout up from the land'.[184] The promise given is twofold: the population will flourish and increase, and the place where this blessing will be granted will be the land given by Yahweh. The play on the etymology of Jezreel here accords with 2:25, a salvation saying which I have argued above[185] is attributable to Hosea.

In short, nothing in 2:1-2 precludes its attribution to Hosea. The fact that the people of Judah are mentioned before the people of Israel in v. 2 is insufficient to warrant the view that it must come from Judean circles,[186] especially in view of northern elements which have already been noted. It may be that the order has been influenced by Judean hands, but the essence of the saying is entirely consistent with Hosea's circumstances and outlook, a point underlined when we turn to consider the evidence we have concerning his attitude to the reunion of the kingdoms.

Excursus: Hosea's attitude to reunion

In the nature of the case only indirect evidence is available, for the two passages (2:2; 3:5) which refer explicitly to the hope of reunion are *ipso facto* the subject of discussion. The first point I wish to adduce concerns the use of the name Israel. It occurs frequently in the material, usually with reference to the northern kingdom as a political entity distinct from Judah. Occasionally, however, another meaning can be detected. There are in the Old Testament as a whole many instances where the name Israel refers not to the northern kingdom in a political sense but to both northern and southern kingdoms together as the whole people of God.[187] It is

JUDAH AND THE DAVIDIC MONARCHY

the use of the name Israel in this sacral sense in the Hosea material which is significant for the question under discussion here. The clearest example occurs in 5:9 where the saying is addressed to 'the tribes of Israel'. There is thus what might be termed an 'all Israel' perspective to Hosea's message, as he draws on the traditions of pre-monarchic times. The same meaning belongs to the name Israel when it is used in connection with the Exodus tradition in 11:1 and 12:13. That the name Israel in these instances refers to the whole people of God is evident from the fact that when attention is then directed towards the northern kingdom, the prophet's immediate audience, the name Ephraim is used. In the rare 'finding tradition'[188] of 9:10 the same sacral sense is present. Thus, as the prophet recalls Yahweh's saving action in the past, and as he addresses the 'tribes of Israel' in the present, his view extends beyond Israel as a political entity distinct from the southern kingdom, and embraces the entire people of God. That his hopes for the future should have a similar perspective is, therefore, entirely reasonable. The ancient pre-monarchic traditions which have helped to shape Hosea's thought include what R. de Vaux has called the three indivisibles: 'one God, Yahweh, who has chosen one people, Israel, the people of Yahweh, and has given to this people one land, Canaan, the land of Yahweh'.[189] Although traditio-historical criticism has shown that these traditions belonged originally to the Joseph tribes,[190] it is undeniable that they became as much the heritage of Judah as of the northern tribes, and were celebrated in the festal worship of the Jerusalem temple. However this common heritage of the early traditions of Israel is explained, whether by Noth's theory of a tribal amphictyony in the period of the judges,[191] or by reference to an earlier period as Mayes[192] suggests, the great theological work of the Yahwist and the psalmody[193] of Jerusalem temple worship indicate that Judah adopted these traditions as her own.

It has, moreover, already become apparent from our survey of the judgmental sayings which refer to Judah that those which are to be attributed to Hosea himself (5:10, 12, 13, 14; 8:14)

are concerned not with a general condemnation of life and
worship in the southern kingdom but solely with the question
of its disunity with the northern kingdom and the sad
consequences of their mutual hostility. It seems justifiable,
therefore, to regard as an integral part of the primary material
a concern with the unity of God's people. On a broader front,
it is clear from the Old Testament in general that, despite
periods of political rivalry and open hostility, the fundamental
religious ties between the two kingdoms were never entirely
forgotten. One may instance as an example of this relationship
the ease with which Amos, a prophet from Judah, was able to
deliver his message in the northern kingdom. The cause of his
expulsion was not that he was a foreigner from Judah, but that in
pronouncing doom upon the reigning monarch and his house he drew
to himself the charge of treason.[194] The fact that the same
condemnation can be directed against Zion and Samaria simultan-
eously (Amos 6:1), and that sanctuaries in both north and south
are included in the same indictment (Amos 5:5; 8:14),
illustrates how close was the association between the two
kingdoms. Other examples can be adduced. One, however, must
suffice. That Jerusalem is regarded as heir to the ancient
traditions which had belonged to the northern sanctuary at
Shiloh is clear from the comparison drawn between them in
Jer. 7:12ff. Leaving aside the disputed question of the
relationship of this passage to the message of Jeremiah himself,[195]
it is significant that 'my place that was in Shiloh' can be
compared without further explanation to 'this house which is
called by my name' in Jerusalem. Nor is this true only from
Judah's side. Long after the fall of Samaria pilgrims from the
north came to Jerusalem to worship.[196] It seems abundantly
clear, then, that despite political hostilities the underlying
religious bonds remained.

In short, it is difficult to justify the categorical
assertion made by Harper in his comment on 2:2 that 'its vision
of Israel's future passes beyond Hosea's horizon',[197] and modern
commentators have tended to recognise this. Only if a narrow

nationalism had taken precedence over his commitment to the
ancient traditions of Yahwism could Judah have been excluded
entirely from Hosea's concern. We have seen that this is not so.
Yahweh's past saving action was seen as extending to the whole
people of God. The same might therefore be expected of his
future saving action. For this reason I suggest that in the
triumphant expression with which 2:2 concludes, גדול יום יזרעאל,
we have a familiar nationalistic expression of popular hopes
taken up by the prophet and given a new and deeper meaning.[198]
The 'day of Jezreel' is no longer a day of national triumph in
a militaristic sense. It signifies instead the restoration to
unity of the people of God. That this is the correct understanding of the expression is evident from 1:4 where also we
have a reference to Jezreel. Here bloodshed which took place
at Jezreel is seen as the cause of the doom pronounced on Jehu's
dynasty and on kingship in Israel. I have set out below[199] my
reasons for believing that the event referred to is the assassination by Jehu of the reigning kings of both Israel and Judah,
and the implications for the prophet of that episode. The future
hope envisaged in 2:2 is thus to be seen as the counterpart to
the past history of guilt alluded to in 1:4. There the two
separate kingdoms were associated in circumstances of violence
and crime. In 2:2 a day of triumph is envisaged when they will
be associated in a new future as the people of God.

3:5

We return now to the salvation sayings. The third of these
which makes reference to the southern kingdom is 3:5 with its
expectation of a time to come when Israel will renew its
allegiance to the Davidic king. For the most part commentators
have attributed this saying to Judean influence. A notable
exception is I. Engnell[200] who sees here an example of the
Messianic hope which he believes to be a central idea in Hosea's
message. Although I have argued above that Hosea's hopes for
the future included Judah also, it is an entirely different
matter to suggest that he might regard the Davidic king as the

legitimate ruler of the reunited kingdoms. Undoubtedly it seems more plausible at first sight to regard this as Judean interpretation. Even were Hosea to have held such a hope, it may rightly be queried whether he could have expressed it openly without incurring the charge of treason while Israel existed as an independent nation. We have, therefore, the following alternatives: i. that the saying is to be attributed to Hosea despite all the difficulties inherent in the view; ii. that the idea of Israel's renewed allegiance to the Davidic king is simply an expression of Judean aspirations; iii. that the saying is a Judean interpretation in different terms of what Hosea may have expressed otherwise, perhaps envisaging a common leader somewhat after the style of 2:2. In attempting to resolve this question we must take account both of the evidence of the structure of the saying and of the broader issue of Hosea's attitude to monarchy in general and to the Davidic kingship in particular.

The linguistic evidence of v. 5 is not itself sufficient to resolve the question of the provenance of the saying. R.E. Clements' reasons for regarding the entire verse as a redactional addition are not linguistic, but based on other premises.[201] I have already in my earlier comments on this passage[202] given my reasons for rejecting this view. Hosea's action towards the woman concerned is not, as Clements holds, primarily a sign of divine discipline and judgement, and vv. 3-4 are not an adequate conclusion to the passage. In essence at least, the salvation saying of v. 5 is required, for Yahweh's command to the prophet is not to punish but to love, and it is within that context that the discipline has its place. It is, however, generally agreed by those[203] who attribute the essence of the saying to Hosea that two elements in it, namely the reference to 'David their king' and the expression באחרית הימים, are Judean supplementation. Yet this solution to the problem, simple though it appears to be, raises on reflection serious difficulties, not least in that it disturbs the balance of the passage. Since the deprivation described in v. 4 is twofold, that is to say both political[204] and cultic, it is to be

expected that restoration should concern those two aspects of the
nation's life. In its present form v. 5 satisfies this
requirement, but if it is emended and the reference to the
Davidic king excised, it fails to do so. In the present form of
the text a chiastic arrangement is apparent in vv. 4-5: Israel's
deprivation will consist in the loss of the institutions of her
political and religious life; her restoration will embrace the
return to true religion ('to Yahweh her God') and to stable
government ('to David her king'). It seems reasonable, therefore,
to assume that some reference at least is required here to the
restoration of adequate political leadership. For this reason I
believe that we must exclude the second alternative suggested
above, that the reference to 'David their king' is simply an
addition expressing Judean nationalistic aspirations. We have
yet to consider whether it may be a Judean formulation of what
Hosea expressed in different terminology. Before we turn to this,
however, note must be taken of the arguments adduced by Wolff to
support his view that the reference to David their king is later
comment.[205] He argues that these words form an unlikely second
object after בקש which properly refers to seeking Yahweh, and
therefore deems it to be a secondary and rather clumsy insertion.
Yet although בקש is used in 5:6 of seeking Yahweh in cultic
worship, as frequently elsewhere in the Old Testament,[206] it is
certainly not limited to such contexts but used with other
personal objects. In 2:9, for example, it is used of the woman's
search for her lovers.[207] Of more immediate relevance for our
purpose here is its occurrence in 2 Sam. 3:17 of seeking David
as king: היִתם מבקשים את־דוד למלך עליכם. This passage is
significant; there is no reason to doubt that it represents an
early tradition reflecting the situation when David and Saul's
son Ishbaal were rival claimants to the throne. It is clear
that in some quarters at least in the northern kingdom
allegiance to David as the stronger leader was in evidence,
undoubtedly on the grounds of self-preservation.[208] Is it not
conceivable that this early tradition has influenced the
sentiment expressed in 3:5, and that here, too, the motivation

is deliverance from hostile powers? Wolff's argument from
language is not convincing. Indeed, the balance of the sentence
in which פחד is followed by two nouns should make us hesitate
before excising one of the two nouns which follow בקש. The
occurrence of the identical phrase 'Yahweh their God and David
their king' in Jer. 30:9 cannot be used as an argument against
attributing the expression in Hos. 3:5 to the northern prophet.
The book of Jeremiah contains many echoes and reminiscences of
Hosea, and it is, in any event, always hazardous to try to
establish in which direction dependence lies.

In short, I believe there are serious problems in the view
that the reference to 'David their king' is simply secondary
Judean comment which originated perhaps in Josiah's time when
hopes began to reawaken of establishing once again the
boundaries of the extensive Davidic kingdom. The content of v. 1
requires a concluding salvation saying if it is to be anything
but ironic. The content of v. 4 requires that the hoped for
restoration should extend to both cultic and political
institutions. The expression באחרית הימים is not an obstacle
to this view, for it does not necessarily denote a developed
eschatology as, for example, in the book of Daniel.[209] There
are instances in the Old Testament where it signifies merely the
future,[210] and thus in Hos. 3:5 forms a parallel to אחר in a
carefully structured and balanced sentence.

Is the third suggestion set out above to be accepted, that
these words are Judean interpretation of a hope expressed by
Hosea in rather different terms? This is the view of van Selms[211]
who considers that it represents Hosea's thought, though such
outspoken language is unlikely. The argument is not as convincing
as it might appear. Considerations of tact and diplomacy do not
seem to have inhibited the prophets. Amos laid himself open to
a charge of sedition by proclaiming not only the destruction of
Israel's cult but disaster for her reigning king (7:11).
Jeremiah was equally outspoken about the downfall of Judah's
kings (22:11, 18f.). Both suffered for their frankness. We
cannot therefore determine the question as far as Hosea is

concerned on these grounds. Was it, in fact, more treasonable for Hosea to refer to a future ideal ruler in terms of David who had been their king at the time of their greatest territorial expansion than to declare that their own monarchy owed, not only its fall, but its very origin to the wrath of God? (13:11). Much has been said of the loose attachment of the northern tribes to the Davidic dynasty, but it must be remembered that there is in the Old Testament, as noted,[212] evidence of a strong desire on the part of at least some northerners to affirm their allegiance to David, and a jealous assertion of their right to claim him as their king (2 Sam. 19:41ff.).

Finally, is it possible that the first alternative is correct, and that the saying is to be attributed to Hosea despite the apparent difficulties inherent in this view? Gordis[213] attributes the saying to Hosea and, in an interesting discussion of its possible situational context, dates it after the fall of the northern kingdom, at which time Hosea might be expected to offer hope and encouragement to those still remaining in the land. The suggestion is attractive, but the main obstacle to its acceptance is the absence of any indication that Hosea continued to minister after the disaster of 721 B.C. It is true that this is an argument from silence, and must be viewed with caution, but had his ministry continued surely some reference to the fall of Samaria might have been expected. It is at this point that the broader issue must be faced of Hosea's attitude to monarchy, and especially to the Davidic kingship.

Excursus: Hosea's attitude to monarchy

As far as Hosea's view of the contemporary monarchy in northern Israel is concerned there can be no doubt.[214] These kings who owe their throne to intrigue and revolution (7:3, 5f.) are without divine sanction (8:4). The result, evident in the society of his day, was impotent and ineffective leadership (10:3, 7, 15; 13:10) and, ultimately, anarchy (7:7). It is more difficult, however, to determine Hosea's attitude to kingship as an institution. He disapproves of what it had in

practice become in the northern kingdom. But does he also
disapprove of it as an institution? I should like to pose three
questions: i. Does he condemn Israel's kings on pragmatic
grounds that the monarchy had failed to provide adequate leadership and had led instead to factions and to revolt? ii. Are his
reasons theological, on the grounds that the only legitimate
kingship having divine sanction is Davidic, and that Israel's
kingship was in origin schismatic? iii. Is his objection based
on the belief that the only legitimate kingship is Yahweh's, so
that he rejects kingship itself as an institution in favour of
some pre-monarchic form of leadership? Wolff puts the question
admirably in his discussion of 1:4: 'Does Hosea threaten the end
of the *kingship* in Israel or the kingship in *Israel*? That is,
does Hosea take up pre-monarchic or Judean traditions?'[215] Wolff
himself opts for the former.

Two passages (8:4; 13:11) are particularly relevant to the
question. 8:4 states categorically that Israel's king-making is
without divine approval. It is carried out in defiance of
Yahweh. But beyond this the statement is unfortunately ambiguous
and provides no clear answer to the questions posed above. Is
the comment concerned only with the instability of the monarchy
as it had become in practice, or is the condemnation directed
against the original instituting of Israel's monarchy in the
time of Jeroboam I? The fact that a reference to the calf image
follows immediately (v. 5) seems to point to the latter, since
Jeroboam was responsible both for Israel's schismatic kingship
and for her religious institutions which rivalled those of
Jerusalem. The verb השירו, however, presents a difficulty. Its
vocalisation indicates that the Massoretes derived it not from
שרר meaning 'they made princes', but understood it as a by-form
of הסירו, 'they have set up kings but not by me; they have
removed them and I knew it not'. In this case the reference
would clearly be not to the institution of monarchy under
Jeroboam I but to the revolutions and assassinations which
disrupted stability in the northern kingdom. Rudolph[216] adopts
this view, as does Gelston[217] who supports it against the meaning

'they made princes' by pointing out that 'nothing is known of any
formal appointment of princes such as would be suggested by such
an interpretation'. Yet it must be noted that considerable
prominence is given in the Hosea material to the office of שר
alongside that of king,[218] which strongly suggests that this
reflects the organisation of society in northern Israel. The
association of השירו with שרר must not be too readily discarded.
In this case it should be vocalised as הְשִׂרוּ. It may well have
been a failure to understand fully the situation in the northern
kingdom which led Judean circles, followed by the later
Massoretes, to connect the verb form with הסירו, a verb used
specifically of deposing a monarch (1 Kings 15:13), and an
altogether more familiar root. If this suggestion is correct,
it seems likely that, in view of the following reference to the
calf image, the allusion is not only to the northern monarchy
as it had become in practice but to the original establishment of
political independence under Jeroboam I. The prophet's objection
is then to the whole institution of kingship in the north, and
in this context the rather obscure expression למען יכרת is
clarified as a probable reference to the schism.[219]

13:11 is also fraught with ambiguities. 13:10b has
overtones reminiscent of the account of the institution of
monarchy in the time of Saul (1 Sam. 8:6). Is the comment of
13:11 intended as a condemnation of kingship *per se*? Against
this the tense of the verbs אתן and אקח seems decisive, and
indicates that the allusion is to the oft repeated situation
in the north whereby kings were set on the throne and deposed
by revolution and intrigue. The implicit allusion to the
incident of 1 Sam. 8 may be intended as a reminder that the
God who gave them their king at the beginning still holds the
initiative. His is still the power to give and to withhold, but
now for Israel's punishment, not her salvation. Is the view
expressed here, that the instability of Israel's monarchy is
the direct result of Yahweh's intervention in wrath, incompatible
with 8:4 which was discussed above, where the enthroning of kings
was described as defiance of Yahweh? Gelston[220] comments that

'this inconsistency may encourage the view that the two passages are making different points, viii 4 being directed against the succession of dynastic revolutions, while xiii 10f. expresses a fundamental objection to the establishment of a human monarchy in the first place'. We have noted already, however, that the imperfect verbs in 13:10f. suggest that this is not the meaning intended. The apparent difficulty is probably to be resolved by recognising that 8:4 describes the situation from the human standpoint, man acting without reference to Yahweh, whereas 13:10f. affirms that whatever man may purpose, the initiative is God's, whether in salvation or in judgement, as it was in the institution of kingship at the first.

To summarize: we have found no evidence to support the view that Hosea condemns kingship as an institution. We have found in 13:10f. strong criticism of Israel's actual kingship as in practice it had become. This was true also of 8:4, though the context suggested that the setting up of monarchy in the northern kingdom under Jeroboam I was included in the condemnation. Thus the prophet objects not only to what Israel's kingship was in practice, but to its very existence.

Other less direct evidence must now be considered. The criticism of Gilgal in 9:15 has sometimes been regarded as a reference to Saul's anointing, and is thus seen as condemnation of kingship as an institution.[221] This seems unlikely, not only because an allusion to an event almost three centuries earlier without some reference to the situation in Gilgal in the 8th century seems strangely out of keeping with the prophetic function of bringing the divine word to bear on the present moment, but also because the two other references in the material to Gilgal (4:15; 12:12) clearly show that Hosea is concerned with the form of cultic worship practised there. On balance, therefore, it seems reasonable to believe that 9:15 is also concerned with Israel's present, and is a reference to practices at Gilgal of which the details are now lost.[222] Indeed the language of divorce (שנא and גרש[223]) used in 9:15 recalls the motif of harlotry of chs. 1-3 which in Hosea belongs to the cultic

JUDAH AND THE DAVIDIC MONARCHY

sphere.[224]

The two rather obscure references to Gibeah (9:9; 10:9) which have also been understood by some[225] to imply condemnation of the monarchy as an institution, by referring to its inauguration in the time of Saul, hardly provide sufficient evidence that such is the prophet's intention. It is true that Gibeah was the residence of Saul,[226] but the context of both references, and especially the mention of war in 10:9, points rather to the events recorded in Jud. 19-21.[227] Closely following the reference to Gibeah in 10:9 is the expression 'their double iniquity'. It is tempting to see here a twofold condemnation of both cult and kingship, such as we find in 8:4, but this is to go beyond the evidence of the text for there is no hint of this in the passage itself. Wolff's suggestion that 'Gibeah's former sin is doubled by Gibeah's present guilt' seems appropriate.[228]

The most that can safely be asserted is that the northern monarchy as it was in Hosea's time was condemned by him without reserve. The two unequivocal statements are that their kings lack divine sanction (8:4) and that the rise, as well as the fall, of their kings is a sign of Yahweh's wrath (13:11). It is likely that the implication of 8:4 goes beyond this, in including in the prophet's condemnation also the beginnings of the northern monarchy. Throughout the history of monarchy in the northern kingdom, dynasties had been founded on political intrigue and on revolution. Jeroboam I's dynasty was brought down by the assassination of Nadab.[229] The 9th century witnessed the assassination of Elah,[230] of Zimri,[231] and of Joram.[232] The same was true of Hosea's own period, during which the dynasty founded by Jehu fell. Yet the absence of explicit condemnation of the institution of an independent monarchy in the northern kingdom suggests that Hosea's primary concern is with the practical considerations of the contemporary situation.

We must now take up the question posed by Wolff to which I referred above:[233] does Hosea take up pre-monarchic or Judean traditions? Since the non-dynastic principle of monarchy in northern Israel[234] had failed to create adequate leadership, and had, as a direct consequence, fostered intrigue and revolution, it seems unlikely that Hosea would have preferred to set in its place the charismatic leadership of pre-monarchic days. Argument for the contrary view rests particularly on the use of the word ראש in 2:2, which is sometimes understood as an expression of polemic against the institution of kingship.[235] It is dangerous, however, to draw this conclusion in the absence of further evidence to substantiate it, for ראש is applied on occasion to a king,[236] and describes his function rather than his office as מלך does.[237] We have no evidence at all to suggest that Hosea would have approved of a pattern of charismatic leadership after the manner of the judges.[238] It is to be noted that the verb used in 2:2 of appointing the leader (שים) occurs in 1 Sam. 8:5 specifically of appointing a king, and in Ps. 18:44 of appointing the king לראש גוים. In contrast, it is not used of appointing the pre-monarchic leader (ראש) in Num. 14:4 and Jud. 11:8.

Can we deduce, then, in the light of the arguments set out above, that, northerner though he is, there is a place in Hosea's thought for the Davidic kingship? I suggest that this is in fact the case. Since, as was noted above, his objections to north Israelite kingship seem to be based not on ideological but on pragmatic grounds, it remains an open possibility that approval of the stable Davidic kingship might have rested on similar pragmatic considerations, that a hereditary monarchy is desirable in order to sustain stable government. There is no need to accept as a corollary to this that Hosea accepted the Jerusalem kingship ideology in its entirety with all its theological implications. Is there solid evidence to support my contention? I believe that the implications of 1:4 support this view. There Yahweh declares: 'I will punish the house of Jehu for the blood of Jezreel, and I will put an end to the kingship[239] of the house of Israel'. The incident alluded to here which took place at Jezreel has such deep significance for Hosea that he regards it as the cause not only of disaster to the ruling dynasty but of the end of kingship in Israel. How are we to understand the allusion? It may be thought to refer to the sum total of violence perpetrated in Jezreel, but we have in the Old Testament the recollection of two significant incidents of bloodshed at Jezreel, both of them associated with a king. The first concerns the perversion of justice in the story of Naboth's murder,[240] an event of much deeper significance than mere covetousness on Ahab's part or callousness on Jezebel's. There are theological considerations involved in this view of kingship not subject to the law of God.[241] Yet this can hardly be the crime alluded to in 1:4 where judgement is pronounced against Jehu's dynasty in particular, with which Ahab had no connection.

The second incident is more relevant. It is the recollection of the massacre of Joram and Ahaziah perpetrated at Jezreel, by which Jehu himself claimed the throne.[242] In this connection it is significant that the judgmental saying refers to 'the house of Jehu' rather than to the reigning king[243] by name. But the question arises, why should this incident, brutal though it was, be regarded by Hosea as of sufficient importance to merit such judgement, and why should an event of a previous century seem to him the cause of the disaster now threatening the nation? The reason for Hosea's condemnation of Jehu's bloodthirsty deed is not to be found in the realm of psychology as U. Cassuto supposes, that 'the upright, gentle spirit of Hosea could not approve of the means he employed'.[244] The violent, bloodthirsty language which Hosea employs to proclaim Yahweh's judgement against the nation hardly justifies this.[245] Nor is it likely to have been motivated by sympathy for the house of Omri which Jehu had exterminated by his action. Even if one allows for the fact that the account in the Deuteronomistic history of how idolatry flourished at the royal court of this period[246] may be biassed, undoubtedly the strength and stability of that time was sustained largely by foreign alliances, a policy consistently denounced by Hosea.[247] Wolff[248] suggests as a solution to the problem of why the judgmental saying of 1:4 should have been pronounced against 'the house of Jehu' that Hosea may have held Jehu responsible for not preventing the internal canaanization of Yahweh worship, referring for corroboration to the criticism of Jehu in 2 Kings 10:28ff. Against this J.M. Ward[249] argues convincingly that the accusation in this passage refers only to the fact that he perpetuated the schism begun by Jeroboam I and cannot be taken as evidence of overt Baalism.

It is clear, then, that we must look elsewhere for the motivation of Hosea's denunciation of this action by Jehu which occurred so long before his own time. Hosea's estimate of the deed differs from that attributed to Elisha[250] and the Deuteronomistic comment in 2 Kings 10:30, where the emphasis is on the effect of Jehu's action as an attack on Baal worship. Hosea's attitude, in contrast, may be a political evaluation of the deed,[251] for not only was Jehu's act a flagrant example of the founding of a dynasty on bloodshed and violence, but he alone of Israel's kings had threatened the throne of Judah with like instability. By Jehu's action the principle of stable dynastic succession in Judah was endangered, with the immediate consequence that Athaliah seized the throne by bloodshed,[252] an action which in turn spawned more violence and intrigue when Joash was restored as the lawful king.[253] Thus Jehu's action came close to involving Judah in intrigue and violence such as had disrupted society in the northern kingdom.

A further implication of Jehu's deed must also be taken into account. It is perhaps to be understood as an attempt to reunite the kingdoms under his own authority.[254] I have argued above[255] that Hosea was committed on theological grounds to reunion of the kingdoms. But reunion demands stable government, not a throne such as Jehu's, founded as it was on violence. May it not be, then, that the hope expressed in 3:5 of Israel's renewed allegiance to the Davidic king may have been formulated as a deliberate counterbalance to ambition such as Jehu's which is categorically condemned in 1:4?

To conclude: Hosea clearly condemns north Israelite kingship as it had in practice become, and possibly also in principle. He does not, however, object to kingship as an institution. To suggest that he has a commitment to the ideology of Davidic kingship as we find it expressed in Jerusalem temple worship is certainly to go beyond what the evidence warrants. It is not, however, implausible to suggest that on purely pragmatic grounds the prophet preferred the principle of dynastic succession. Just as his hopes for the maintenance and transmission of Yahwistic tradition seem to have lain with Judah's cultic worship, so his hopes for political stability seem to have turned to Judah's hereditary monarchy. This is not to suggest that Hosea accepted the Jerusalem traditions of kingship, but that as the Deuteronomists were prepared to accept monarchy as expedient provided that it was subject to the Sinai covenant,[256] so possibly was Hosea before them.

To return then to the question of the provenance of 3:5: both literary considerations as to the structure of the passage and a wider survey of evidence for Hosea's attitude to kingship suggest that we ought not too readily to assume that the reference to 'David their king' must be due to Judean influence. It is arguable that it belongs to the primary stratum of the material.

12:1

We come finally to the last of the references to Judah. 12:1 confronts us with one of the most difficult exegetical problems in Hosea. Its meaning is so uncertain that it is unclear whether the attitude to Judah expressed here is favourable or unfavourable.[257] Although, as I argued above,[258] the criterion of content, whether the attitude shown to Judah is favourable or otherwise, is not adequate as a guide to the provenance of a saying, but can serve as a supplementary indicator when taken together with other evidence, in this instance the extent of the ambiguity of meaning robs us of even this help. Any conclusion reached concerning this saying must therefore be especially tentative.

First we must consider the structure of the saying. Does it in any way indicate that the name Judah belongs to the original

form of the saying, or are the indications that it is secondary
in origin and belongs to the application of the message to the
southern kingdom? The position of יהודה suggests that it is
integral to the saying. Were it a substitution we should have to
assume that it replaced the name Jacob, since Ephraim and Israel
already appear in v. 1a. However, as Wolff comments, 'the
inverted sentence order emphasises the subject by placing it
first. This makes sense only if the subject is not identical with
the subject in v. 1a, thus making an intentional distinction'.[259]
The name Judah appears to belong to the original form of the
saying, and the emphasis on Judah by virtue of its position in
the sentence implies a contrast with the statement concerning
Ephraim/Israel.

We turn now to the meaning of the terms used, of which both
רד and קדושים are problematic. The latter has three possible
meanings. It may be an intensive plural referring to Yahweh as
the most holy,[260] or as genuinely plural in meaning and
referring either to divine beings[261] or to earthly saints.[262]
The third meaning is hardly appropriate in view of its
parallelism with אל (clearly here meaning Yahweh, not the head
of the Canaanite pantheon[263]), whether the parallelism of the
clauses is intended synonymously or antithetically. If the
second possibility is adopted we are faced with the question
whether the divine beings are attendants of Yahweh or members
of the Canaanite pantheon. This problem is increased by the
fact that רד too is of uncertain meaning. Is Judah here
spoken of with approval or disapproval? If it is with
disapproval, קדושים must refer to false gods. If it is with
approval, קדושים will refer either to Yahweh himself (an
intensive plural) or to his divine attendants. The answer can
only be tentative in view of the uncertain meaning. But it is
a priori unlikely that in a polemical context where Canaanite
deities are seen as rivals for the devotion of God's people the
word קדושים would be used to designate them. Yahweh is קדוש
(11:9). This is to some extent corroborated by the usage of
נאמן elsewhere in the Old Testament where it signifies praise-

worthy devotion, not commitment to false gods. The vocalisation
of רד suggests that the Massoretes connected it with a root רוד,
though the only known meaning of such a root is 'to wander'. If
this *is* the intended meaning the parallelism of the two clauses
in v. 1b must necessarily be antithetic, as in the NEB
translation:

> Judah is still restive under God,
>   still loyal to the idols he counts holy.

However, the intrinsic unlikelihood that נאמן and קדושים should
have a pejorative meaning here (concealed somewhat in the NEB
paraphrase 'idols he counts holy') makes this interpretation
improbable. The RSV, too, regards רד as meaning 'he roams', but
considers it inappropriate and emends to ידע. To connect רד
with the root רדה 'to rule' hardly solves the problem both in
view of the difficulty of accounting for the form of the verb
and of its not entirely appropriate meaning, 'Judah still rules
with God'.[264] Widengren[265] is correct, I believe, in recognising
that רד and נאמן are synonymous, for El and the Holy Ones
together constitute the divine assembly, and no opposition is
intended between them. He therefore translates: 'but Judah is
seeking pasture[266] with El, and with the Holy Ones she is
faithful'. On balance, then, although the precise meaning of
רד has been lost, either through textual corruption or from some
other cause, it seems preferable to understand the two clauses
of v. 1b as in synonymous parallelism. This holds true equally
whether קדושים is understood as an intensive plural referring
to Yahweh, or as a reference to his heavenly court. The
conclusion to which I come, therefore, is that in its present
form the saying expresses approval of Judah in contrast to the
accusation levelled against the northern kingdom in v. 1a. The
final difficult question is the origin of such a saying. Is it
to be attributed to Hosea himself or to redactors? An answer
can be offered only tentatively on the basis of the general
conclusions reached thus far. Nowhere have I found evidence that
the use to which the redactors put the originally northern

material was to encourage complacency in Judah. Its intention was to warn and challenge. From Hosea, on the other hand, comes criticism of Judah in one particular respect, namely its disunity with Israel. I have argued above[267] in discussing 1:7 that there is evidence that Hosea looked to Judah for the continuity of the people of God. Likewise in considering 3:5, despite the many difficulties involved, the conclusion to which I came[268] was that, northerner though he was, there was a place in Hosea's thought for the Davidic kingship, not on ideological but on pragmatic grounds. It may be that the expression of approval of Judah in 12:1 is to be understood, in the light of this, as having a place in Hosea's message. From the Judean redactors, in contrast, comes comprehensive criticism of Judah's life and worship.[269]

In conclusion, the idea that pro-Judean passages are likely to have come from the hand of Judean redactors and that those which express criticism of Judah come from Hosea has proved to be a highly questionable assumption. It is an altogether too simplistic view of the matter. Hosea expresses criticism of Judah, but it is limited and specific, relating to her relationship with Israel. On theological grounds the prophet is committed to reunion of the kingdoms at the one people of one God. From Judean redactors who applied the prophet's message anew to the circumstances of Judah comes more wide-ranging criticism of life and worship. It is not possible to date this redactional activity closely, but general similarities to the message of Jeremiah[270] suggest that it belongs, in part at least, to the seventh century when a fate similar to Israel's began to threaten the southern kingdom.

CHAPTER III

ISRAELITE WORSHIP: ITS SANCTUARIES AND CULT PRACTICES

That one of Hosea's chief concerns was to voice a consistent protest against the syncretistic religion practised by his contemporaries and the fertility rites which degraded Israelite worship in the last decades of the northern kingdom is immediately evident. This polemical note pervades the material and only an unwarranted scepticism as to the reliability of the tradition in essence could lead to a denial that it originated with Hosea himself. Indeed, it is to a great extent this primary concern with cultic abuses which distinguishes his message from that of his near contemporary Amos. The latter, it is true, does not ignore this aspect of the nation's life, but condemns the empty sham of a religion which meticulously encourages the celebration of festivals and the requirements of sacrificial offerings but makes no demands upon the worshippers in the sphere of human relationships as an expression of commitment to God, thus denying the very nature of the God it professes to worship.[1] Nevertheless, the primary motivation of Amos' indictment of his contemporaries is not cultic but ethical, and the main thrust of his message concerns the disregard of the obligations of social justice on the part of the wealthy and powerful in Israelite society of the time.[2] It is not without significance that in the story of his encounter at Bethel with Amaziah the priest - although he proclaims the destruction of Israel's sanctuaries and high places, and the end of cult and monarchy alike (7:9) - yet there is no polemic specifically against the calf image installed at that very sanctuary. The words to which Amaziah takes exception concern the death of Jeroboam and the exile of the nation (7:11).[3] It is in this respect that the contrast

between Amos and Hosea is most striking, for in the message of
the latter the emphasis is reversed. The requirements of social
justice are not forgotten,[4] but concern with cultic affairs takes
precedence, and with Hosea we find the first explicit denunciation
of the existence of a calf image.[5] R.P. Carroll notes that
'strangely it is only in Hosea that a trenchant criticism of
idolatry was maintained by an eighth-century prophet .....
The prophets of that period were more intent on condemning social
injustice than on criticizing idolatry'.[6] It is significant that
precisely in the context of his polemic against the contemporary
cult in Israel some of Hosea's distinctive characteristics are
evident, such as the harlotry motif[7] and the emphasis on דעת as
Yahweh's requirement of his people.[8] The difference of emphasis
in the message of the two prophets Amos and Hosea, so nearly
contemporary with each other and alike ministering in the
northern kingdom, lends credence to the reliability of the
tradition and vindicates the position which I have adopted,[9]
that, despite undoubted redactional influence which has
contributed to the final form of the material, the essence of
the prophetic message has been faithfully preserved. The work
of later redactors has not left us with a mere amalgam of the
messages of many prophets. Their individuality and distinctive
characteristics have survived.[10]

Nonetheless, despite this confidence that the core of the
material which has been transmitted faithfully reflects Hosea's
message, it would be rash not to allow for the possibility,
indeed I would say the probability, of the presence of secondary
comment on the aspect of Israel's life which figures most
prominently in Hosea's concern, the corruption of worship and
religious practice, since the transmission of the material
took place in the southern kingdom with its own hallowed
sanctuaries and its cherished festivals. Two factors in
particular must be taken into account as we endeavour to
estimate the extent to which Judean influences may have
contributed to the hostile attitude presented in the book of
Hosea towards Israel's sanctuaries and cult practices. The one

ISRAELITE WORSHIP: ITS SANCTUARIES AND CULT PRACTICES

arises from a deliberate theological stance, the other unwittingly from an unconscious attitude of mind. The importance of both of these factors must not be underestimated. The former is associated with the emphasis on the centralisation of worship characteristic of the Deuteronomists.[11] We are obliged to take seriously the possibility that this commitment to centralisation may have helped to heighten, and thus to distort, the polemic expressed by Hosea himself against the sanctuaries and cult practices of the northern kingdom. The books of Kings, for example, provide ample evidence of the influence exerted by the Deuteronomists with their particular theological stance on the presentation of historical material. The criterion of commitment to the central sanctuary in Jerusalem has excluded the possibility of a positive evaluation of the reign of any northern king, and has undoubtedly shaped the record, if not the event itself, of the Josianic reform and its purge of Israel's sanctuaries and cult personnel.[12] That Hosea's polemic against the cult of his day in the northern kingdom should have remained entirely free of such influence is unlikely. There is, however, a second factor which may also have contributed to the final form of the material. There were both religious and political reasons why the people of Judah should feel a degree of distrust, if not of outright hostility, towards the schismatic northerners who had not only rejected the Davidic dynasty and the sanctuary which was the focus of the Jerusalem ideology of kingship and had established a rival monarchy and royal sanctuary, but had also from time to time allied themselves with Judah's enemies.[13] It is reasonable, therefore, to suggest that, in addition to conscious polemical aims motivated by a particular theological stance, there may also unwittingly have been a failure in Judean circles rightly to understand the nature and purpose of certain north Israelite cult practices. We must allow for the possibility that misunderstanding of this kind as well as deliberate and determined polemical motives may have contributed to the way in which Hosea's own protest against cultic abuses is now presented. It is clear, on the one hand, that criticism of

Israel's cult was prominent in Hosea's message, and, on the
other, very probable that powerful influences in Judah have,
deliberately or inadvertently, shaped the present form of the
material. It is my intention, therefore, to examine a number
of passages in which attention is directed towards Israel's
sanctuaries and cult practices in order to assess, as far as
possible, the nature and extent of redactional influence, and
to determine whether it has merely applied Hosea's original
message to a new situation or whether in any material respect
it diverges by the introduction of new and alien elements.

Sanctuaries

i.   Passing references: I shall concern myself mainly in
this study with the important sanctuaries at Bethel and Gilgal.
A number of other sanctuaries are, however, referred to in the
material and require a brief mention. Among these are Mizpah,
Tabor and possibly Shittim (5:1-2), though the MT is difficult
at this point.[14] Little more can be deduced from the brief
passage than that the priests, together with others of the
nations leaders,[15] have merited rebuke, though it seems clear
from the reference to priests that the place names are those of
sanctuaries. The location of Mizpah is unclear,[16] as is also
the nature of the sin in question. The ambiguity of the passage
is increased by the difficulty of determining whether משפט
refers to the administration of justice[17] by the parties
mentioned, or to the threat of judgement against them.[18] With
these we can include Ramah which similarly receives only passing
mention (5:8). In this instance it is not clear whether the
reference is in fact to a sanctuary. The passage is frequently
understood as a reference to military attack either during or
in the aftermath of the Syro-Ephraimite war.[19] E.M. Good,[20]
however, argues that the music and shouting referred to are not
warnings of military invasion but belong in a liturgical
context. In this case the reference must be to Ramah as a
sanctuary town. He differs from most scholars in identifying

this Ramah with the place at which Samuel had his headquarters where he built an altar to the Lord (1 Sam. 7:17), and follows Hertzberg[21] in the view that only later was the Samuel tradition attached to a more northerly location. Whether or not Good is correct in understanding 5:8 to refer to a liturgical procession from one sanctuary to another, the passage has no contribution to make to the present study. The same uncertainty as to whether a sanctuary is intended attaches to the reference to Gibeah which is linked with Ramah in 5:8. E.M. Good stresses that as the seat of Saul's kingship it was a sanctuary town, but in general its significance here is seen to lie in the fact that it was a border town and a cause of contention between the northern and southern kingdoms. Gibeah is mentioned also in 9:9 and 10:9 where 'the days of Gibeah' are specified as a particularly heinous example of corruption in Israel's past history. Unfortunately the allusion here also is unclear and it is not possible to speak with any certainty about the historical episode intended, though from the evidence available it is possible to surmise that the shameful incident mentioned in Jud. 19-21 is in mind.[22] This receives some corroboration from the fact that there is a reference to war in 10:9, since the result of the crime committed at Gibeah in the period of the Judges resulted in battle. Yet doubts remain about this interpretation of the passage, and I am not myself convinced that the intended reference is to this event since the guilty party in this episode was the tribe of Benjamin, and it was Israel through whom justice was done and the evil requited. Certainly the view expressed by Mays[23] that a double allusion may be intended, both to the events of Jud. 19-21 and to the inauguration of Saul's kingship whose home was at Gibeah, hardly carries conviction, for the passage cannot be held at one and the same time to express a rejection of the institution of monarchy and an indictment of the pre-monarchic period. In any case, none of these passages provides evidence for the present study.

The same is true of the two references to Gilead (6:8; 12:12). Here too it is not clear whether a sanctuary is intended. The name Gilead is generally applied to the region in north Transjordan. In 6:8, however, it is clear that a city is meant; but its identity is uncertain, as is also the sin of which its inhabitants are accused. The expression used here (פעלי און) can refer to sins either of a political[24] or of a cultic[25] nature. One cannot be dogmatic in this instance on the basis of so brief a comment. It is possible that the reference is to Pekah's assassination of the reigning king Pekahiah in 737 B.C. in which fifty men from Gilead were implicated.[26] If cultic sin is in mind, the tracks of blood (6:8) may refer, as Wolff suggests,[27] to child sacrifice, to which there may be a possible allusion in 5:7 also. In 12:12 the text is difficult, and the meaning of this reference to Gilead cannot be considered in isolation from the accompanying saying concerning Gilgal which was clearly an important sanctuary. I shall return to this passage presently.

Several times reference is made to Samaria. As Israel's capital city it was undoubtedly the scene of some of Hosea's activity. Reference to the royal court in 5:1-2, and the implication of 10:13-15 that political leaders are addressed make it likely that the setting of these sayings is Samaria.[28] Wolff suggests that the sayings in 5:8 - 7:16 are also perhaps to be associated with Samaria, in particular with a cultic celebration with penitence and sacrifices.[29] Be that as it may, the book of Hosea gives no firm evidence of Hosea's attitude to a sanctuary at Samaria. The only temple there of which we have evidence was the Baal temple built by Ahab[30] and destroyed by Jehu.[31] The royal sanctuary and dynastic temple of the northern kingdom were situated at Bethel, not Samaria, and where there is a reference to the calf of Samaria (8:5) it seems clear that the sanctuary concerned is the famous one at Bethel.[32]

There remains only one possible reference to a sanctuary to be considered before we turn to consider the attitude of the

prophet towards Gilgal and Bethel. In 6:9 we have the expression
דרך ירצחו־שכמה. The syntax is unusual in the apparent separation
of the construct דרך from its *nomen regens* שכמה. Hirschberg[33]
argues that the word שכמה means not Shechem but 'viciousness',
and is to be compared to the Arabic *shakama,* on which כי זמה is
a gloss, so that we read ושכמה עשו בביתי. More commonly the
passage is understood as referring to the ancient sanctuary at
Shechem, famous in Israel's history. Opinion is divided,
however, as to whether the accusation is directed against the
activity of priests on the road to Shechem, or whether Shechem
itself has been defiled by evil deeds. If the former is the
correct understanding of the passage it appears that Shechem alone
of all the sanctuaries in the northern kingdom is exempt from
the prophet's criticism. This view is held by Wolff,[34] for
example, who considers that Shechem was a centre for faithful
levites to whom the official priesthood were opposed, and that
it still represented a true adherence to Yahweh. E. Nielsen[35]
similarly holds that Shechem and its cult were exempt from the
prophet's criticism. In contrast, E.W. Nicholson inclines to
the view that Shechem also had been corrupted, and that the
priesthood of that very sanctuary are here portrayed as brigands
and murderers.[36] N.W. Porteous[37] is of a similar opinion, and
this is the implication also of the textual emendation suggested
by G.R. Driver:[38] דרכו ירצחו שכמה. One has reluctantly to
conclude that the evidence of these ambiguous words is altogether
too fragile to support the argument that Shechem alone of northern
sanctuaries had remained untainted by Canaanite religious
practices. It is more likely that the significance of the
saying lies in the juxtaposition of the verb ירצחו with שכמה,
for Shechem was one of the cities of refuge[39] set apart for the
protection of those who themselves had shed blood. Thus with a
dreadful irony the priests themselves are guilty of murder
before ever the city of refuge is reached.

We turn now to the two major sanctuaries, Bethel and Gilgal,
of which alone we have sufficient evidence in the material to

provide a basis for an evaluation of Hosea's attitude towards them and a possible comparison with Judean attitudes.

ii. Bethel: Although the name Bethel appears only twice in Hosea (10:15; 12:5), the designation Bethaven which is used in 4:15; 5:8; 10:5 is generally understood as referring also to that sanctuary. There can be little doubt that this is so.[40] The association of Bethaven with Gilgal in 4:15 implies that both are prominent Israelite sanctuaries, and the closely similar saying in Amos 4:4 and 5:5 has Bethel and Gilgal. The identification of Bethaven with Bethel is substantiated by Hos. 10:5 with its reference to the calf image, which had from the time of Jeroboam I been associated with the famous sanctuary at Bethel. There is little room for doubt, therefore, that Bethaven is intended as a designation of Israel's royal sanctuary, commonly interpreted as an ironical formulation by which Hosea expressed his fierce condemnation of the sanctuary at Bethel.[41] Although the exact connotation of און is open to discussion, and Bethaven has been variously interpreted as 'house of wickedness',[42] or, with specific reference to cultic matters, 'house of idolatry',[43] or, connecting און with אין, 'house of nothingness, unreality',[44] it is commonly assumed that Hosea derived this pejorative designation from Amos 5:5: ובית־אל יהיה לאון and that it epitomises his repugnance to the sanctuary. It is, however, precisely this assumption which merits examination. Hosea's attitude to Israel's cult in general, and to the Bethel sanctuary in particular, must be re-examined on the basis of the material as a whole. Only then, when the prophet's attitude towards the religion practised by his contemporaries has been considered, shall we be in a position to assess whether the derogatory connotation of Bethaven appropriately expresses Hosea's attitude to Bethel, or whether it is to be understood as the expression of Judean hostility towards a northern sanctuary. The point at issue is whether the rejection of a sanctuary which had formerly been a notable Yahwistic shrine[45] originated from Hosea himself, or whether, despite his undoubted opposition to the cult practices of his contemporaries, his attitude towards the sanctuary itself was of a more positive nature.

I shall take as the starting point in this discussion the saying in 4:15 which is generally understood as an explicit statement of the prophet's hostility towards both Bethel and Gilgal, and his desire to prohibit the people from worshipping there:

> Though you play the harlot, O Israel,
>   let not Judah become guilty.
> Enter not into Gilgal,
>   nor go up to Bethaven,
>   and swear not, 'As the Lord lives'.

I have already[46] set out my reasons for regarding as redactional the oblique reference to Judah (אל־יאשם יהודה), which interrupts the direct address to Israel with which the verse opens and closes, and for concluding that the prophetic saying in its original northern Israelite form was not intended as a total prohibition of worship at the two sanctuaries mentioned. The arguments need not be repeated here, but I should like to consider the different approach to the text offered by Wolff,[47] who regards only the name Judah as redactional. Following the LXX he argues that אל תאשם stood in the text originally, and that the change to the third person came with the introduction of the reference to Judah. He understands the meaning of the passage to lie in the distinction which the prophet makes between the guilty priests who have adopted Canaanite forms of worship and the innocent people who are in danger of being misled by their religious leaders. The prophet's warning is, according to Wolff, addressed to the people as distinct from their leaders, and urges them to avoid contamination by separating themselves from 'the cult that now stands under judgement'[48] (*dem Gericht verfallenen Kultus*). He warns them against taking part in cultic rituals to avoid sharing in the guilt of their leaders. Interesting though this suggestion is, the distinction in the prophet's thought between guilty priests and innocent people which forms the basis of this argument is difficult to enforce. It is true that the priests are accused specifically in 4:4-5 for their failure to instruct the people faithfully, but the evidence of the material as a whole suggests that all alike are implicated in the guilt. It is the community as a whole who are indicted: ריב ליהוה עם־יושבי הארץ (4:1). Whereas Wolff understands 4:13b and 14b as excusing the people as a whole because the priests, their leaders, are primarily to blame, the words are surely ironic, exculpating the brides and daughters for their adultery because of the guilt of the whole community.

In short, the most natural explanation of the threefold prohibition lies in the sad spiritual condition of the nation, described by the prophet as 'adultery'. The prophet is not concerned to condemn the existence of the sanctuaries at Gilgal and Bethel any more than he is opposed in principle to the oath formula חי־יהוה. He is concerned rather with an apostate nation whose practices defiled ancient and honourable sanctuaries hallowed in Israel's past history as they also dishonoured the oath taken in Yahweh's name. Certainly if the prophet's prohibitions were to be heeded the result would be the cessation of worship at these sanctuaries.[49] Yet it must be recognised that, far from implying hostility on the prophet's part to the sanctuaries concerned, this might rather indicate respect for the honourable past of holy places now defiled by his contemporaries. The motivation of the prophet's words, I suggest, is comparable to that of Mal. 1:10 where no antagonism against the Jerusalem temple is implied, but solely a desire to safeguard it from further abuse. I believe Hosea is to be understood, not as condemning the sanctuaries themselves but as castigating the guilt of those who worship there. It is not without significance that the following verses (16-19) speak, not of judgement on the sanctuaries themselves, but of the fate of the apostate people. Superficially this saying in Hos. 4:15 may appear to resemble that of Amos 5:5:

ISRAELITE WORSHIP: ITS SANCTUARIES AND CULT PRACTICES   127

> Do not seek Bethel,
>   and do not enter into Gilgal
>   or cross over to Beersheba.

On closer examination, however, the difference in emphasis is the more noteworthy. Amos' prohibitions express hostility against the sanctuaries themselves. Indeed, the words which follow pronounce judgement on them explicitly:

> Gilgal shall surely go into exile,
>   and Bethel shall come to naught.[50]

In contrast, Hosea directs his protest against the nation whose apostasy profanes a legitimate oath and, by implication, lawful sanctuaries. Whether or not the above is a correct assessment must now be tested by examining the other references to this sanctuary.

The first passage to be considered is 10:5 where Bethel is again referred to as Bethaven. It is to be noted that here, too, the prophet's polemic is directed not against the sanctuary itself but specifically against the calf image.[51] Vv. 5-6 are concerned with the doom which awaits this impotent idol. The word כבוד in v. 5 is best taken as a reference to the calf image itself, and the third singular masculine pronominal suffixes as referring to עם, rather than understanding the suffixes to refer to עגל understood,[52] and taking כבוד to mean, as Mays suggests, 'the costly ornamentation and gilding decorating the idol',[53] the language having ironical overtones. The expression על־כבודו כי־גלה ממנו is reminiscent of the lament over the loss of the ark in 1 Sam. 4:21-22. כבוד is there used of the ark which symbolised the presence of God in Shiloh. Here that which was considered to represent the presence of the deity, namely the calf image, is ironically referred to as כבוד. Significantly, the saying contains no expression of hostility against the sanctuary; attention is focussed on the impotence of the image to avert disaster, and on the subsequent shame of the people. Again the evidence seems to indicate that, although the prophet is uncompromising in his protest against the rites practised at the Bethel sanctuary, no polemic is directed against the existence of the sanctuary. This feature stands in marked contrast to the explicit threat of destruction uttered against certain shrines, in particular those designated as 'high places'[54] (v. 8). It is these, not Bethel, which are described as 'Israel's sin' (חטאת ישראל), and there can be no doubt about Hosea's opposition to *their* existence.

Another important reference to Bethel occurs in 12:5, but here unfortunately the passage is fraught with ambiguities. The context broadly speaking is an indictment of the nation, and a parallel is drawn with certain events in the life of the eponymous ancestor Jacob. However, the meaning of the Jacob references in vv. 4-5 and in v. 13 are highly ambiguous and have proved to be something of a *crux interpretum*. Despite the considerable literature which has been produced on the subject, there is no consensus of opinion even on the primary question as to whether the Jacob tradition is used here with a positive or negative evaluation.[55] Some have argued that Jacob's God is here identified with Yahweh, and thus the God who addressed himself to the nation's ancestor is the one who now addresses the community.[56] Others have understood the point to lie in the contrast between Jacob's God, an inferior, and Yahweh.[57] Among these scholars is P. de Boer,[58] who argues that 'the prophet denies that Jacob's god is Yhwh', and believes that the point of the sayings lies in the prophet's opposition to the syncretism of his time which wrongly identified the God of Moses with the gods of the patriarchs. However, more convincing is the view of P.R. Ackroyd[59] that whatever the historical relationship between the religion of the pre-exodus period and later Israelite religion, Israel herself clearly did not regard them as separable. One of the central features of the Exodus tradition in its present form is the identity of the God of Abraham, Isaac and Jacob with Yahweh who revealed himself to Moses. Moreover, Hosea's polemic seems to be based, not on the belief that the god worshipped at

Bethel was an alien deity, but on the fact that Israel had lost
touch with God who revealed himself there. I believe Ackroyd is
correct in his arguments that the treatment of the Jacob
tradition in vv. 4-5 is not a negative one, and that the prophet
is not telling his hearers, 'The story you love is not one of
which you should be proud, for it is a story of deceit. You are
condemned because you are one with your father Jacob in your
falsity'.[60] On the contrary, the tradition is used positively,
and the prophet is affirming, 'The success of your father Jacob
was due to divine favour, and to the closeness of the relationship
which was his with God'.[61]

On the basis, then, that the Jacob tradition is regarded in
a positive light, the meaning of the passage can be set out as
follows. The theme is stated in v. 2: the pursuit of wealth
and power is futile apart from God. It is illustrated by the
reference to Jacob which follows, and continued throughout the
series of sayings in vv. 8-14. The prophet reminds the nation
that Jacob strove for pre-eminence and power, first in the womb
in conflict with his brother, then in his maturity in conflict
with God. But the encounter with God showed him where true
strength and resources are to be found. However, the meaning
of the statement בית־אל ימצאנו ושם ידבר עמנו is problematic, for
the subject of ימצאנו and of ידבר is unclear. We have noted
already that it is unlikely to be Bethel understood as the name
of a deity;[62] the following שם indicates that the reference is
to the sanctuary, not to a deity. Is the subject, then, God
or Jacob? A consideration of the Pentateuchal traditions
suggests that in ימצאנו the prophet is alluding to the
tradition in Gen. 28:11, where פגע is in effect a synonym of
מצא here,[63] and Jacob is therefore the subject. Despite this,
however, I cannot escape the conviction that God is intended as
the subject of ידבר. The tradition that God addressed Jacob at
Bethel is a persistent one, and in Gen. 35:13, 15 Bethel is
called specifically 'the place where he (God) had spoken with
him'. One might perhaps account for the confusing omission of
an explicit indication of the change of subject by the

familiarity of the tradition to the prophet's hearers. Hosea makes no reference to the content of the conversation between God and Jacob at Bethel, but its significance appears clearly in the Pentateuch:

> I am El Shaddai: be fruitful and multiply; a nation and a company of nations shall come from you .... The land which I gave to Abraham and Isaac I will give to you (Gen. 35:11f.).

This passage is attributed to the P strand,[64] but the earlier source in Gen. 35:14-15 also emphasises that Jacob was addressed by God. Moreover, in the tradition associated with Bethel in Gen. 28:13-15, which is commonly ascribed to the J strand,[65] the theme of the promise to Jacob of land and posterity is also found. The theme of Hos. 12, concerned as it is with the nation's pursuit of wealth through injustice and oppression, suggests that Hosea has in mind not only the tradition of the encounter at Bethel between God and Jacob but specifically the promise given there to the nation's ancestor of future well being.[66] Hosea's treatment of the traditions is allusive and not explicit, and consequently it is obscure to the modern reader. As part of the *hieros logos* of the Bethel sanctuary the traditions would be familiar to the prophet's hearers; by alluding to them he thus brought a strong reminder of the significance of the sanctuary.

It is clear, then, despite difficulties of exegesis, that the purpose of the prophet in 12:5 is not to denigrate the sanctuary at Bethel, but to remind his hearers of its true significance. He affirms that it is the place where a significant encounter took place between their ancestor Jacob and his God. The tradition with which Hosea is familiar is consistent with that of the Pentateuch, and it is reasonable to assume that the content of the divine word spoken to Jacob at Bethel is the promise of future blessing such as is found in Gen. 28 and 35. The prophet thus reminds his hearers that only in encounter with God and in laying hold on his promise can their

future be secured. Accordingly, the prophet makes no attack on
the Bethel sanctuary itself. God's ריב is with his people (v. 3)
who, forgetting the ground of their hope in God's promise to
their ancestor, have turned to oppression in order to secure
wealth. To them the prophet brings a reminder of the honourable
origins of the sanctuary at which they are worshipping and of
the God who is there to be encountered.[67]

The passages studied thus far lead to the same conclusion:
that the prophet is opposed not to the Bethel sanctuary itself
but to those who in their worship are untrue to the God whom
their ancestor there encountered, in which event the origins of
the sanctuary lie.[68] There is, however, one passage which seems
to speak explicitly of the great wickedness of Bethel and, by
implication, of the prophet's hostility to the sanctuary itself:

> The tumult of war shall arise among your people,
> and all your fortresses shall be destroyed,
> as Shalman destroyed Beth-arbel on the day of battle;
> mothers were dashed in pieces with their children.
> Thus it shall be done to you, O Bethel,[69]
> because of your great wickedness (10:15).

Here if anywhere we might expect to find the pejorative
designation Bethaven used if it indeed originated with Hosea
himself to express the wickedness and futility of Israel's major
sanctuary. If Bethaven had originally stood in the text here
it would be difficult to explain the change to Bethel. In all
probability the name Bethel is to be understood as a textual
corruption of בית־ישראל, an emendation which is widely accepted[70]
and agrees with the LXX. It is true that Ackroyd[71] argues for
retaining the reading Bethel on the grounds that comparison is
drawn with one particular city, Betharbel. The immediate
context (vv. 13-15), however, suggests that the prophet has in
mind the nation as a whole rather than one particular city.
The mention of 'your warriors', 'your people', 'your fortresses',
and the reference to the king of Israel, all support this view.
A comparable threat of judgement through the ravages of war is

to be found in 11:5-6, where the disaster is regarded as co-extensive with the nation; not one but many cities will be destroyed. It seems on balance, therefore, justifiable to prefer the reading of the LXX to that of the MT on the grounds that it is more appropriate to the context. What is not legitimate is to adduce as an additional reason for rejecting the reading Bethel the fact that Hosea usually calls Bethel Bethaven,[72] for a statement such as this merely prejudges the issue.

How, then, did the reading of the MT, with Bethel in place of an original 'house of Israel', arise? Are we to understand it as an example of Judean polemic against Israel's royal sanctuary which had been claimed as a rival to Jerusalem, or is it the accidental result of textual corruption with no implications for redactional activity? It is impossible to be certain. The LXX witnesses to the fact that long after the Deuteronomistic hostility to northern sanctuaries had manifested itself in the presentation of historical material a tradition of reading 'house of Israel' was known. This may, however, be evidence of a genuinely divergent tradition, and need not be taken to imply that the change to Bethel belongs to a date later than the LXX. Both readings can be construed as polemic against the northern kingdom, the LXX general, the MT specific. It may well be that the LXX preserves the original, while the MT has, as it were, capitalised on the scribal error caused by assimilation to the specific reference to the city of Betharbel in the previous lines. Whatever decision is reached on this point, however, the evidence indicates that the original form of the saying did not include specific polemic against Bethel. The wickedness with which the prophet is concerned is the wickedness of the nation.

To summarize: an examination of the passages in which Bethel/Bethaven is named does not suggest an attitude of hostility on the part of the prophet towards the sanctuary itself consistent with the pejorative meaning inherent in Bethaven. He protests against the cultic rites practised there, and castigates the nation for their apostasy, but does not

oppose the sanctuary *per se*. There is, however, other evidence
of a more indirect kind which must also be considered if a
balanced view is to be obtained. There are certain passages
where it is arguable that Bethel is alluded to, although not by
name. The first of these is the reference to 'Yahweh's house'
in 8:1. This expression, which occurs also in 9:4, and the
related expressions 'my house' (9:15) and 'the house of his
God' (9:8), are usually understood to refer not to a sanctuary
but to the land of Israel.[73] I have previously set out[74]
detailed arguments for my view that only in 9:15 does the
expression 'house' refer to the land of Israel, where it occurs
in a particular context in which Israel is portrayed as an
unfaithful wife and Yahweh as a betrayed husband; such is the
implication of the use here of the verbs שנא and גרש, both of
which occur elsewhere in a similar context of divorce.[75] It is
appropriate that here the land should figuratively be described
as 'Yahweh's house', from which the aggrieved husband expels his
unfaithful spouse. The figurative use of the expression cannot
be extended automatically to the related expressions in 8:1;
9:4; 9:8. In all these passages there are cultic associations
which make a reference to a sanctuary entirely appropriate.[76]
In 8:1-3 in particular, considerations of both form-criticism
and literary criticism have led me to the view that the reference
is not, as is commonly supposed, to a situation of military
danger but to a cultic ceremony. The difficult syntax of the
MT כנשר is eased by vocalising the word as נַשָׁר [77] 'herald', with
the resultant meaning 'Set the trumpet to your lips as a herald
[making a proclamation] against the house of the Lord'. Thus
the reference to 'Yahweh's house' is seen to refer to a major
sanctuary. The emphasis on the calf of Samaria (vv. 5-6)
suggests, in the light of 10:5, that Bethel is the sanctuary in
question. If this is correct, we have here further evidence
that Hosea's polemic is not directed against the Bethel sanctuary
itself. For him Bethel is not Bethaven but Yahweh's house, an
authentic and legitimate Yahweh sanctuary. But proclamation is

made against it on account of the nation's sin, just as in Jer. 7 disaster is proclaimed against the Jerusalem temple, because of the nation's disregard of their obligations to Yahweh.

Two other passages, 14:3 and 7:10, must also be taken into account. Their ambiguity is too great to permit them to be used as direct evidence of Hosea's attitude to Bethel, but if the above assessment of Hosea's attitude to the sanctuary is correct, their meaning is thereby elucidated and they lend some support for the hypothesis. Leaving aside for the moment the *crux interpretum* of 14:3, namely whether פרים שפתינו refers to offerings of praise or to animal sacrifice,[78] it is clear that the prophet has a sanctuary in mind as the place at which the nation is to express its penitence and renew its devotion to Yahweh, for nowhere does he conceive of worship or penitence in purely individual and private terms. It is the action of the nation as a whole which is his concern. Bethel, Israel's major sanctuary, was the place at which her apostasy was expressed in worship of the calf image bitterly repudiated by the prophet, yet also the place where God encountered Jacob and would encounter the nation (12:5).[79] I would suggest that it is this very sanctuary, purged of its apostate rites, which the prophet has here in mind as the place where Israel's penitential offerings will be made. This suggestion permits a fresh significance in the vow, 'We will say no more, "Our God", to the work of our hands'. Seen in the context of association with Bethel, this is no vague, general renunciation of idols, but an explicit and total rejection of the calf image.

Consistent with my understanding of Hosea's attitude to Bethel is the statement in 7:10, with its parallel in 5:5: וענה גאון־ישראל בפניו. I have argued above[80] that גאון־ישראל in its original northern context referred not to Israel's arrogance in general but specifically to the expression of that pride in Israel's major sanctuary Bethel. But in what sense can the sanctuary be said to testify against the nation, to act as a witness for the prosecution? Surely the answer lies

in the discrepancy between the ancient traditions of the
sanctuary's origin as the place of encounter between the
patriarch and his God and the apostate worship practised there
by Hosea's contemporaries, from which God is absent (5:6). In
short, it is not only the prophet who indicts the nation; her
own chief sanctuary, the source of her pride, itself stands as
a witness against her. It is an ancient and honoured shrine,
but the rites practised there by Israel are not consistent with
that which is enshrined in the traditions of the holy place. The
true significance of 5:5 and 7:10 is appreciated only when due
recognition is given to the prophet's positive attitude towards
the Bethel sanctuary itself, as distinct from the cult practised
there, which he repudiates.

To conclude: a careful survey of the evidence suggests that,
far from denigrating the sanctuary at Bethel, Hosea is not
unmindful of its honoured past. It is a legitimate sanctuary,
which, far from constituting a defilement of the nation, is
itself defiled by Israel's apostasy. Bethel is still Yahweh's
house, although proclamation is made against the sanctuary
because of the sin of the worshippers (8:1). It is the place
where God would yet encounter his people (12:5). It testifies
through the ancient traditions associated with it against
Israel's faithlessness (5:5; 7:10). It is perhaps the sanctuary
at which the prophet envisages the repentant nation repudiating
idols and renewing her devotion to God (14:3).

For these reasons the pejorative designation of Bethel as
Bethaven scarcely seems consistent with Hosea's attitude and
is unlikely to be his deliberately ironical formulation. To
whom, then, is this hostile designation to be attributed, If
we are to understand it as an expression of Deuteronomistic
hostility to a northern sanctuary, reflected in the account of
2 Kings 23, we are faced with the difficulty that in other such
passages which express extreme opposition to northern
sanctuaries the name Bethel and not Bethaven is used.

Superficially the traditional view that it is Hosea's formulation appears less problematic, for it is in Hosea alone of the prophets that this designation occurs. Yet we have found this to be inconsistent with Hosea's attitude to the sanctuary. Now, it is noteworthy that the designation Bethaven occurs in four other passages in the Old Testament: Josh. 7:2; 18:12; 1 Sam. 13:5; 14:23. Wolff[81] suggests that in these instances traditionists have been influenced by Hosea's usage. Yet the question must be raised why such influence should have taken effect in these four instances alone, none of which is in any way polemical but merely a geographical reference. Indeed, whether Bethaven is to be identified with Bethel in these four passages is not clear. Certainly the place is distinguished in the present form of the MT in Josh. 7:2 as lying 'east of Bethel'. S.R. Driver[82] accepts this at its face value, and places it a couple of miles from Bethel. More commonly one or other of the names is regarded as a gloss. J.A. Soggin[83] holds the view that the words 'Bethaven east of' are an interpolation, whereas J. Gray[84] is of the opinion that the gloss comprises either 'which is near Bethaven' or 'east of Bethel'. The details are not important for the purposes of my argument, and indeed the gloss may possibly have arisen from confusion in failing to recognise the identity of Bethaven, and thus having to locate it in relation to Bethel. It is, however, significant for my argument that we have in these four passages evidence of the form Bethaven. In view of its derogatory meaning[85] it is unlikely to have been the original form of the place name, but a revocalisation of Beth-on which would have the meaning 'house of wealth/strength'. This is the view proposed by J. Bright,[86] for example. I wish to suggest that it is this name Beth-on which has been contemptuously revocalised by redactors, thus giving rise to the form Bethaven in Hos. 4:15; 5:8; 10:5, expressing Judean hostility to the famous northern sanctuary. This in its turn may have influenced the form of the name in the non-polemical passages in Joshua and Samuel. It seems to me that we have a pointer in the direction of this hypothesis in Amos 5:5 which is

frequently quoted as the basis of Hosea's formulation of the name
Bethaven. Mistaken though I believe this view to be, (as I have
argued at length above), Amos 5:5 is indeed, rightly understood,
the source of the form Bethaven by which Judean polemic was
voiced against this northern sanctuary, for underlying this
saying, and giving force to it, is a familiarity with the name
Beth-on. The saying of Amos 5:5 is clearly intended as a
powerful word of judgement against Gilgal and Bethel: כי הגלגל
גלה יגלה ובית־אל יהיה לאון. The play on the name Gilgal is
forceful and effective. In comparison there is no powerful play
on the name Bethel, such as might have been produced, for example,
by the use of the word אליל which would provide an ironical play
on the word אל and convey the idea of impotence and futility.[87]
If, however, Bethel, as Israel's principal and royal sanctuary,
was also known as Beth-on, 'house of wealth', then Amos 5:5 does
indeed contain an example of a play on words matching that on
the name Gilgal in its effectiveness, for the prophet is saying:
'Bethel shall no longer be Beth-on as you call it, but Bethaven'.
Indeed the pronunciation of the two may have differed little,
approximating to 'awn', if at this period the reduction of
diphthongs had not yet taken place.[88]

If the suggestion is accepted that Bethel was also
familiarly known as Beth-on, we have a solution to the problem
why the derogatory form should occur in Hos. 5:8, which is a
non-polemical passage merely identifying a geographical
location. Beth-on nowhere occurs, for the traditionists have
been consistent in interpreting 'house of wealth' everywhere
as 'house of wickedness'. In contrast, the form Bethel,[89] not
Bethaven, occurs in 12:5 since this is the name in the Jacob
tradition on which the prophet draws.

In short, it seems plausible to suggest that it is the
form Beth-on, not Bethel, which underlies the present
vocalisation as Bethaven not only in Hosea but elsewhere in
the Old Testament. Although this can be presented as no more
than a hypothesis, it derives credibility from the fact that it
provides an explanation why the derogatory designation Bethaven

occurs not only in polemical passages but also as a purely geographical indicator. Although the name Beth-on is preserved in the LXX it occurs nowhere in the MT but has consistently been revocalised to carry a derogatory connotation. Whether we owe this to the influence of Deuteronomistic circles, of whose hostility to Bethel the Old Testament provides ample evidence, or whether it is a convention adopted in later centuries by the Massoretes, one cannot be certain.[90]

iii. Gilgal: Evidence that Hosea's own attitude to Bethel has been overlaid and distorted by greater opposition to the sanctuary emanating from Judean circles encourages us to consider whether the same development may have taken place in relation to Gilgal. Indeed we already have evidence of this in its association with Bethaven in 4:15 discussed above.[91] Only two other references to Gilgal occur in the book of Hosea. The first of these in 9:15, despite some obscurity in meaning, seems to support the conclusion that Hosea is opposed not to the sanctuary itself but to the practices of an apostate people which dishonour ancient and hallowed places. The verse in question contains a severe indictment:

> Every evil of theirs is in Gilgal;
> there I began to hate them.

The nature of the evil here referred to is not easy to determine. Is it an allusion to Israel's past sin, in particular the inauguration of Saul's kingship at Gilgal, with all the implications of that event for the Israel of Hosea's time?[92] Or is a reference to contemporary cultic abuse more likely?[93] The question need not detain us here, for the significance of the passage for the present study is the fact that again the prophet's polemic is directed not against the sanctuary itself but against the sin of those who worshipped there:

> Because of the wickedness of their deeds
> I will drive them out of my house.[94]

I will love them no more.

It is instructive to compare this saying with the words of Amos 5:5, which pronounce judgement against the sanctuary itself: הגלגל גלה יגלה.

The remaining reference to Gilgal in 12:12 is the one with which I am particularly concerned here, with a view to the possibility that redactional shaping has had an effect on its interpretation. The presence of a serious exegetical problem becomes apparent when the variety of interpretations offered by scholars is noted. It is for this reason that one is led to suspect that we may have here an example of two levels of meaning, the first originating from Hosea and addressed to the northern kingdom, the second a later reapplication of the prophetic message to Judah. The cult practised at Gilgal is the target for severe criticism:

בגלגל שורים זבחו
גם מזבחותם כגלים על תלמי שדי

The exact nature of the offence committed is unclear, and we must first define the form of the saying. There are two possibilities; it can be understood as indictment followed by pronouncement of judgement, or the two parts of the saying may both be taken as accusation. As an example of the former view we may cite the translation offered by Wolff:

> In Gilgal they sacrifice bullocks,
>   thus their altars shall also become stone heaps
>   on the furrows of the field.[95]

A number of scholars agree though they differ in certain other details.[96] As an example of the second view we have the NEB:

> (they) sacrificed to bull-gods in Gilgal;
> their altars were common as heaps of stones beside a
>   ploughed field.

Clearly, this rendering differs from that cited above not only as to the form of the saying but also in what it understands

to be the nature of the offence committed. The exegetical points
involved here will be discussed below. It is sufficient at this
juncture to note that the offence referred to here has two
aspects, first the offering of sacrifices to bull-gods, and
second the undue proliferation of altars. Leaving aside for
the moment whether the emendation to לשורים required by this
rendering is justified, it is clear that the second objection
to the proliferation of altars and, by implication, overemphasis
on the role of sacrifice, can be paralleled elsewhere in the
material.[97] Yet I believe it to be an incorrect interpretation
of the verse in question. There are not two reasons for the
accusation, but one followed by proclamation of judgement. I
have come to this conclusion regarding the form of the saying on
the grounds that the terms used in the second part of the saying
have a significant correspondence to those of the first part,
a relationship which is meaningless if two separate accusations
are intended, but highly significant if the accusation is
matched by the pronouncement of judgement. The impact of the
saying is heightened as sin is matched by punishment. Not only
is בגלגל echoed by כגלים, but זבחו by מזבחותם, and it is surely
not coincidental that a connection exists between שורים and
תלמי שדי.[98] There is here a deliberate note of irony, and the
highly structured form of the saying indicates that the second
part is a response to the first. They are not simply co-ordinate
statements as would be the case if they were both understood as
indictments: the second is consequent upon the first. Thus גם
is to be understood not as 'also' but as 'even', adding
emphasis to the word מזבחותם.

A second, less important, exegetical problem (which ought
to be noted since scholarly opinion differs on the point)
concerns the meaning of the preposition כ in the expression
כגלים על תלמי שדי. The exact nuance of prepositions is
frequently difficult to determine for, as J. Barr has rightly
emphasised, 'in any one language the meaning of the prepositions
is a highly subtle, difficult, and idiosyncratic structure of
possibilities and choices'.[99]

ISRAELITE WORSHIP: ITS SANCTUARIES AND CULT PRACTICES   141

ב expresses likeness, but is it in this case similarity or identity?[100] Is the saying declaring that Israel's altars are (or will be) comparable with the heaps of stones which are gathered from a field in preparation for ploughing, either in their abundance[101] or in their utter lack of significance,[102] or is the meaning that Israel's altars will themselves be destroyed and become mere rubble heaps?[103] This point I shall take up presently.

We come now to the fundamental exegetical problem in the saying. What is the nature of the offence to which objection is made and as a result of which judgement is pronounced? The MT states quite simply: בגלגל שורים זבחו. Hosea elsewhere makes explicit the reasons for his strictures on his contemporaries.[104] This is true even of the passages where the particular allusion to a sinful practice or event is unclear to us owing to our lack of background information.[105] What is now obscure to us after 28 centuries would appear in a very different light to the prophet's contemporaries. Why, then, is the prophet so reticent in the passage under discussion? Or perhaps the question ought to be framed differently: Is the prophet really as reticent as he appears to be? In the light of this query we must seriously consider the possibility that the prophet's original intention has been obscured in the process of transmission, not by textual corruption but by being interpreted in the different context, and from the different point of view which transmission in the southern kingdom gave to the material. It is clear that both in ancient times, as the Versions indicate, and among modern commentators a problem has been felt. The Versions show no consistent tradition concerning the nature of the sin at issue, and there is similar disagreement among scholars today. It is evident that some commentators have felt that the phrase בגלגל שורים זבחו is not of itself sufficient as an accusation. They have resorted to emendation, with the implication that corruption of the text has obscured the meaning. Two plausible suggestions have been made; the first that this corruption is a simple case of haplography where the preposition ל has been lost

before שורים under the influence of the preceding בגלגל. Such is
the approach adopted, for example, by the NEB.[106] There is one
instance in the Old Testament where שור is used of an image,[107]
and one might cite the frequent use in the Ugaritic texts of the
cognate *tr* as a designation of El.[108] But elsewhere in the Hosea
material we find עגל used to denote the image at the Bethel
sanctuary.[109] The main objection to this emendation, however,
is the fact that the Old Testament provides no evidence whatsoever
which would enable us to associate worship of 'bull-gods' with
Gilgal.[110] The second suggestion is that שורים is a corruption
of לשדים, and the question at issue is the worship of demons,[111]
a practice attested in two instances in the Old Testament.[112]
Yet this emendation is not easy to defend in this particular
instance[113] and rests simply on the premise that the MT does not
provide a sufficient reason for the prophet's objection. Mays,
in contrast, rejects the resort to emendation and seeks to
elucidate that to which the prophet takes exception by observing
'the sacrifice of steers was not wrong in itself; the cult was
pagan and the offerings dedicated to Canaanite deities'.[114] This
is undoubtedly true in general, and evidence can be adduced from
the material.[115] The question I wish to raise is whether this is
the point of the statement in 12:12. If so, why is Hosea so
reticent here in specifying the sins of his contemporaries? By
assimilating the meaning of this passage so readily to others
where such an accusation is made explicit are we not in danger
of losing its distinctiveness and of supposing that what is
undoubtedly true of Hosea's attitude to Israel's cult in general
is true of this passage in particular? In this passage we have
no reference to pagan rites or to Canaanite deities, and there
is no mention here of Israel's apostasy, but only of sacrificial
activity at a named sanctuary.

I propose to look at the statement first in a Judean
context. The accusation includes three elements: the place of
sacrifice (בגלגל), the victims of sacrifice (שורים) and the act
of sacrifice (זבחו). To the act of sacrifice as an element in
worship there is unlikely to be objection since it was a

prominent feature of Jerusalem temple worship. Nor is there likely to have been objection to the שׁוֹר as a sacrificial victim. It was indeed a costly sacrifice.[116] It appears likely, therefore, that exception is taken to the place of sacrifice, a reasonable deduction in the light of Deuteronomistic emphasis on the centralisation of sacrificial worship at Jerusalem. The context indeed corroborates this suggestion, for the reference to the offering of sacrifices at Gilgal is preceded by the words אִם־גִּלְעָד אָוֶן אַךְ־שָׁוְא הָיוּ. The presence of אִם here is problematic;[117] leaving this point aside, however, it is the designation of Gilead as אָוֶן which is significant. One can compare the references to Bethaven discussed above. In a Judean context the statement בַּגִּלְגָּל שְׁוָרִים זִבֵּחוּ is sufficient accusation in itself in circles under Deuteronomistic influence. On worship at the Gilgal sanctuary judgement is pronounced; the very sanctuaries of the northern kingdom fall under judgement. Yet what of the primary level of meaning in its original northern context? I have already argued[118] that Hosea's attitude is not one of hostility to the sanctuary itself. To what offence does he voice a protest in 12:12? It is unlikely that he repudiates sacrificial activity as such. Some scholars have argued, chiefly on the basis of 6:6, that Hosea is opposed in principle to the offering of sacrifice.[119] I believe those to be correct who understand Hosea's rejection of sacrifice to be relative, not total, that his opposition is not to the institutions of worship as such but to their corruption and misuse.[120] Hosea repudiates sacrificial worship which takes place in disregard of Yahweh's demands (4:6-10; 8:11-13) and without loyal devotion (6:6; 10:1-2). If this view is correct, that Hosea does not reject sacrificial activity as such, but only its substitution for true commitment, we are left with שְׁוָרִים as the target of his protest. It is here that I believe later Judean interpretation has overlaid and obscured the original meaning. As a key to that meaning we must turn first to the parallel reference to Gilead: אִם־גִּלְעָד אָוֶן אַךְ־שָׁוְא הָיוּ. What is the point of this saying? The variety of weak renderings produced, of which the RSV can be taken as an example, highlights the difficulty:

> If there is iniquity in Gilead
> they shall surely come to naught.[121]

The NEB makes a valiant attempt to produce something more forceful:

> Was there idolatry in Gilead?
> Yes: they were worthless ....

A consideration of the context, however, suggests a solution. In 12:8-10 a contrast is drawn between the nation's pursuit of wealth (מצאתי און לי) and the intervention of God in judgement. A similar theme can be traced in the preceding verses also. Ephraim makes treaties[122] with foreign nations but it is merely a pursuit of the elusive wind (v. 2). And Jacob strives with God באונו, but in the end he seeks God's favour with tears and God addresses him (vv. 4-5). The presence of this theme, the futility of man's efforts apart from God, and the occurrence of the word און in vv. 4 and 9, suggest the possibility that this is the meaning intended in 12a. We have no longer a weak statement but the emphatic declaration, entirely appropriate to the context,

> though[123] Gilead was wealthy, they have indeed become nothingness.

The revocalisation of אוֹן as אָוֶן may have been assisted by the fact that Gilead is described in 6:8 as קרית פעלי און, and the original meaning thus obscured. All man's wealth cannot secure his future when God acts in judgement. It is as a parallel to this that the reference to cultic activity at Gilgal is to be interpreted. The prophet is not opposed to the Gilgal sanctuary, nor to the act of sacrificing, but the point of his protest concerns the offering of שורים, not because they are unacceptable on technical grounds, but because he wishes to remind his hearers that their wealthy offerings are merely a symbol of their affluence[124] and not immune from the judgement of God. Man's offerings cannot avert the consequences of his sin, and the very altars on which these costly sacrifices are offered will become mere rubble heaps.[125] In short, in its original northern context the saying is concerned with the futility of man's wealth apart from God. God maintains his sovereign freedom to act whether in judgement or salvation. What God requires of his people is a personal encounter with himself. But when God acts in judgement the affluence of the nation and its sacrificial offerings are as nothing. In its later Judean context, in contrast, the saying is motivated by opposition to the Gilgal sanctuary itself. It is on this level of interpretation that the vocalisation of זבחו as Piel can be held to signify, as BDB comments,[126] sacrifice 'in unlawful places'. Thus in this instance we have evidence not only of a development of Hosea's message but of a distinct change in meaning attributable to its new context in Judah during the process of transmission. Two distinct levels of interpretation must be taken into account.

The offering of sacrifices

Thus far we have considered references in the material to the great sanctuaries of Bethel and Gilgal in an attempt to determine to what extent Hosea's own attitude has been overlaid by that of later interpreters in the southern kingdom. The evidence has indicated that hostility to the sanctuaries themselves belongs to the secondary material. Hosea's own attitude to the ancient sanctuaries of his own country is of a more positive kind.

The fact that the exegetical problem of 12:12 was resolved by allowing for two distinct levels of interpretation, the one belonging to the original northern context of the saying, the other arising during the process of transmission in Judah, suggests the need to consider whether other exegetical difficulties should perhaps be approached in this way. This is not to deny, of course, that some problems may have arisen through textual corruption, but before we resort to emendation the possibility that later Judean interpretation may have obscured the original meaning and have created ambiguity should at least be taken into account. This possibility ought, indeed, to be reckoned with throughout the material, not merely where difficulties appear to exist. I have selected by way of example two passages for examination on the grounds that they are of special interest in view of the problems they present for exegesis. The expressions which I wish particularly to consider are זבחי אדם in 13:2 and פרים שפתינו in 14:3.

13:2

This saying has proved highly problematic to commentators and translators. The variety of approaches adopted and of meanings proposed indicates the extent of the difficulty. I shall consider first examples of translations offered by those who wish to retain the MT and to avoid resorting to emendation. Among these is the

NEB:
> Men say of them,
> 'Those who kiss calf-images offer human sacrifice'.

There are, however, several objections to this rendering. The translation of the pronoun הם is unnatural, for it seems to refer more naturally to the subject of the preceding verbs. But since this is the apostate worshippers themselves it is inappropriate. If, nevertheless, we accept the proposed rendering, what does it mean? Is it to be understood as a rumour that human sacrifice is offered without necessarily any basis in fact? If so, it seriously weakens the impact made by the accusation in the previous lines, and is a strange prelude to the pronouncement of doom which follows in v. 3. And who are those who spread this rumour? There is no suggestion of a division of opinion within the nation whereby one section of the community expresses disapproval of the cultic activities of others. To suppose that it is intended to refer to the opinion of surrounding nations is also highly improbable.

The rendering offered by Wolff[127] avoids this particular

difficulty:

> They say to themselves:
> "Those who sacrifice men kiss calves".

Although he finds corroboration for this translation in 7:2 ובל־יאמרו ללבבם, the meaning is not entirely appropriate. Wolff suggests that it is intended as an ironical cultic precept to 'disclose the complete absurdity of the fertility rites'.[128] The most serious objection to this translation, however, as to that of the NEB above, is the improbability that the prophet would dismiss with such brevity so grave a perversion of the legitimate means of approach to God as the offering of human sacrifice. The context in which the saying appears is concerned with the foolishness of worshipping man-made images, a theme which is taken up elsewhere in the material.[129] There is also much evidence of the prophet's protest against the immorality of Israel's cult practices.[130] If, however, human sacrifice formed part of those rituals it is strange that this brief passing reference alone should have been preserved.[131] One is aware that in general an argument from silence is to be regarded with suspicion, but there are times - and this is, I believe, one of them - when what is not said is highly significant. It must also be noted that the Old Testament provides no evidence that human sacrifice was a concomitant of calf worship. The only passage where the two practices are referred to together is 2 Kings 17:16-17,[132] but this is a Deuteronomistic passage which summarizes in sweeping generalisations the many sins committed by Israel for which 'the Lord was very angry with Israel, and removed them out of his sight'. In fact the Old Testament provides more evidence of this practice in Judah than in the northern kingdom. Specific instances of human sacrifice are recorded in connection with the Judean kings Ahaz[133] and Manasseh,[134] but in the narrative account of Josiah's reform in 2 Kings 23 among Israel's many misdeeds there is no reference to the practice of offering human sacrifice. On the contrary, it is Josiah who is said to have slain the priests of the high places upon their altars.¹³⁵ It seems unlikely, then, that Hosea is here concerned to condemn an evil of such enormity.

This difficulty is obviated if אדם is understood not as an objective genitive but as explicative of the preceding noun. The meaning of the phrase will then be 'men who sacrifice'.¹³⁶ Many instances of this use of a genitive of nearer definition can be adduced. In none of them, however, does the *nomen regens* have such a strongly verbal element. The closest parallels are: נסיכי אדם 'men who are princes' (Mic. 5:4), אביוני אדם 'men who are poor' (Is. 29:19) and כסיל אדם 'a man who is a fool' (Prov. 15:20).¹³⁷ However, in none of these instances is there any ambiguity of meaning; it is open to question whether the genitive in זבחי אדם can be taken as explicative since it would be open to misunderstanding as an objective genitive. The solution to the problem cannot plausibly be sought in this direction.

Others have sought a solution by emendation. The reconstruction suggested by Harper¹³⁸ is a rather drastic one and entirely conjectural. He suggests that זבחי is the sole remaining fragment of a three word line corresponding to אדם עגלים ישקון. He proposes to read עם זבחים לשדים, arguing that עם has been lost through its resemblance to הם and to the ending of אמרים, and that לשדים has dropped out through its resemblance to אדם. A neat text is produced, but on a very insecure basis.

Simpler and altogether more convincing is the widely accepted emendation of זבחי to זבחו. As an example we may take the RSV:

Sacrifice to these (i.e. the idols), they say.
Men kiss calves!¹⁴⁰

The balance of the sentence is good and the meaning appropriate. The entire meaning of v. 2 is ironical. Out of silver men make their idols according to their own understanding¹⁴¹ (viz. of what God is) (כתבונם עצבים ¹⁴² מכספם). Then in pride at their own craftsmanship (מעשה חרשים כלה) they say, with emphasis falling on להם, 'Sacrifice to these'. And, comments the prophet, 'Men kiss[143] calves'! The juxtaposition of אדם and עגלים is deliberately ironical.

The simplicity of this emendation, the appropriateness of the meaning, and the balanced structure which results from the necessary redivision of the sentence: להם הם אמרים זבחו // אדם עגלים ישקון all serve to lend credibility to the view that this was the original form of the saying. It is entirely consistent with Hosea's polemic elsewhere. There is no sudden and isolated reference to human sacrifice but a protest barbed with irony against the foolishness of men who pay worship to their own craftsmanship. This, then, is the meaning of the saying in its primary northern context.

How then did the present form of the text arise? There are three possibilities: that it is due to scribal error; that it arose from misunderstanding of the situation in the northern kingdom; that it is a deliberate change in order to heighten the polemic against apostate practices. To take the first possibility: if זבחי arose from an accidental corruption of זבחו, its subsequent interpretation as a construct participle would require a following noun in the genitive, supplied by אדם and leading to a redivision of the sentence. In support of this view are the easy confusion of י and ו in the square, though not in the ancient Hebrew script, and the LXX θύσατε. If this view is adopted the reading of the MT is without significance for the subject of this study. Before accepting this easy solution too readily, however, it must be noted that the LXX hardly supports the text produced by the suggested emendation. It seems likely that the LXX translators were themselves wrestling with a difficult text, and have given to the saying a very different meaning: αὐτοὶ λέγουσιν θύσατε ἀνθρώπους μόσχοι γὰρ ἐκλελοίπασιν.

'They say, "Sacrifice men, for the calves have failed".'

But the main objection to the suggestion of textual error is the difficulty of explaining how so simple a text should have given rise to so difficult a reading. The principle of *lectio difficilior* is applicable here.

The second alternative posed above, that the reference to human sacrifice arose from Judean misunderstanding of Israel's religious practices associated with the calf image, has more to commend it. The reading of the MT זבחי אדם which is problematic in the context of Hosea's ministry becomes explicable when interpreted in the context of Judah, for among the evils abolished in the Josianic reform was the practice of offering human sacrifice in the valley of Hinnom.[144] It is a plausible suggestion that a saying of Hosea's should, in the light of Judah's own experience of the evils of apostasy, have been misinterpreted as referring to human sacrifice. I believe some support for this argument can be derived from the account of Josiah's reforming activity in 2 Kings 23. Whatever the historical basis of the account, is it not significant that Josiah is reported not only to have slaughtered the priests of the high places, but specifically to have 'slaughtered (them) (ויזבח) ..... upon the altars, and burned the bones of men (אדם) upon them' (v. 20)? This action is stated explicitly to have been 'according to all that he had done at Bethel' (v. 19), the site of the calf image. Was this in a macabre way intended as a punishment to fit the crime of which Israel's priests were presumed guilty, the crime of human sacrifice? At any rate the possibility must be acknowledged that there existed in Judah a belief that Israel's calf image was associated with the practice of human sacrifice, an association implied in the measures taken by Josiah against the priests of Israel's high places, and apparently of Bethel also, and probably the source of the present form of the saying in 13:2. Whether this belief exerted its influence on the saying unconsciously, or whether the reinterpretation was deliberate as seems to have been the case in the reinterpretation of Bethel as Bethaven, one cannot say. Certainly by the time of Ezekiel[145] we find Israel linked with Judah in the accusation of practising human sacrifice. The same is true also of Ps. 106:37-38. Both of these instances

ISRAELITE WORSHIP: ITS SANCTUARIES AND CULT PRACTICES   151

belong to a time long after the fall of the northern kingdom[146] and are consistent with the suggestion I have made above that human sacrifice was not a part of the Israelite cult associated with the calf image but was attributed to the worship of the northern kingdom by Judeans, to whom the present form of the saying in 13:2 is due rather than to Hosea himself.

14.3

In this instance, too, a fundamental question of meaning is at issue. The problem is well illustrated by a comparison of the RSV: 'We will render the fruit of our lips',[147] with the NEB: 'We will pay our vows with cattle from our pens'.[148] The saying forms part of the unit vv. 2-4[149] of which there is little doubt that it comes from Hosea. The chief pointers to this are the reference to Assyria as a powerful force in international politics, and to the place of idols in Israel's worship, both now to be repudiated if the prophet's exhortation is heeded. Thus the sins confessed embrace the spheres of politics and cult which are so prominent a concern of Hosea's. As corroborative evidence, though insufficient to stand on its own, are the many connections with Hosea's vocabulary.[150] The likelihood that the saying relates to Bethel was noted above.[151] The passage contains a number of problems, but the phrase on which I wish to focus attention here is פרים שפתינו. In the present form of the text there can be little doubt that שפתינו must be taken as indicating how פרים, that is to say the offerings, is to be understood. The paraphrase of the RV captures the meaning: 'So will we render as bullocks the offering of our lips'. The words פרים and שפתינו appear to stand in apposition, the one defining the other.[152] Yet the very strangeness of the saying with its odd juxtaposition of פרים and שפתינו compels us to ask what is the probable original form of the saying, and whether the present form has arisen through the error of a singularly inept scribe or here, too, redactional influence is to be reckoned with.

First, the probable primary form of the saying: it is this

that the RSV and the NEB, in contrast to the RV, have attempted
to recover, though the conclusions to which they have come are
diametrically opposed to each other. Does the prophet consider
animal sacrifice a worthy expression of repentance, or is he, as
Mays holds, 'categorically against the sacrificial approach to
Yahweh .... Prayer is to be the means of their access to God'.[153]
The question cannot be resolved on grammatical grounds alone. To
posit the presence of enclitic מ,[154] unrecognised by the
Massoretes and thus giving rise to the present text, does not
resolve the problem. The text could equally well be vocalised
as פָּרִים or פְּרִים. If the latter is adopted, שפתינו will be
understood in the sense of 'pens' or 'folds' and connected with
שפתים,[155] or משפתים,[156] the latter being a possibility by
redividing the words פרי משפתינו without resorting to enclitic מ.
The question must, therefore, be resolved in the wider context of
Hosea's attitude towards sacrifice, and to this we must now turn.

I have argued above[157] that Hosea is not opposed to the
offering of sacrifice as a valid element in worship, but only to
the substitution of sacrifice for חסד and דעת, and to undue
emphasis on such activity. It is going beyond the evidence to
suggest that Hosea categorically rejects the validity of
sacrifice. A number of passages are adduced by Mays[158] in
support of his contention to this effect. However, a closer
examination of the passages concerned suggests a different
conclusion. Thus 4:8:

> They feed on the sin of my people;
> they are greedy for their iniquity,

hardly warrants the conclusion that this is a total condemnation
of sacrifice. The saying is set in the context of condemnation
of a priesthood which rejects knowledge and ignores the law of
God (v. 6). Far from warning against sin, they derive personal
gain from much sin which requires much sacrifice. It is,
therefore, the distortion of the purpose of sacrifice at which
the prophet protests.[159] The implication of 5:6, to which Mays
also refers, is similar. Observing the normal cultic requirements

cannot avail in the abnormal situation to which the prophet is addressing himself. God has withdrawn from his people, and more than the ritual offering of sacrifices is necessary to restore the relationship. I have already noted above[160] that 6:6 is not to be understood as a total rejection of sacrifice. The contrast is posed starkly between חסד and זבח for emphasis, and is not to be taken in an absolute sense as the parallel expression, 'knowledge of God rather than[161] burnt offerings' indicates. The last passage which Mays adduces is 8:13, but here again the love of sacrifice[162] is juxtaposed with disregard of Yahweh's laws. It is in this context that the prophet says יהוה לא רצם. To this we may add the evidence of 10:1, a protest against the proliferation of altars. But here again the reason for the prophet's objection is not his opposition to sacrifice, but the fact that Israel's altars are built as an expression of her wealth, a symbol of her affluence, and not as an expression of her need to approach a holy God. This is surely the significance of the words (10:2) עתה יאשמו. Israel's altars are not a means of expiating sin, but a cause of sin. In 3:4 a word of judgement is pronounced on the nation. Cultic as well as political activity will cease. Is this perhaps evidence that the prophet regarded sacrifice as unacceptable? It seems not, in view of v. 3. The unnamed woman whose life is symbolic of the nation is to be deprived of legitimate as well as illegitimate relationships, suggesting that such is true also of the nation. Finally 9:4 must be taken into account. This statement is set in the context of threat of exile, the inability to celebrate Yahweh's festival (v. 5). The implication of the saying is, however, that under different circumstances they might acceptable 'pour libations of wine to the Lord' and 'please him with their sacrifices'.[163] It is for these reasons that I believe it to be an incorrect understanding of Hosea's message to attribute to him a total repudiation of sacrifice. In the context of a right relationship with God sacrifice has a legitimate place, but it should be noted that in 14:3 the offering of sacrifice is in response to God's forgiveness,[164] not the motivation of it.

Yet the objection may be raised: is not the context concerned particularly with the expression of penitence, indicating that 'fruit of lips' is the likely meaning of פרים שפתינו? Israel, in returning to the Lord, is urged קחו עמכם דברים. This is followed by the words אמרו אליו, and a further reference to verbal expressions is seen by some in the rather difficult phrase וקח־טוב, whereby טוב is derived from a root טבב and carries the meaning 'word'.[165] This last is unconvincing, but in any event word accompanied sacrifice in cultic celebration.

It remains to be enquired how the text reached its present form. Is it due to textual corruption or are redactional influences to be traced here? Wolff[166] describes the MT פרים as a misreading. The very strangeness of the reading, and the fact that פרים and שפתינו stand in surprising juxtaposition makes accidental corruption unlikely. Scribal error can more reasonably be posited when the words form a familiar phrase. I am conscious of moving here in the realm of conjecture, but I cannot escape the conviction that redactional influence is at work. The two words stand apparently in apposition, with שפתינו indicating that פרים is to be understood metaphorically: the offering is not a material one. It is possible that such theologically motivated reinterpretation is Deuteronomistic. The northern prophet had spoken of an offering of פרים to be made by the nation in response to God's forgiveness, but for the Deuteronomists, with their emphasis on the centralisation of worship at the Jerusalem temple, no material offering made at a northern sanctuary could be acceptable.[167] This suggestion is not entirely without problems. Clearly, it leaves open the question why in this particular instance the call to repentance שובה ישראל עד יהוה אלהיך should continue to have been regarded as referring solely to the northern kingdom, in contrast to the many sayings which, as we have seen, were reapplied to Judah. Given this new situational context, animal sacrifice would have been appropriate to Jerusalem temple worship, and the expression of penitence would appear to be compatible with the Deuteronomistic account of Josiah's reform.[168] There remains also the problem of why פרים has remained unchanged, and not reinterpreted as פרי, if for theological reasons שפתינו has been reinterpreted to indicate that the offerings referred to are of a spiritual, not a material, kind. The conclusion to which I have come is that we must be dealing here with a written text, a question which has up to this point remained outside the concerns of this study.[169] The change from שְׁפָתֵינוּ 'pens' to שְׂפָתֵינוּ 'lips' required no consonantal change. In contrast, to reinterpret פָּרִים 'bulls' as פְּרִי 'fruit' would have necessitated a change from plural to singular, since a plural of פְּרִי is not found in the O.T.[170] For the period in which this reinterpretation is to be located we should probably look not to the Deuteronomists but to the Babylonian exile with its enforced cessation of animal sacrifice. This suggestion derives corroboration from the apparently inconsequential statement with which v. 4 ends: אשר־בך ירחם יתום. As Mays comments, 'the affirmation of trust ..... is attached to the vow sequence quite awkwardly in the Hebrew text, and looks like an addition to the original saying'.[171] He goes on to interpret the saying with reference not to the individual but to the community, to Israel 'now desolate as an orphan'.[172] That this saying may have as its background the Babylonian exile is suggested to me by Lam. 5:3 יתומים היינו.

To conclude: both AV and RV are true to the MT, though the rigidly literal translation of the former requires comment to be intelligible. The NEB, in contrast, represents Hosea's meaning, though in disregarding the vocalisation of the MT it raises a fundamental question of the correct approach to Bible translation. It is the canonical form of the text with which the translator is concerned. It is the exegete who is concerned to elucidate the meaning of the text at its various levels. The RSV, in contrast to the other translations instanced above, represents neither the primary northern form nor the final meaning of the saying, but in adopting the LXX reading has taken the process of spiritualising still further.

CONCLUSION

The process by which the book of Hosea reached its present form is a highly complex one, the latest stages of which are represented by its present framework comprising the title of the book and the final solemn admonition to the reader to respond which ends the book. No attempt has been made in this study to raise many of the issues involved. My sole concern has been to explore in depth from the standpoint of redaction criticism three important areas of the material, namely salvation sayings, references to the southern kingdom and the Davidic monarchy, and attitudes expressed towards sanctuaries and cult practices in the northern kingdom. Within these specified areas I have attempted to assess the nature and extent of Judean influence on the final form of the material. The terms 'primary' and 'secondary' have been applied to the material in a purely chronological sense only, and do not imply that material which is unlikely to have originated in Hosea's northern milieu is of less importance, for the process of redaction is to be seen as a 'living remodelling'[1] of the tradition in the conviction that what was addressed to a previous generation as a word from God still has relevance for a later time and for a new situation. The main question at issue, however, is this: does the final Judean form of the material constitute merely a development and extension of the prophet's message to suit the circumstances of a later time, or is it more aptly described as a reshaping and reinterpretation of the message under the influence of Judean religious traditions undergirded with a difference of theology? In short, is the distinction between material of northern and of southern origin to be explained on purely historical and circumstantial grounds, or is the difference of a theological kind?

The attempt to distinguish between primary and secondary material, and thus to evaluate the importance of redactional influence on the formation of the text, is bound to be a

CONCLUSION

difficult if not hazardous undertaking. All too easily issues are prejudged by unconscious preconceptions of what is consistent or inconsistent with the message of a northern prophet, and consequently the study ceases to be truly objective. For this reason I have not relied on content as a criterion in attempting to distinguish between primary and secondary material, but have looked instead to sentence structure, since this may serve as an indication of the presence of supplementary material which has not been completely integrated into its context, together with historical setting which may indicate compatibility or otherwise with the circumstances of Hosea's ministry. At best the results can only be tentative. It is, however, possible to impose some external control on them in that they can be checked against findings in a related field of Old Testament study. Should my results prove to be compatible with these, they may be said to derive from this some measure of support. I have in mind the comparison which can be drawn with conclusions reached in the field of studies in Deuteronomy, which provide a useful check on the credibility of my results.

In the area of salvation sayings I found little material which on grammatical or historical grounds appeared to be secondary. Taking as my starting point two salvation sayings (2:16-17; 3:5) which are, I argued, integral to their present context and cannot be detached from it without doing despite to the structure and meaning of the text, I came to the conclusion not only that expressions of future hope form a consistent element in Hosea's message but that a distinctive theology of repentance is discernible in the primary material. Here Israel's penitence is not regarded as the prerequisite to Yahweh's saving action; the initiative lies always with Yahweh, and from his saving, rather than his judgmental action will come the nation's repentance and transformation. In the one instance (11:10) where the language of the saying showed clear traces of the traditions of Jerusalem temple worship, and was for that reason attributed to later Judean influence, in content it seemed consistent with Hosea's thought, and there was no discernible

change in theological emphasis. It was simply an extension of
the range of the prophet's message to meet the situation of a
later time. Elsewhere, however, and perhaps unconsciously, a
subtle shift in emphasis was apparent. A number of salvation
sayings were clearly fragmentary and detached from their
original context. In these instances the present arrangement
of the material, with the new contextualisation which it created,
proved to be of particular interest. The idea was conveyed,
not overtly but by implication, that repentance must precede
salvation, was indeed its *sine qua non*. The initiative lay,
therefore, not with God but with the nation. It is at this
point, in the theology which seems to be implicit in the present
arrangement of the sayings, that a significant divergence from
Hosea's thought can be detected. For the prophet, as we have
seen, the initiative is always Yahweh's, and it is his saving
action rather than his judgement which will awaken the nation to
repentance and thus effect its transformation. That this
editorial activity with its different theological emphasis was
more reasonably to be attributed to Judean influence than to a
northern traditionist closely associated with Hosea was
demonstrated particularly from the collection of sayings in
2:18-25 where this divergent theology was much in evidence.
Here the recurrent use of the formula 'in that day' suggested
that the same editorial hand was at work as in 1:5. Since this
saying unquestionably destroys the elaborate schematic structure
of ch. 1, a passage which probably originated with one of the
prophet's intimate associates, the present disrupted arrangement
of the material can hardly be said to derive from the same
milieu, but must belong to another stage in the redactional
process.

The second area selected for examination, the references to
Judah and the Davidic dynasty, also produced unexpected results.
The material fell into three broad categories: i) limited
criticism of Judah relating specifically to its hostile
relationship with the northern kingdom; ii) a sense of nostalgia
for, and confidence in, the Davidic dynasty in the south, whose

CONCLUSION   159

stability contrasted with the anarchy increasingly prevalent in
the northern kingdom during its last years; iii) wide-ranging
criticism of Judah's cultic worship and religious life as a whole.
On the basis of the criteria adopted in the study, that we should
be guided not by the content of the sayings but by historical
considerations and by the evidence of sentence structure and
linguistic features, the conclusion was reached that the first
two categories of sayings belong to the ministry of Hosea in
contrast to the third which is the result of Judean supplementation and reshaping of the material. This conclusion is at
variance with the widely accepted view that sayings which evince
a favourable attitude to Judah and the Davidic monarchy are of
southern origin.

   The third area examined concerned attitudes expressed or
implied towards the sanctuaries and cult practices of northern
Israel. Here the evidence indicated that, in spite of his
unremitting and uncompromising criticism of the cult as
practised by his contemporaries, Hosea was not antagonistic
towards the major sanctuaries at Bethel and Gilgal, but
displayed a positive attitude towards them. These were
sanctuaries which had an honourable history associated with the
great traditions of Israel's past. In the present form of the
material, however, a different more hostile attitude appears.
Polemic is directed against the very existence of the
sanctuaries, as for example in the hostile designation of Bethel
as Bethaven. This attitude does not stem from the northern
prophet but is attributable to Judean influence with its concern
to centralise sacrificial worship at the Jerusalem temple. The
hostile attitude expressed in certain passages comes close to
the total rejection of northern sanctuaries which is found in
the Deuteronomistic account of the Josianic reform. Hosea's
attitude, in contrast, may be compared to that of Malachi in a
later century with regard to the Jerusalem temple, where the
sanctuary itself is held in honour while the practices by which
it is desecrated are condemned. By his positive attitude
towards these two major northern sanctuaries Hosea is

distinguished from his close contemporary Amos, despite the superficial resemblance of certain of their sayings. This is itself significant in view of Amos' Judean origins, and lends credibility to the view that the hard polemic against the northern sanctuaries themselves, and the negative light in which they are regarded, originate in the southern kingdom. In a few instances the possibility was explored that a number of problems and ambiguities may have arisen not from textual corruption but from the overlaying of primary northern material by later Judean interpretation, though the question had sometimes to be left open whether this had occurred accidentally through failure to understand correctly the cult practices of the northern kingdom or deliberately through hostility to them.

We turn now to the need to provide, if possible, some form of external control against which the plausibility of these conclusions may be checked. Here the comparison which can be drawn between the books of Hosea and Deuteronomy is of value. The origins of Deuteronomy are themselves highly complex, and it, too, includes both northern and southern traditions. It is at the same time the deposit of sacral and cultic traditions which betray a northern origin and is also closely associated with the Jerusalem temple and a concern for centralisation of worship in the 7th century, a demand never advocated as far as we can tell by any, whether priests or prophets, in the northern kingdom.[2] To account satisfactorily for both aspects of Deuteronomy has been, and indeed still is, a major concern of scholarship.[3] Nevertheless, the existence of a close relationship between Hosea and Deuteronomy is widely recognised, even though there is disagreement as to the precise origins of each.[4] In view of this it is reasonable that the conclusions to which I have come concerning those aspects of the Hosea material which belong to northern and southern traditions respectively should be compared with results reached on this same question in the field of Deuteronomy research. If there appears to be an irreconcilable conflict between them my

CONCLUSION 161

conclusions must inevitably be called into question. If, on the other hand, there appears to be consistency between them, some degree of corroboration will thus be provided for the views which I have expressed.

I have emphasised as an element in the primary northern stratum of the material the prophet's concern for the reunion of the divided kingdoms and his commitment to the ideal of the one people of God. Similarly the unmistakable 'all Israel' orientation of Deuteronomy has been associated with its northern origins and not attributed to Judean influence.[5] There seems no reason, therefore, to reverse my judgement that this is a fundamental element in Hosea's thought. I have suggested also that the positive attitude to Judah which is evident in the material belongs to the primary northern stratum, on the grounds that Hosea's hopes for the continuity of the authentic traditions of Yahwism came to centre on the southern kingdom. It is indeed a *priori* unlikely that if Hosea had been anti-Judean, as he has sometimes been represented, his sayings would have been preserved in Judah. On this point, too, my conclusion is in line with evidence drawn from Deuteronomy. The attitude which I have postulated for Hosea is consistent with the view of those whose reform programme is enshrined in Deuteronomy, for it appears that they themselves came to Judah after the fall of the northern kingdom there to preserve their cherished traditions in the belief that the future of the people of God lay in the southern kingdom.[6]

In departing from the widely accepted view and arguing that Hosea had a positive attitude towards the Davidic monarchy I again find corroboration in Deuteronomy. Hosea's attitude towards kingship was, I believe, a pragmatic one. Valuing the stability of monarchy established, as it was in Judah, on the dynastic principle, he did not adopt the Jerusalem ideology of kingship, but regarded it as a means of maintaining order, and of avoiding anarchy such as had disrupted the last years of the northern kingdom. Similarly, kingship has a place in

Dt. 17:15ff., though also there is no commitment to the sacral kingship ideology of Jerusalem.[7] Indeed Deuteronomy firmly reasserts the Sinai covenant tradition which had become in effect subordinate to the tradition of the Davidic covenant in the Jerusalem cult.

In these respects an analogy can be drawn between Hosea and Deuteronomy. In his attitude to the southern kingdom and to the Davidic monarchy Hosea appears as the pre-cursor of Deuteronomy whose roots also lie in the northern kingdom. When we turn to those elements in the book of Hosea which I have argued are to be attributed to its transmission in Judah, we find them consistent with aspects of Deuteronomy which seem to belong to its promulgation in Judah. Among these is the concern with the centralisation of worship, explicit in Deuteronomy, implicit in Hosea in that it manifests itself in opposition to the sanctuaries of the northern kingdom. As E.W. Nicholson argues, the northern provenance of Deuteronomy does not account for 'the demand for the centralization of the cult which, as far as we know, was never advocated by any northern circle whether priestly or prophetic'.[8] This seems to be in some sense a concession to the traditions of Jerusalem, though acceptable to the authors of Deuteronomy 'as a vital means of securing the cultic purity for which they strove'.[9] For the authors of Deuteronomy in the 7th century the situation was becoming increasingly grave, for disintegration within the southern kingdom politically and religiously threatened the sole remaining representatives of the people of God. It is to this urgent situation in Judah that the reshaping of Hosea's message, with its outright condemnation of northern Israel's cult and sanctuaries, is addressed.

Finally it remains for us to consider how the two theologies of repentance which can be traced in the Hosea material in its present form relate to the book of Deuteronomy. I have argued that for Hosea the emphasis lies on Yahweh's saving action as that from which the nation's penitence will come. The initiative is always Yahweh's. In contrast, the

CONCLUSION 163

Judean reshaping of the message shifts the emphasis. The prelude to forgiveness is repentance. It is this latter emphasis which is prominent throughout Deuteronomy with its repeated exhortation to obedience. It is true that Dt. 30:6 affirms the primacy of God's action in effecting the transformation of the nation. Yet this gracious act of God depends on the prior response of the people. When they return to the Lord and obey his voice, then the Lord will have compassion on them (30:2-3). This challenge to obedience which is so prominent in Deuteronomy is undoubtedly to be associated with the Sinai covenant tradition with its continual reminder of the obligations laid upon the nation, and is probably a reflection of covenant renewal ceremonies. This is a distinctively northern tradition in contrast to the emphasis on the Davidic covenant which is distinctive of Jerusalem. How then are we to account for the contrast in this respect with Hosea from whose sayings, as Muilenburg notes,[10] the conditional is strangely absent? It must be emphasised that Hosea is no less concerned than are the authors of Deuteronomy with the need for repentance. The difference lies in the place they accord to the possibility of a change of heart on the part of the nation. For the authors of Deuteronomy response by the nation still remained a possibility, and to this end they strove for the survival of the people of God. For Hosea in the last years of the northern kingdom the only hope for a nation which persisted in its apostasy lay in the gracious action of God. Such was in fact the pre-requisite of the nation's repentance, not its consequence. That the difference is due to the change in historical situation is corroborated by the fact that when Judah, too, reaches the point of no return and exile is inescapable, both Jeremiah[11] and Ezekiel[12] proclaim the initiative of God as the ground of future hope. The promise of restoration is no longer bound to the prior repentance of the people, but is an act of God's grace. It seems reasonable, then, to hold that the emphasis on the prior need for repentance which belongs to the redactional material in Hosea and is comparable to the stance adopted in Deuteronomy arises from the different needs of the situation to which it was addressed. It is not the theology of repentance in response to a crisis arising from the nation's obduracy in rebellion against Yahweh.

The Judean redaction of Hosea has, therefore, introduced a fundamental change in the content of the material, not by turning a prophet of doom into one of salvation, nor by adopting an alien pro-Judean stance for indeed it extends the scope of criticism directed against the southern kingdom, but by overlaying a theology of repentance in which the initiative lies solely with the forgiving love of Yahweh with the call for man's prior response. But Hosea's theology is overlaid, not obliterated, and the same note re-emerges eventually when Judah is faced with the extreme catastrophe of exile. In this period, as by Hosea in an earlier time, the nation's history is seen by both Jeremiah and Ezekiel as altogether failure, and the new and transforming action is Yahweh's alone.

It is important that the book of Hosea should be allowed to address us theologically, not only as a totality but in its different strands of tradition. The different emphases of the two theologies of repentance are both alike necessary, and are indeed complementary to each other. They serve as a reminder that the divine word is always rooted in history. Changed circumstances require a different aspect of the truth. The emphasis of the primary stratum which comes from Hosea in the 8th century concerns God's sovereign freedom to act in salvation even when man is totally undeserving. The later Judean emphasis concerns the importance of man's response to the summons to repent, the need for an act of will. It is significant that in that basic article of Israel's faith, the Sinai covenant, the two aspects are combined. Heavy obligation is laid upon the nation to respond, but the covenant itself is rooted in the divine initiative. Continuance of the relationship lies with man's volition: the offer of the relationship rests solely on the grace of God. But to explore further the inter-relationship of these two factors must belong to another study.

NOTES TO INTRODUCTION

1. For a discussion of the evidence see especially the recent commentaries by H.W. Wolff, *Hosea* (ET 1974), xxii; W. Rudolph, *Hosea* (1966), 20ff.; J.L. Mays, *Hosea* (1969), 1f.; also the earlier commentary by W.R. Harper, *Amos and Hosea* (1905), cxl, 202f. Among the evidence adduced is the following: the prophet addresses himself primarily to the political and religious situation of the northern kingdom with which he is clearly familiar; the cities and sanctuaries mentioned are those of the north; certain distinctive features of his language are best explained as dialect.
2. For the majority view see, for example, O. Eissfeldt, *The Old Testament. An Introduction* (ET 1965), 385, who holds that 'Hosea was a native of the northern kingdom, or at any rate worked there exclusively'; G. Fohrer, *Introduction to the Old Testament* (ET 1970), 419; also such varied works as G.R. Driver, 'Studies in the Vocabulary of the Old Testament', *JTS* 36, 1935, 294; N.H. Snaith, *Mercy and Sacrifice. A Study of the Book of Hosea* (1953), 50; J. Bright, *A History of Israel* (revised ed. 1972), 260; P.R. Ackroyd, 'Hosea', *Peake's Commentary on the Bible* (revised ed. 1962), 603. For a strongly dissenting view see I. Engnell, 'Hosea', *SBU* (1962), cols. 978f.; N.H. Tur-Sinai, *Halashon Vehasefer*, II (1950), 304-323. (For a discussion of this view see p. 57.
3. Cf. E. Day, 'Is the Book of Hosea Exilic?' *AJSL* 26, 1909-10, 106.
4. Cf. H.L. Ginsberg, 'Hosea, Book of', *EJ* (1971), cols. 1016ff., who argues that only chs. 1-3 contain the message of Hosea, whom he dates at the beginning of Ahab's reign, and that chs. 4-14 come from an unknown author in the reign of Menahem.
5. Cf. Wolff, *Hosea*, xxxif.; Mays, *Hosea*, 5; Rudolph, *Hosea*, 25; S. Mowinckel, *Prophecy and Tradition* (1946), 67, 72; Fohrer, *Introduction to the Old Testament*, 419; D.A. Knight, *Rediscovering the Traditions of Israel* (1973), 8; J. Lindblom, *Prophecy in Ancient Israel* (1962), 280.
6. The chronology followed here is that of Albright. For this and alternative chronologies see J.H. Hayes and J.M. Miller (eds.), *Israelite and Judean History* (1977), 683.
7. That Hosea's prophetic activity continued after the stability of Jeroboam II's reign had ended is evident from passages such as 7:3-7; 13:10-11, for example, which seem to reflect a situation verging on anarchy. Wolff, *Hosea*, xxi, regards the present arrangement of the material as broadly chronological and considers that from 5:8 onwards it relates to a time later than Jeroboam's reign.

8. Hosea's ministry seems to have spanned a period of about thirty years. The latest texts are probably to be dated either immediately before or at the beginning of the siege of Samaria, when Hoshea had already been imprisoned by the Assyrians (13:10-11). There is apparently no reference, however, to the fall of the northern kingdom in 721 B.C. On this see Wolff, *Hosea*, 224. For a different view see F.I. Andersen and D.N. Freedman, *Hosea* (1980), 33ff., who locate Hosea's ministry mainly in the period 755-740 B.C.
9. Much recent discussion has centred on the question of the date at which the prophetic traditions were committed to writing. The matter is not significant for the present study and I shall not enter the debate. There is, however, some reason to believe, especially in the case of Hosea, that the tradition was committed to writing soon after its first expression in the prophet's ministry. The general uncertainty of the times and the impending crisis of 721 B.C. may have precipitated the formation of a written text in order to safeguard the prophet's message for the future. On this question see, for example, G. Widengren, *Literary and Psychological Aspects of the Hebrew Prophets*. UUÅ (1948), 77f., who considers that the prophecies of both Hosea and Amos are preserved in a better text than would have been possible by purely oral transmission. He stresses that the prophets operated in an urban civilisation where writing was the natural medium for preserving a spoken message. Cf. also Wolff, *Hosea*, xxix ff., who believes that some of the traditions were already fixed in writing during the prophet's lifetime; J.M. Ward, *Hosea: A Theological Commentary* (1966), 246f.; G. Fohrer, *Introduction to the Old Testament*, 359f. A.H.J. Gunneweg, *Mündliche und schriftliche Tradition der vorexilischen Prophetenbücher als Problem der neueren Prophetenforschung* (1959), 77 ff., argues for the co-existence of written and oral transmission, locating the former at sanctuaries, the latter in the private sphere. The uncertainty attaching to this question is illustrated, however, by the fact that, in contrast to the scholars cited above, E.M. Good, in his study, 'The Composition of Hosea', *SEÅ* 31, 1966, 23ff., holds that the method of compilation points primarily to a process of oral transmission.
10. See R.E. Clements, *Prophecy and Tradition* (1975), 48f., who argues for a thoroughgoing influence of the Deuteronomists on the prophetic books. Cf. also Wolff, *Hosea*, 4; Mays, *Hosea*, 17, 20.

NOTES TO INTRODUCTION

11. *Hosea*, 15.
12. Cf. Rudolph, *Hosea*, 25; Wolff, *Hosea*, xxxi f.; J. Mauchline, 'Hosea', *IB* 6 (1956), 563f.; Fohrer, *Introduction to the Old Testament*, 422f.
13. *Introduction to the Old Testament* (revised ed. 1948), 570; he comments pessimistically that these secondary interpolations 'obscure Hosea's own thoughts, which, moreover, are set down in chaotic confusion'. See also R.E. Wolfe, 'The Editing of the Book of the Twelve', *ZAW* 53, 1935, 91f., for the view that many of the Judah references are to be attributed to redactors.
14. 'The Composition of Hosea', *SEÅ* 31, 1966, 21 n. 1.
15. *Hosea*, 16.
16. *Hosea*, xxiii.
17. *Mercy and Sacrifice*, 50.
18. 'A Problem of Theological Ethics in Hosea', *Essays in Old Testament Ethics* (eds. J.L. Crenshaw and J.T. Willis, 1974), 142.
19. *Amos and Hosea*, clix ff.
20. *Prophecy and Tradition*, 42f., 56.
21. Cf. 1 Kings 12:26-33.
22. Another important area is, of course, the question of how the idea of covenant is related to Hosea's message. On this see p. 3 above, and the important contribution to the subject of covenant theology in general made by L. Perlitt, *Bundestheologie im Alten Testament*. WMANT 36 (1969). For an alternative to Clement's view see F.C. Fensham, 'The Covenant-idea in the Book of Hosea', *Die Ou Testamentiese Werkgemeenskap in Suid-Afrika: Studies in the Books of Hosea and Amos* (Potchefstroom, 1966), 35ff.
23. Cf. Wolff, *Hosea*, xxx f.; Eissfeldt, *The Old Testament. An Introduction*, 391; Fohrer, *Introduction to the Old Testament*, 423, who prefers to speak in more general terms of friends or adherents of the prophet rather than of disciples.
24. Indeed it might be argued to the contrary that the description of widespread apostasy in 4:1-2 precludes the existence of such a group. This is, however, to be understood as the hyperbole of emphasis, and it would be over-prosaic to infer from this passage that Hosea alone had remained faithful to Yahweh.
25. It is reasonable to assume that it comes from someone intimate with the prophet. So, for example, Wolff, *Hosea*, 11; Mays, *Hosea*, 24. F.S. North, 'Hosea's Introduction to his Book', *VT* 8, 1958, 429-432, argued on the basis of textual variants that ch. 1 was originally autobiographical in form, a view which has not found support. On the question of the role of disciples in preserving memories of the prophet see also Widengren, *Literary and Psychological Aspects of the Hebrew Prophets*, 92f., 115f., 121.
26. *Hosea*, xxxi.

27. On this question cf. Engnell's view in 'The Book of Hosea', *SBU* I, col. 983, who argues that to seek for the *verba ipsissima* of the prophet is methodologically unacceptable since the prophet and his disciples together constitute an indissoluble unity, with the view of S. Mowinckel, *Prophecy and Tradition,* 88, who maintains equally vigorously that 'with such a dogma "tradition history" has become a *"Zutritt verboten"* of a police (*sic*), a prohibition of the very carrying on of tradition history'. He does accept, however, that in practice 'in many cases we have perhaps to give it up; the voice of the prophet sounds there more like a powerful backing melody or as a deep undertone in the chorus of the tradition, or more subdued, flooded by the many-stringed accompaniment of tradition'. Cf. also E.M. Good, 'The Composition of Hosea', *SEÅ* 31, 1966, 57, who admits to finding himself increasingly in sympathy with Engnell's view.
28. Cf. Clements, *Prophecy and Tradition,* 6f.
29. *When Prophecy Failed* (1979), 134.
30. *Pace* Clements, *Prophecy and Tradition,* 7. I find myself in agreement with the view of Mowinckel, *Prophecy and Tradition,* 78f., who admits the possibility that a shift may occur in the presentation of a prophet (the example he gives is Amos) and that tradition may be untrue to the original meaning. Clements himself seems to admit this in his later work, *Isaiah and the Deliverance of Jerusalem. A Study of the Interpretation of Prophecy in the Old Testament.* JSOT Supplements 13 (1980), 85ff.
31. 'The Canonical Approach to Introducing the Old Testament: Prodigy and Problems', *JSOT* 16, 1980, 36. See also J. Barr, 'Trends and Prospects in Biblical Theology', *JTS* NS 25, 1974, 270, and in the same volume J.F.A. Sawyer, 'Notes and Studies. The Meaning of בצלם אלהים ('in the image of God') in Genesis i-xi', 418f., who stresses the opposite but equally valid point to that made by Landes, that 'there is no scientific reason why the earliest level should have priority'. See also G. von Rad, *Old Testament Theology* II (1965), 46ff.
32. *Introduction to the Old Testament* (1975), 208ff.
33. Cf. E. Hammershaimb, *Some Aspects of Old Testament Prophecy from Isaiah to Malachi* (1966), 29.
34. *Hosea,* xxiii.

NOTES TO CHAPTER I

1. See p. 3 above. Harper, *Amos and Hosea,* clix ff., regards the salvation sayings as 'unquestionably from exilic times', though he recognises on cliii that Hosea 'contributed a conception of Yahweh which made such a future not only possible, but, indeed, probable'. W.F. Stinespring, 'A Problem of Theological Ethics in Hosea', *Essays in Old Testament Ethics,* 133ff., emphasises the non-fulfilment of the salvation oracles for the northern kingdom as evidence against their authenticity: 'if Hosea had promised success and salvation for the Northern Kingdom, he would have been a very poor predictor, for that kingdom fell, never to rise again ..... The only oracles of hope that make clear sense to me historically are oracles on the restoration of Judah after the exile'. That this criterion of literal historical fulfilment is, however, a far from adequate guide to authenticity is clear from the salvation oracles of Deutero-Isaiah. The ultimate eschatological meaning of such oracles is an altogether different matter. The whole question of the non-fulfilment of prophecy is discussed by R.P. Carroll in his stimulating work, *When Prophecy Failed. Reactions and Responses to Failure in the Old Testament Prophetic Traditions.*
2. See A.S. Kapelrud, *God and His Friends in the Old Testament* (1979), 104, who comments that it is 'Western logic at its worst' to think that a prophet cannot give oracles of both weal and woe. Cf. J.M. Ward, *Hosea. A Theological Commentary,* 194; R.E. Clements, *Prophecy and Tradition,* 52.
3. I have followed here the view of Wolff, *Hosea,* xxix ff., that the book consists of three main complexes of tradition. There is, however, little agreement as to the way in which chs. 4-14 have been compiled. For a different division of the material in chs. 4-14 see Eissfeldt, *The Old Testament. An Introduction,* 386, and the detailed, but hypothetical reconstruction proposed by Good, 'The Composition of Hosea', *SEÅ* 31, 1966, 21-63. There is, on the other hand, general agreement that chs. 1-3 form a distinct complex, at first transmitted separately from chs. 4-14. So Mays, *Hosea,* 15ff.; Eissfeldt, *The Old Testament. An Introduction,* 387, 391; Fohrer, *Introduction to the Old Testament,* 423. J.Lindblom, *Prophecy in Ancient Israel,* 242ff., however, expresses scepticism on this point.
4. The symbolic names can be taken as evidence for Hosea's message even though, as is widely acknowledged, the biographical form of ch. 1 suggests that it comes not from Hosea himself but from a close associate who was familiar with the circumstances of his life and the burden of his ministry. On this point see n. 25 above. Cf. Fohrer, *Introduction to the Old Testament,* 423, who suggests that

the third person account 'may go back to Hosea himself
despite its style'. Similarly Rudolph, *Hosea*, 39, comments,
'Die Verschiedenheit der Stilform braucht nicht auf
Verschiedenheit des Autors zu führen. Wie ein Ichbericht
fingiert und ein Erbericht autobiographisch sein kann, so
kommt auch bei *demselben* Verfasser der Wechsel der Stilform
vor, ohne dass sich sachlich etwas ändert'.

5. Here and in the following line יהי is understood as
   equivalent in meaning to, or as a scribal error for, the
   more common איה, not as an apocopated imperfect of היה.
   See KB³ *ad loc*. BDB, 13, suggests here a possible dialect
   form. H.S. Nyberg, *Studien zum Hoseabuche*. UUÅ (1935),
   103ff., regards it as a byform of אהה.
6. In contrast, H.L. Ginsberg, 'Lexicographical Notes', *VTS* 16,
   1967, 79, takes the passage as a salvation saying,
   understanding the opening lines as statements not questions,
   and translating the concluding words, 'Revenge shall be far
   from my thoughts'.
7. I have commented already in n. 1 on the inadequacy of the
   criterion of historical fulfilment or non-fulfilment used
   by Stinespring, 'A Problem of Theological Ethics in Hosea',
   Essays in Old Testament Ethics, 133ff., as a test of the
   authenticity of a prophetic saying. Carroll, *When Prophecy
   Failed*, 75, in commenting on the non-fulfilment of
   salvation prophecies, shows greater perception in his
   suggestion that 'one cannot rule out the possibility that
   prophecy originally attempted to do something new, namely
   the prophets sought to translate into the categories of
   human history the divine activity they perceived on a
   cosmic scale'.
8. See below, pp.101ff.
9. *Prophecy and Tradition*, 30. cf. Rudolph, *Hosea*, 86ff.;
   Pfeiffer, *Introduction to the Old Testament*, 567, who
   asserts that '3:5 is spurious without question'.
10. Pfeiffer, *Introduction to the Old Testament*, 567, argues
    that עוד modifies ויאמר. In contrast, Lindblom, *Prophecy
    in Ancient Israel*, 168, holds the view that עוד is merely
    an editorial link connecting the narratives of chs. 1 and 3.
11. Cf. Clements, *Prophecy and Tradition*, 30: 'the message has
    controlled and determined the account of the events, so
    that the prophet's action and experience are to be
    understood from the message, and not vice versa'.
12. Cf. 2:17; 9:10.
13. There is no need to regard this expression as secondary on
    the grounds that it is Deuteronomic. Hosea's close
    relationship to Deuteronomy leads Wolff, *Hosea*, 60, to
    regard it as 'a genuine Hosean reproach'.
14. Cf. Wolff, *Hosea*, 58.
15. *Ibid*.
16. See below, pp. 101ff.
17. See Mays, *Hosea*, 36; Wolff, *Hosea*, 32.
18. *Hosea*, 32. By 'kerygmatic unit' Wolff signifies a series of
    sayings 'proclaimed by the prophet on one and the same
    occasion' (xxx).

NOTES TO CHAPTER I   171

19. See pp. 22ff.
20. Thus Wolff, *Hosea*, 36, understands it as a divorce suit.
    Cf. also R. de Vaux, *Ancient Israel. Its Life and
    Institutions* (ET 1961), 35; C.H. Gordon, 'Hos 2:4-5 in
    the Light of New Semitic Inscriptions', *ZAW* 54, 1936, 277.
    In the context, however, of the warning, 'Lest I strip her
    naked .....', an action for divorce seems inappropriate. I
    find myself in agreement, therefore, with J.D. Martin, 'The
    Forensic Background to Jeremiah III 1', *VT* 19, 1969, 89.
    See also Andersen and Freedman, *Hosea*, 221ff., who, though
    agreeing that reconciliation not divorce is intended, deny
    that court proceedings are in mind at all. It is a personal
    matter between husband and wife.
21. The reference by name to Jehu suggests that the events of
    2 Kings 9 are intended. For discussion of the passage see
    below pp. 110ff.
22. Cf. Hos. 2:25; Jer. 31:27. It may be objected that in
    Zec. 10:9 judgement is signified, but here again this
    nuance derives from the context with the words עמים and
    מרחקים.
23. The fact that שנא and גרש are used in 9:15 to express
    rejection of the nation serves to emphasise the point.
24. E.g. 4:6, 8, 12; 6:11; 11:7. That the ultimate expression
    of the broken relationship between Yahweh and his people in
    the symbolic name לא עמי is not to be located chronologically
    after the references to Israel as 'my people' is clear from
    the last two references above, both of which reflect the
    background of the later years of Hosea's ministry. Whereas
    the giving of the symbolic name of 1:9 is to be dated on
    circumstantial evidence only some five or six years after
    the beginning of Hosea's ministry, 6:11 belongs probably
    to the events of 733 B.C., and 11:7 is probably, though less
    certainly, to be assigned to the latter part of Hoshea's
    reign. For a detailed consideration of this question of
    historical setting see Wolff, *Hosea*, 112 and 197.
25. *Hosea*, 129. Cf. the comment made by Ackroyd, 'Hosea',
    Peake's Commentary on the Bible, 603, to the effect that
    'with all its variety, the message of the prophet may
    nevertheless be drawn together under two main aspects, the
    intimacy of the relationship between God and his people, and
    the inevitability and utterness of God's judgement. These
    are the two focal points, and the insistence upon the former
    makes the latter all the more vivid, while the relationship
    between the two aspects of the prophet's thought makes
    intelligible his words of hope'.
26. 14.
27. *Prophecy in Ancient Israel*, 365. Cf. also Lindblom's
    earlier work, *Hosea Literarisch Untersucht* (1927), 109f.,
    where he accepts 11:8-9 as also part of the primary northern
    material, locating it with 2:16-17 in the early optimistic
    period of the prophet's career, in contrast to 2:1-3, 18-25
    and 14:2-9 which he considers secondary. See also Pfeiffer,
    Introduction to the Old Testament, 569, who holds that in

chs. 1-3 (written before 744, the date which he assigns to the end of the reign of Jeroboam II and the beginning of a period of anarchy) the prophet still hoped for a conversion of his people, whereas in chs. 4-14 (to be dated between 744 and 735) the nation's condition was seen to be incurable.

28. It is more probable that the omission of לו is stylistic, creating a pattern of increasing brevity as the dramatic climax is reached. Moreover, as v. 9 indicates, the meaning of the symbolic name refers not to the child but to the nation. In this connection compare the symbolic names of Is. 7:3 and 8:3, where also the meaning of the name has no reference to the child who bears it but to the historical situation in which it is given.
29. Details of the story such as the bride's name, the sex of the children, the time of conception (v. 8), point in the direction of history rather than allegory.
30. See above, p. 13.
31. Cf. Clements, *Prophecy and Tradition*, 29, where he rightly warns of the danger of going beyond the evidence by appealing to the prophet's own religious experience in order to clarify his message. It is, as he says, 'a methodologically unsatisfactory procedure. It establishes a reconstruction of what the prophet's experience is thought to have been, and then proceeds to use this to interpret the message'.
32. The mutually exclusive reconstructions proposed by scholars using the same evidence are a testimony to this. See, for example, the view, diametrically opposed to Lindblom's, proposed on the basis of the same evidence by J.A. Bewer, *The Literature of the Old Testament in its Historical Development* (1933), 94, that Hosea's personal tragedy transformed him from a prophet of doom to one of love.
33. As in the Talmudic interpretation, b. Pesaḥim 87, that 'the Holy One, blessed be He, commanded Hosea to marry Gomer, the daughter of Diblaim, in order that he might understand the Lord's attitude towards Israel'. For a similar view see, for example, H.H. Rowley, 'The Marriage of Hosea', *BJRL* 39, 1956, 233.
34. See Mays, *Hosea*, 24.
35. E.g. Fohrer, *Introduction to the Old Testament*, 421.
36. See above, pp. 14f.
37. Cf. Eissfeldt, *The Old Testament*, 387: 'Hosea had from the outset a conception of the forgiveness of Israel after punishment'.
38. In this debated question much depends on the significance of עוד. See n. 10 above. Mays, *Hosea*, 55, takes the widely accepted view that the events of ch. 3 are subsequent to those of ch. 1, but adds the warning: 'of what time in the life of Hosea does the report tell? Such questions about the biography of Hosea meet an oblique indifference in the material; it was not formed to assist in the quest for the historical Hosea'.
39. See above, pp. 13f.

NOTES TO CHAPTER I   173

40. E.g. Jer. 2:3, 4, 14; Is. 40:27; 41:8.
41. E.g. Wolff, *Hosea*, 33; Mays, *Hosea*, 47; Lindblom, *Hosea Literarisch Untersucht*, 65ff.; N.H. Snaith, *Mercy and Sacrifice*, 51.
42. See above, pp. 6ff.
43. משם (v. 17) is to be understood in a pregnant sense: 'and (leading her) from there I will give her back her vineyards'. Cf. Mays, *Hosea*, 45. In contrast, R. Gordis, 'Hosea's Marriage and Message; A New Approach', *HUCA* 25, 1954, 23, argues for a temporal not spatial sense.
44. See p. 6.
45. Cf. Gen. 34:3; Jud. 19:3, though it can carry a more general sense as in Ruth 2:13.
46. E.g. Ex. 22:15; Jud. 14:15; 2 Sam. 3:25.
47. Cf. 2:10-11.
48. The phrase is Bonhoeffer's, *The Cost of Discipleship* (1964), 35. Cf. Snaith, *Mercy and Sacrifice*, 48: 'It is sheer sentiment of the most dangerous type which suggests that God, because of his love for Israel, is going to let Israel off from paying the price of her sin'.
49. A view strongly supported by W. Rudolph, *Hosea*, 68f. Cf. also J. Mauchline, 'Hosea', 579; and among earlier commentators H. Oort, 'Hosea', *ThT* 24, 1890, 252f.; O. Procksch, BH^3; A. Condamin, 'Interpolations ou Transpositions?' *RB* 11, 1902, 389f. This view has been incorporated into the translation of JB.
50. 'Hosea 2: Structure and Interpretation', *Studia Biblica* 1978. *JSOT* Supplements 11 (1979), 84ff. Cf. Wolff, *Hosea*, 35; J.M. Ward, *Hosea: A Theological Commentary* (1966), 25.
51. 'Hosea 2: Structure and Interpretation', 86.
52. *Ibid*.
53. See, for example, Wolff, *Hosea*, 47; Mays, *Hosea*, 46f.
54. A variety of terms are used in form criticism to describe types of salvation sayings. For a discussion of the question see C. Westermann's essay in *The Old Testament and Christian Faith* (ed. B.W. Anderson, 1964), 203ff. He distinguishes three categories: 'assurance of salvation' (*Heilszusage*), 'announcement of salvation' (*Heilsankündigung*), and 'portrayal of salvation' (*Heilsschilderung*).
55. V. 19 can scarcely be classed as a salvation saying, and I have not, therefore, included it in the discussion at this point. In function and purpose it is to be compared with 2:13, 15. Its connection with the preceding verse is editorial, by means of the catchword בעלים which is, nevertheless, used differently in the two verses; in the singular in v. 18 with disapproval of its use as a designation of Yahweh; in the plural in v. 19 with reference to the worship of other gods. Thus the former is concerned with the problem of syncretism, the latter with pagan worship.
56. For a discussion of the probable historical background see Wolff, *Hosea*, 48f.

57. E.g. 2:4, 9, 14; 9:15.
58. Cf. E. Jacob, 'L'Héritage Cananéen dans le livre du prophète Osée', *RHPR* 43, 1963, 250-9.
59. For a different view of the meaning of the passage see R.N. Whybray, *Readings in Biblical Hebrew* II (ed. J.H. Eaton, 1978), 35, who finds it strange that איש and בעל are used together, and considers that Bathsheba's mourning for her בעל is intended as irony.
60. *Hosea,* 49. The fact that Wolff describes איש as '*apparently* an endearing expression' (the emphasis is mine) is significant. His exegesis of the passage has been influenced unduly by the meaning attaching to the word בעל in other contexts, a meaning which he has imported into this passage. The comment made by J. Barr, *Biblical Words for Time* (revised ed., 1969), 160, is relevant here, though made in a different context. He stresses that 'the meaning of a vocabulary item is a function both of the item itself and of the item as occurrent in various contexts'. His particular concern is to affirm that 'the question whether καιρός contrasts with χρόνος in New Testament Greek depends entirely on the syntactical environment'. Old Testament usage indicates that the same is true of the contrast between איש and בעל as designations of a husband. In contrast to Wolff, Mays, *Hosea,* 48, emphasises that 'in the context of Hosea's prophecy a cultic and confessional dimension is certainly involved in the use of the word'.
61. Cf. the theological implications of the penitential song in 6:1-3, on which see Mays, *Hosea,* 94ff. There, too, Israel confuses Yahweh with a deity whose activity was a function of the processes of nature.
62. For a detailed discussion of this passage see my article, 'The Structure and Meaning of Hosea VIII 1-3', *VT* 25, 1975, 700-710.
63. I Kings 18:21.
64. Cf. 10:12; and, for the absence of the required response, 4:1-2; 5:1.
65. So prominent is this theme that Wolff, ' "Wissen um Gott" bei Hosea als Urform der Theologie', *Ev Th* 12, 1952-53, 533-554, arguing that it indicates specifically a knowledge of the Sinai covenant, bases on it his view that Hosea's links are with Levitical groups. For a different view of the meaning of 'knowledge of God' see N.W. Porteous, 'Actualisation and the Prophetic Criticism of the Cult', *Tradition und Situation* (eds. E. Würthwein and O. Kaiser, 1963), 97; J.L. McKenzie, 'Knowledge of God in Hosea', *JBL* 74, 1955, 22f.
66. See p. 6.
67. Probably not here to be understood with a sexual connotation although it is in the context of the marriage metaphor, but, as Mays comments, *Hosea,* 52, 'in the context of the thematic and crucial use which Hosea makes of 'knowledge of God', the expression is best interpreted in terms of its theological meaning. ..... It means the whole response of Israel to the acts and words of Yahweh'.

NOTES TO CHAPTER I

68. They are attributes of Yahweh, not of Israel, the bridal price paid by Yahweh for his bride. See Wolff, *Hosea,* 52. Cf. 2 Sam. 3:14; Dt. 22:29 for evidence of this custom in ancient Israel.
69. Cf. 6:4.
70. This is indeed the consensus of modern scholarship, contra J. Lindblom, *Hosea Literarisch Untersucht,* 68. See, for example, Wolff, *Hosea,* 48f.; Mays, *Hosea,* 47; Mauchline, 'Hosea', 589; Eissfeldt, *The Old Testament,* 388f. In this connection it is not without significance that whereas in BH³ 2:18-25 are printed as prose, in BHS they are regarded as poetic in style.
71. *The Old Testament,* 388.
72. The name Jezreel has probably been lost from the beginning of v. 25 through homoioteleuton, though it is futile to speculate what else has been lost. The feminine suffix of וזרעתיה is difficult since Jezreel in 1:4 is clearly a masculine name. It may be due simply to scribal error of which we already have evidence in the loss of the first part of the saying. More likely it is due to the fact that the symbolic names here refer not to Hosea's children but to the nation which is frequently presented as feminine in the Hosea material. That the reference is to Jezreel's mother is unlikely since the two symbolic names which do appear, לא רחמה and לא עמי, need to be balanced by the name Jezreel.
73. See W. Rudolph, 'Eigentümlichkeiten der Sprache Hoseas', *Studia Biblica et Semitica Theodoro Christiano Vriezen Dedicata* (1966), 315.
74. See p. 15.
75. On this see Wolff, *Hosea,* 48.
76. See above, n. 22.
77. Cf. 2 Kings 11:17 where Jehoiada is represented as making a covenant between Yahweh as one partner and king and people as the other, and also between king and people, thus acting as a covenant mediator. See also *ANET,* 482, for an instance of a third party mediating a covenant in Mari.
78. E.g. Wolff, *Hosea,* 47f.; Mays, *Hosea,* 47; Mauchline, 'Hosea', 589f.
79. See above, p. 29.
80. See, for example, Ps. 91:14-16.
81. Cf. Wolff, *Hosea,* 53f.
82. See J. Lindblom, 'Wisdom in the Old Testament Prophets', *Wisdom in Israel and in the Ancient Near East,* VTS 3, 1955, 203.
83. Cf. also 2:6, 10, 14.
84. Mays, *Hosea,* 47, summarizes the position thus: 'the inner connection of the material in every verse with the rest of Hosea's prophecy leaves no reasonable basis for doubting that the sayings are his'. Cf. also Ward, *Hosea: A Theological Commentary,* 41.
85. See above, pp. 5f.
86. For a discussion of 1:5 see Wolff, *Hosea,* 19, who has no hesitation in regarding it as originating with Hosea and secondarily inserted at this point.

87. *Hosea*, 11f., 48.
88. *Hosea*, 47.
89. There is no reason to regard these details as unhistorical although as I have indicated on pp. 17ff., the primary purpose is theological not biographical.
90. See below, pp. 89ff. Cf. Wolff, *Hosea*, 19.
91. E.g. 2:20; 3:7, 18; 4:1, 2; 5:30; 7:18, 20, 21, 23 and *passim*.
92. For full discussion of the meaning of the expression 'in that day' see P.A. Munch, *The Expression Bajjôm Hāhû': Is it an Eschatological Terminus Technicus?* (1936).
93. Cf. 2:8.
94. Cf. 8:2 where the people claim allegiance to Yahweh but fall under the prophet's condemnation.
95. It is unlikely to imply that the fall of the northern kingdom has already taken place, for of this there is no trace in the rest of the material. That such a traumatic experience should have left no other trace in the prophet's sayings is improbable.
96. Cf. also Jer. 34:16 where שוב signifies changing one's course of action.
97. *Hosea*, 194.
98. In addition to the following verse 11:11 see also as examples 9:3; 10:6; 11:5; 12:2.
99. See Wolff, *Hosea*, 197. Rudolph, *Hosea*, 217f., also recognises the probability that 11:8-9 belongs to the original northern core of the material.
100. For a discussion of the meaning of this very difficult and obscure verse see below, pp. 113ff.
101. See, for example, Is. 10:20; 12:6; 31:1. This idea reaches its fullest expression in the message of Deutero-Isaiah, e.g. 41:14; 48:17; 49:7.
102. Cf. Wolff, *Hosea*, 126ff., who adduces the historical situation and also the resemblance to the annals of Tiglath-pileser as evidence supporting a date in 733 B.C.
103. See above, pp. 21f., 30ff.
104. So Wolff, *Hosea*, 194f.
105. Dt. 29:33.
106. See n. 101 above. The comment by Mays, *Hosea*, 157, is apt: 'the actions and feelings of Yahweh can be translated into representations of human, and even animal, life ..... But he transcends the metaphor, is different from that to which he is compared, and free of all its limitations'.
107. The power of this statement is not diminished by the problematic בעיר with which the verse ends. The opening statement is in any case clear and emphatic. There is general agreement as to the essential meaning of the saying, despite the radically different view of Nyberg, *Studien zum Hoseabuche,* 90, where, by understanding v. 9 as a series of questions, he produces a statement of extreme vengeance. Cf. Andersen and Freedman, *Hosea*, 589f., who regard לא here as asseverative, 'registering the renewed determination of Yahweh to carry out his threatened judgements'.

108. Cf. Mays, *Amos*, 21.
109. I am grateful to J.F.A. Sawyer for this comment.
110. Cf. L.C. Allen, *The Books of Joel, Obadiah, Jonah and Micah* (1976), 31.
111. 5:14; 13:7.
112. See for example Is. 11:14; 24:14, 15.
113. The only other examples occur in 6:1-3 and 12:7. 10:12 is not a summons to the prophet's audience, but a reference to Yahweh's past requirement of his people.
114. As, for example, by Mays, *Hosea*, 184; Wolff, *Hosea*, 233f.; Mauchline, 'Hosea'. 721ff.
115. A point correctly understood by J.H. Eaton, *Vision in Worship* (1981), 85, though he shows an uncritical acceptance of the present arrangement of the material without allowing for redactional influence.
116. So RSV and NEB. Cf. also Wolff, *Hosea*, 232; Mauchline, 'Hosea', 723; Mays, *Hosea*, 189.
117. Cf. Num. 14:9; Is. 30:2, where there is a reference to בצל מצרים.
118. Cf. J.H. Eaton, *Vision in Worship*, 85, who translates:
    Inhabitants will gather under his shade,
    again they shall grow corn.
    The RSV, in contrast, not only emends בצלו as noted above, but reads כגן for דגן.
119. Cf. especially the Song of Songs *passim*. The fact that such imagery belongs to the language of love songs is significant, cf. Mays, *Hosea*, 188.
120. See above, p. 6.
121. E.g. Wolff, *Hosea*, 234; G.R. Driver, 'Linguistic and Textual Problems: Minor Prophets. I', *JTS* 39, 1938, 165f.; R.B. Coote, 'Hosea 14:8: "They who are filled with grain shall live"', *JBL* 93, 1974, 173 n. 52, who attributes vv. 5-8 to Hosea without reservation, and goes so far as to suggest that, in the light of this, v. 10 also, in contrast to the generally accepted view, may be attributed to Hosea. I mention Coote only in support of the Hosean origin of the material. His interpretation of the passage as based on an ancient banquet motif differs from mine.
122. Cf. Ps. 51:10; 126:5f.
123. 'Hosea', 721.
124. *Ibid.*
125. *Vision in Worship*, 85.
126. See also pp. 53f.
127. M.J. Buss, *The Prophetic Word of Hosea*, 128, comes to a similar conclusion on form critical grounds.
128. Cf. Jer. 3:22, even though here a call to return precedes.
129. I am indebted to J.F.A. Sawyer for this observation.
130. See p. 46.
131. Cf. J. Gray, *The Legacy of Canaan*. VTS 5, 1965, 177, n. 1, who comments: 'the sacred tree as a fertility symbol is one of the most familiar motifs in native Canaanite art, being represented as a palm-tree, natural or stylised, often flanked by rampant caprids which reach up to its fruit. That

the tree represents the mother-goddess is indicated by the fact that on the relief on the lid of an ivory unguent box from Minet el- Beida (14th c.) the mother-goddess is represented between two caprids, to whom she offers plants'.
132. For a discussion of this question see E. Jacob, 'L'Héritage Cananéen dans le livre du Prophète Osée', *RHPR* 43, 1963, 250-259.
133. My own translation. Cf. Eaton, *Vision in Worship,* 85, who renders:
    I myself have answered
    and will watch over my promise.
134. Cf. Ackroyd, 'Hosea', *Peake's Commentary on the Bible,* 613. Wolff, *Hosea,* 233, on the other hand, dismisses it as too audacious, and Harper, *Amos and Hosea,* 415, regards it as 'a freak of the imagination'.
135. Cf. Ex. 34:13; Dt. 12:3, and especially Dt. 16:21, לא תטע לך אשרה כל־עץ. For further discussion of this see W.L. Reed, *The Asherah in the Old Testament* (1949); R. Patai, 'The Goddess Asherah', *JNES* 24, 1965, 37-52, who believes an artefact, not a natural tree, is intended.
136. See above, p. 50.
137. See above, p. 37f.
138. See above, pp. 22ff.
139. E.g. 6:4-6; 8:12-13; 13:12-13.
140. See also 4:12.
141. Cf. Rudolph, 'Eigentümlichkeiten der Sprache Hoseas', *Studia Biblica et Semitica,* 313.
142. So RSV, though the exact nuance of the verb is difficult to determine. In 14:1 it seems to refer rather to the bearing of punishment. Good, 'Hosea 5:8-6:6: An Alternative to Alt', *JBL* 85, 1966, 279f., prefers the meaning 'bring a guilt offering' in view of בקש and שחר both of which have cultic relations and seem to point to cultic activity.
143. See below, pp. 72f.
144. E.g. in 2:18-25. See above, pp. 37f.
145. *Hosea,* 92f.
146. 'Hosea', 721.
147. *The Prophetic Word of Hosea,* 138.
148. *Introduction to the Old Testament,* 425.
149. 'The Concept of Grace in the Book of Hosea', *ZAW* 70, 1958, 105.

NOTES TO CHAPTER II

1. See above, p. 1.
2. 1:1, 7; 2:2; 4:15; 5:5, 10, 12, 13, 14; 6:4, 11; 8:14; 10:11; 12:1, 3.
3. 3:5.
4. 1:1; 2:4, 5; 7:12.
5. 9:11, a verse generally considered to be secondary.
6. Amos 1:1.
7. *Das Dodekapropheton* (1903), 8.
8. *Amos and Hosea,* clix. Cf. R.E. Wolfe, 'The Editing of the Book of the Twelve', ZAW 53, 1935, 91f.
9. *Studies in the Name Israel in the Old Testament* (1946), 139.
10. 'Profetia och Tradition', SEÅ 12, 1947, 130ff.
11. As, for example, in 1:7; 2:2; 3:5; 4:15; 6:11. See also N.H. Tur-Sinai, *Halashon Vehasepher* II, 304-323, who regards Hosea as a Judean hostile to the northern kingdom.
12. 'Hosea', SBU I (1962), cols. 978f.; *Critical Essays on the Old Testament* (1970), 141 n. 43.
13. The influence of A. Alt, 'Hosea 5:8 - 6:6. Ein Krieg und seine Folgen in prophetischen Beleuchtung', *Kleine Schriften* II, (1959), 163ff., has been particularly significant in this respect. For a brief summary of various views of the extent of redactional influence see Ward, *Hosea,* 246f.
14. A particularly noteworthy example is to be seen in the NEB's cavalier treatment of 1:7.
15. 'Lexicographical Notes', VTS 16, 1967, 76 n. 2. On the question of abbreviations in general in the MT see G.R. Driver, 'Abbreviations in the Massoretic Text', *Textus* I, 1960, 112-131; 4, 1964, 76-94.
16. 5:12, 13, 14; 6:4; 10:10; 12:3.
17. Ginsberg's arguments are set out briefly in his essay on Hosea in *Encyclopedia Judaica* (ed. C. Roth, 1971), col. 1016.
18. See p. 1f.
19. Cf. M. Noth, *The Laws in the Pentateuch and Other Studies* (1966), 167ff.
20. A.D.H. Mayes, *Israel in the Period of the Judges,* SBT, Second Series 29 (1974), 2.
21. Cf. G. von Rad, *Old Testament Theology* II, 43; G. Fohrer, *Introduction to the Old Testament,* 423f.; Mays, *Hosea,* 16f.
22. See above, p. 8.
23. *Hosea,* xxiii.
24. 'Eigentümlichkeiten der Sprache Hoseas', *Studia Biblica et Semitica,* 313-317.
25. Cf. Wolff, *Hosea,* xxxi.
26. *Amos and Hosea,* 376.
27. So A. Gelston, 'Kingship in the Book of Hosea', OTS 19, 1974, 80. Cf. Wolff, *Hosea,* xxxif. who believes that the redaction which speaks of salvation for Judah is earlier than the one which applies to that kingdom the prophet's judgmental sayings; Rudolph, *Hosea,* 25ff.

28. See above, pp. 1f.
29. 'Kingship in the Book of Hosea', 79. Cf. also A. van Selms, 'The Southern Kingdom in Hosea', *Studies on the Books of Hosea and Amos* (ed. A.H. van Zyl, 1965), 110, who accepts the reference to Judah as original, though without detailed examination of this particular passage.
30. *Hosea*, 206.
31. *Ibid*.
32. Cf. Is. 2:3; Mic. 3:9-10; Jer. 2:4; 31:11; Ps. 14:7; 20:2.
33. See above, pp. 57f.
34. As, for example, in Amos 3:1; 8:2 in their later Judean context.
35. 'The Masorah and the Levites', *VT* 10, 1960, 282f., who considers the allusion is not redactional but original to the prophet. He also accepts the reference to Judah in v. 1 as belonging to the primary stratum of the material and sees in it an allusion to the story of Judah and Tamar which is preserved in Gen. 8.
36. See as examples Wolff, *Hosea*, 95; Mays, *Hosea*, 84; Rudolph, *Hosea*, 117; van Selms, 'The Southern Kingdom in Hosea', 105, comments that the reference here to Judah 'hangs loosely and rickety'.
37. *Amos and Hosea*, 270. The only other reference to Judah which Harper attributes to Hosea himself is 4:15.
38. Harper can hardly be said to have argued the case sufficiently in this instance.
39. For a similarly loose attachment of a supplementary comment, though not as here asyndeton, see 4:5.
40. The use of *Qal* in the perfect and *Niphal* in the imperfect seems to be characteristic of this verb. See Andersen and Freedman, *Hosea*, 393, for statistics.
41. It is generally recognised that the second occurrence of the name Israel overweights the line and destroys the balance between Israel and Ephraim which is a feature of the previous lines. See, for example, Mays, *Hosea*, 82.
42. The same expression occurs in 7:10.
43. Cf. BDB 145; T.K. Cheyne, *The Book of Hosea*. CBSC (1913), 72.
44. *Hosea*, 84. Cf. Wolff, *Hosea*, 100; Mauchline, 'Hosea', 618; Harper, *Amos and Hosea*, 270.
45. *Studies in the Name Israel in the Old Testament*, 117f.
46. *God and Temple. The Idea of the Divine Presence in Ancient Israel* (1965), 55 n. 1.
47. Cf. for example the usage in Jer. 2:3, 14; 3:20; 4:1.
48. 'Hosea 5:8-6:6. Ein Krieg und seine Folgen in prophetischen Beleuchtung', *Kleine Schriften* II (1959), 163ff. In contrast Andersen and Freedman, *Hosea*, 34f., 402ff., locate the events earlier, in the time of Uzziah, on the grounds that the attack must have been initiated by Judah. As an example of the earlier more sceptical attitude towards the Judah references see R.E. Wolfe, 'The Editing of the Book of the Twelve', *ZAW* 53, 1935, 91. E.M. Good, 'Hosea 5:8-6:6: An Alternative to Alt', *JBL* 85, 1966, 281ff., understands the passage liturgically, relating it to the covenant festival.

NOTES TO CHAPTER II   181

49. Cf. Mays, *Hosea*, 87, who comments: 'this long sequence of course does not represent one oral unit, as the shifts in style and form make clear; it is held together by its setting within the same complex of events'.
50. Cf. Dt. 19:14; 27:17; Prov. 22:28; 23:10; Job 24:2.
51. שרים here, as commonly, is to be understood as referring to military leaders. In contrast, Harper, *Amos and Hosea*, 275, identifies them with בית המלך of v. 1.
52. See J.H. Hayes and J.M. Miller, *Israelite and Judean History*, 432.
53. This is generally accepted by commentators. See, for example, Mays, *Hosea*, 89f.; Wolff, *Hosea*, 112ff., who regards it as a response by the prophet to the objections of his hearers to his previous words in vv. 8f.
54. Ginsberg,in a personal letter to me dated 23/11/1969, stresses this point particularly. Cf. 'Hosea, Book of' *EJ*, 1019.
55. Cf. 2 Kings 16:5; Is. 7:1-6. It is to this event that Hos. 5:11 refers, whether צו is understood as synonym of שוא meaning 'what is worthless' (cf. Wolff, *Hosea*, 104), or as a corruption of צר 'enemy' (cf. Mays, *Hosea*, 85).
56. Hayes and Miller, *Israelite and Judean History*, 427.
57. E.g. Wolff, *Hosea*, 111f.; Mays, *Hosea*, 86f. As indicated above, the normative work on this subject is that of Alt, 'Ein Krieg und seine Folgen in prophetischen Beleuchtung', 163ff.
58. Cf. Mays, *Hosea*, 91. Rudolph, *Hosea*, 124, understands וישלח as a corruptoon of (sic) וירושלם. The unintelligible מלך ירב is to be understood as מלכי רב with *yod compaginis*, the equivalent of the Akkadian šarru rabu used as a designation of the king, for which see *KAI* 1, 42. Cf. Wolff, *Hosea*, 104
59. *Amos and Hosea*, 275ff. Note in contrast Wolff, *Hosea*, 115; Mays, *Hosea*, 91.
60. Cf. 7:8-9; 12:2 as examples.
61. See Mays, *Hosea*, 85f.; Wolff, *Hosea*, 104ff.
62. *Hosea*, 87. Mays recognises that the composition in its present form is the work of redactors, but he believes that the material itself has an inner coherence since it belongs to the same complex of events. Cf. Wolff, *Hosea*, 116f., who also attributes the composition to redactors. He argues that a song of penitence already in use was added to Hosea's sayings by traditionists in order to make the rhetorical questions of 6:4 understandable.
63. Cf. Wolff, *Hosea*, 116f.
64. *Hosea*, 117.
65. See above, pp. 53f.
66. *Hosea*, 116. It is true that טרף occurs both in the proclamation of judgement in 5:14 and in the penitential song of 6:1, but this is not an integral connection but another example of linking by catchword.
67. It should be noted that where מקום is used in Jer. 4:7 it applies not strictly to the lion's lair but to the destroyer represented figuratively by the lion.

68. *Hosea,* 92.
69. *Ibid.*
70. See above, pp. 22ff.
71. *Hosea,* 119.
72. Wolff nevertheless affirms that in 6:4, just as in 5:10-14, Hosea is concerned with all the tribes of Israel, and consequently he accepts the reference to Judah as original.
73. Cf. F. Hvidberg, *Weeping and Laughter in the Old Testament* (1962), 126ff.
74. R. Hentschke, *Die Stellung der vorexilischen Schriftpropheten zum Kultus,* BZAW 75 (1957), 91.
75. Mays, *Hosea,* 94.
76. *Hosea,* 109. He compares 5:12, 13b; 7:13b, 15.
77. See below, pp. 77f., 87.
78. For a detailed treatment of this chapter and reasons for regarding vv. 1-13 as a unit and not as a compilation of sayings see my article, 'The Structure and Meaning of Hosea VIII 1-3', *VT* 25, 1975, 705f.
79. See above, p. 6.
80. *Hosea,* 146. See also his remarks on 136.
81. *Hosea,* 115 and 124.
82. See above, p. 6.
83. Cf. Wolff, *Hosea,* 136, though he does incline to the view that the saying originates with Hosea himself.
84. Cf. Mays, *Hosea,* 124.
85. So Wolff, *Hosea,* 146, who comments that 'Hosea sees a danger in the civilisation of the cities in general'.
86. So Mays, *Hosea,* 124.
87. *Hosea,* 146.
88. The widely accepted emendation of דרך to רכב has been adopted here by the RSV.
89. For the meaning 'palaces' in preference to 'temples' see BDB 228:1. A number of palaces in the northern kingdom are referred to in the Old Testament: by implication that of Jeroboam I (1 Kings 12:25); the palace in Tirzah (1 Kings 16:18); Ahab's palace (1 Kings 21:1).
90. Contrast Wolff, *Hosea,* 146, who considers that the contrast between Israel's palaces and Judah's fortified cities is merely stylistic and has no particular significance.
91. For a further discussion of Hosea's attitude to the reunion of the kingdoms see below, pp. 98ff.
92. See above, pp. 59f.
93. *Amos and Hosea,* clix and 262f.
94. 2 Kings 8:18; 16:3; Ezek. 23:13.
95. *Hosea,* 77.
96. 'The Southern Kingdom in Hosea', 105.
97. M. Dahood, 'Hebrew-Ugaritic Lexicography I', *Biblica* 1963, 293f.
98. Contrast Wolff, *Hosea,* 72 and 89, who prefers the LXX.
99. It should be noted that an inner Greek variant exists, and that some mss read ὁ for οὐ in 4:14. This however, does not affect the point I am making.

100. συμπλέκω is used of sexual intercourse. See H.G. Liddell and R. Scott, *A Greek-English Lexicon* (revised ed. 1940) 1684.
101. See Barr's salutary remarks in *Comparative Philology and the Text of the Old Testament*, 266ff.
102. E.g. 4:16.
103. Or at any rate the account of that reform given in 2 Kings 23:15ff.
104. The conjunction in ואל-תבאו is superfluous and is probably to be explained as a necessary addition when the reference to Judah was included.
105. See further on this question pp. 124ff. below. Cf. also my study of 8:1 in 'The Structure and Meaning of Hosea VIII 1-3', 709, which led me to a similar conclusion. For a different point of view see Wolff, *Hosea*, 89.
106. *The Bible in Aramaic* III (ed. A. Sperber, 1962).
107. *Hosea*, 78.
108. *Ibid*.
109. The sentiment expressed coincides, therefore, with that of Jer. 4:2; 5:2.
110. See below, pp. 135ff.
111. Cf. T. Worden, 'The Literary Influence of the Ugaritic Fertility Myth on the Old Testament', *VT* 3, 1953, 290.
112. 2 Kings 23:15ff.
113. The translation adopted here is that given by Mays, *Hosea*, ad loc., apart from the fact that I have left לו untranslated as befits the English idiom. I regard it as an ethic dative. Cf. Wolff, *Hosea*, 180, textual note n. The LXX regards the reference to Judah as a threat, and understands the verb in the first person as παρασιωπήσομαι 'I will pass over in silence'.
114. *Prophecy and Tradition*, 72f.
115. *Hosea*, 145. Cf. also Nyberg, *Studien zum Hoseabuche*, 81, n. 1; NEB, though this differs in regarding Judah as a corruption of הוא, not as a substitution for Israel.
116. *Hosea*, 185.
117. So Mays, *Hosea*, 144f.; Wolff, *Hosea*, 182f.
118. See for example 5:9 and the discussion on the prophet's attitude to reunion 135ff. below.
119. It is likely that the difficult עברתי על is a corruption of עברתי על על 'I laid a yoke upon .....'
120. 2:17.
121. 11:1.
122. For the view that Judah is never addressed directly by Hosea see above, p. 74.
123. See above, p. 64.
124. Cf. Amos 7:2, 5 and Mic. 1:5 where Jacob and Samaria are contrasted explicitly with Judah and Jerusalem.
125. Taking שת as impersonal, 'one has appointed'.
125. E.g. RSV, NEB, TEV. The AV in contrast retains the sentence division of the MT.
127. LXX has a different approach and connects the first two words of 7:1 with 6:11.

128. For a similar loose connection of redactional comment cf. 4:5.
129. Thus Mays, *Hosea*, 102; Wolff, *Hosea*, 106, who considers that the expansion of the saying took place in two stages; Ward, *Hosea*, 127. Mauchline, 'Hosea', 631, is less prepared to commit himself on the question of either provenance or meaning.
130. Cf. Jer. 51:33; Joel 4:13.
131. Note should be taken here of JB which regards the mention of Judah as a later addition but differs from other recent translations in its sentence division:
    Judah, I intend a harvest for you, too, when I restore the fortunes of my people.
132. There is no reason why the expression שוב שבות should be considered later than Hosea's time, and v. 11b attributed to redactional influence, for the noun שבות is to be connected with the root שוב, with the meaning 'restoration', and not with שבה, which would give the specific meaning 'captivity'. Cf. A.R. Johnson, *The Cultic Prophet and Israel's Psalmody* (1979), 208; J.H. Eaton, *Psalms* (1967) 285.
133. Cf. also Jer. 3:8ff.
134. Cf. NEB; Wolff, *Hosea,* 20f; Mauchline, 'Hosea', 572, and commonly. In contrast Andersen and Freedman, *Hosea,* 194, understand 1:7 as a judgmental saying, taking the negative of v. 7b to apply to the whole saying.
135. Cf. Wolff, *Hosea,* 63; Snaith, *Mercy and Sacrifice,* 50, who states baldly, 'No northerner in his senses would write or say a thing like that'. It is interesting to note that E.H. Maly, 'Messianism in Osée', *CBQ* 19, 1957, 217, is far more cautious and admits that he hesitates 'to say with some authors that Osée *could* not have expressed this idea'.
136. E.g. Wolff, *Hosea,* 27f., who believes the background of the verse to be the time before the collapse of the northern kingdom; Mays, *Hosea,* 31, considers that 'if it does not derive from Hosea, it must come from his period and the circles sympathetic to his prophecy'.
137. *Studies in the Name Israel in the Old Testament,* 145ff.
138. *Hosea,* xxxi and 20f.
139. See pp. 113ff.
140. V.5 also interrupts the carefully structured passage, and its present position is certainly secondary, whatever its origins may be.
141. Cf. Jer. 7:1-15 for a portrayal of the nation's complacency and a prophetic protest against it.
142. Cf. Wolff, *Hosea,* 11f.; Mays, *Hosea,* 24.
143. Cf. 2 Kings 19:32-37. For an interesting discussion of later treatment of this event see R.E. Clements, *Isaiah and the Deliverance of Jerusalem* (1980), 60, 86.
144. Thus Wolff, *Hosea,* 21, sounds a warning on this point, in contrast to J. Mauchline, 'Hosea', 572.
145. *When Prophecy Failed,* 34.

NOTES TO CHAPTER II 185

146. Cf. G. von Rad, *Der heilige Krieg im alten Israel* (1958), 42ff., 56ff.
147. Cf. R. de Vaux, *Ancient Israel. Its Life and Institutions* (ET 1973), pp. 258-264, especially 262.
148. *Hosea*, 20.
149. E.g. Dt. 20:4, and frequently in the Deuteronomistic history, as in Jos. 22:22; Jud. 3:9; 6:36f.; 1 Sam. 14:23, 39; 2 Kings 14:27 etc. For an up-to-date discussion of this verb see J.F.A. Sawyer, 'Hôšîaʿ', *TWAT*.
150. It is possible to understand the preposition here as ב essentiae, giving the meaning, 'as the Lord their God', but in the light of the following occurrences of ב to indicate the instrument, it is more likely here the agent.
151. Cf. Num. 36:2; Gen. 9:6. See R.J. Williams, *Hebrew Syntax. An Outline* (1967), 48.
152. E.g. 6:5; 12:14; 14:4 and possibly 12:7.
153. Contrast Jer. 21:4; 51:20 etc.: כלי המלחמה.
154. See above, pp. 30ff.
155. E.g. 1:2; 2:22; 3:1; 4:6, 10, 12; 5:4 etc.
156. On the reasons for attributing this saying to Hosea himself see, for example, A.C. Welch, *Kings and Prophets of Israel* (1952), 179, who rightly emphasises that the fact that Assyria is mentioned as an ally in v. 4 implies that the saying comes from Hosea's time. From the period of Ahaz until the collapse of Judah, Assyria was an enemy. The saying is, therefore, unlikely to have originated in Judah. Cf. Wolff, *Hosea*, 234.
157. See further on this question pp. 110ff.
158. Cf. N. Porteous, 'The Prophets and the Problem of Continuity', *Israel's Prophetic Heritage* (eds. B.W. Anderson and W. Harrelson, 1962), 14f.
159. The reference to Shechem in 6:9 is altogether too uncertain to provide evidence to the contrary, especially in the light of 4:1-3.
160. See as examples Ps. 50 and 81, both of which probably belong to Jerusalem temple worship but draw on the ancient pre-monarchic traditions of Israel. On this see A.A. Anderson, *Psalms* I, 381, II, 587. The great theological work of the Yahwist is also a case in point.
161. *Origins and History of the Oldest Sinaitic Traditions* (1965), 160.
162. See above, p. 89.
163. See above, p. 89.
164. For the reasons for so dating see Wolff, *Hosea*, 66, 76.
165. Wolff, *Hosea*, 224.
166. See above, pp. 16ff.
167. See n. 136 above.
168. *Hosea*, 24.
169. Cf. 2:16.
170. *Hosea*, 26.
171. Cf. Wolff, *Hosea*, 26, on the historical background.
172. Gen. 32:13. Note in contrast the formulation of the promise in the Abraham tradition in Gen. 22:17.

173. *Hosea*, 27.
174. Cf. Jos. 3:10; Ps. 42:2; 84:2.
175. Cf. Hayes and Miller, *Israelite and Judean History*, 427ff.
176. 2 Kings 9:16ff.
177. Cf. Is. 9:3 יוֹם מִדְיָן, where the context is clearly military.
178. 2 Kings 9:27. For further discussion of this passage see pp. 111f. below.
179. Cf. J.R. Bartlett, 'The Use of the Word ראש as a Title in the Old Testament', *VT* 19, 1969, 1-10.
180. Cf. Wolff, *Hosea*, 27.
181. As is done, for example, by Harper, *Amos and Hosea*, 245.
182. So Mauchline, 'Hosea', 576, who nevertheless attributes the saying to Hosea, interpreting it as the reversal of the dispersal threatened in 8:8; 9:3, 6, 17; 11:11.
183. Among the various suggestions are the following: 'they shall go up' in a military sense (Mays, *Hosea*, 33); 'they shall go up' to a festival (Östborn, *Yahweh and Baal*, 64; Ward, *Hosea*, 46 n. 9); 'they will come up' i.e. from the underworld, referring historically to the exodus from Egypt and eschatologically to resurrection (Andersen and Freedman, *Hosea*, 209); 'they shall grow up' like plants (Rudolph, *Hosea*, 58). For arguments against the military sense, 'to gain ascendance over the land', see K. Rupprecht, עלה מן הארץ (Ex. 1:10 and Hos. 2:2) "sich des Landes bemächtigen"?', *ZAW* 82, 1970, 442f.
184. For this view, in addition to Rudolph, *op. cit.* above, see TEV.
185. See p. 28ff.
186. Thus Wolff, *Hosea*, 26, does not doubt the northern origin of the saying, attributing its present position and to some extent its formulation to a close associate of the prophet. He comments, 'It is just as probable that he had some effect on the present form of the passage as it is that the passage's basic content comes from Hosea'. This differentiation, however, lies outside the scope of this study.
187. For a discussion of this subject see Danell, *Studies in the Name Israel in the Old Testament*, 137ff. Cf. also A.D.H. Mayes, *Israel in the Period of the Judges*, SBT Second Series 29 (1974), 1ff.
188. A similar tradition occurs in Dt. 32:10.
189. 'Method in the Study of Early Hebrew History', *The Bible in Modern Scholarship* (ed. J.P. Hyatt, 1965), 22.
190. Cf. J. Bright, *A History of Israel,* 136f. In contrast, Noth, *The History of Israel* (1960), 118f., considers it methodologically wrong to ask which tribes came out of Egypt, since they were formed into such units only when they reached Palestine. He does not, of course, differ on the fundamental point that an 'all Israel' perspective has been superimposed.
191. *Das System der zwölf Stämme Israels*, BWANT III, 10 (1930), the normative study on this subject.
192. *Israel in the Period of the Judges*, 106ff.
193. E.g. Ps. 50 and 81.

194. Amos 7:10ff.
195. See E.W. Nicholson, *Preaching to the Exiles* (1970), 137f.
196. Jer. 41:5. Cf. Clements, *God and Temple*, x.
197. *Amos and Hosea*, 245. In contrast, Gordis, 'Hosea's Marriage and Message; A New Approach', *HUCA* 25, 1954, 34, stresses that concern for a united Hebrew nation is a basic attitude of both northern and southern prophets.
198. Cf. Amos' radical reinterpretation of the 'day of the Lord' (5:18), though there a word of judgement, here of hope.
199. See pp. 111f.
200. 'The Book of Hosea', *SBU*, cols. 983f.
201. *Prophecy and Tradition*, 30.
202. Pp. 12ff. above.
203. E.g. Wolff, *Hosea*, 57; Mays, *Hosea*, 60.
204. Nyberg, *Studien zum Hoseabuche*, 123f., finds here a reference to deities, in contrast to the majority view.
205. *Hosea*, 57.
206. E.g. Dt. 4:29; Pss. 24:6; 27:8 and *passim*.
207. Cf. Cant. 5:6, where it is clearly the language of love.
208. Cf. 2 Sam. 19:42ff. See H. Cazelles, 'The History of Israel in the Pre-exilic Period', *Tradition and Interpretation* (ed. G.W. Anderson, 1979), 297.
209. Cf. Dan. 12:13.
210. For this meaning see Dt. 4:30, 'in days to come' (NEB); 31:29; Gen. 49:1. For a discussion of this question see further G.W. Buchanan, 'Eschatology and the "End of Days"', *JNES* 20 (1961), 188-193; E. Lipiński, 'באחרית הימים dans les textes préexiliques', *VT* 20 (1970), 445-450.
211. 'The Southern Kingdom in Hosea', 103f. As evidence of the northern origin of the saying in essence van Selms draws attention to the unusual use of פחד with the preposition אל, of which an example occurs also in 1 Sam. 16:4.
212. See p. 103.
213. 'Hosea's Marriage and Message: A New Approach', *HUCA* 25, 1954, 30ff. See also Andersen and Freedman, *Hosea*, 307, who comment, 'We hardly know enough of Hosea's political thinking to rule out the restoration of the Davidic kingdom as an eschatological expectation'.
214. Nyberg's divergence from the majority view has already been noted in n. 204 above. A similar view to Nyberg's is held by G. Östborn, *Yahweh and Baal*, 23f. and 54ff. Against this view, however, 13:10f. in particular seems to refer more naturally to earthly rulers. See Gelston,'Kingship in the Book of Hosea', *OTS* 19, 1974, 72ff.
215. *Hosea*, 19.
216. *Hosea*, 157.
217. 'Kingship in the Book of Hosea', 83.
218. See 3:4; 7:3, 5, 16; 8:10; 9:15; 13:10.
219. למען can then be understood in its usual sense to express purpose, avoiding the difficulty inherent in the traditional interpretation, as seen, for example, in the comment in BDB, 775, and Mays, *Hosea*, 113 n. b.

220. 'Kingship in the Book of Hosea', 83.
221. Cf. J. Bright, *A History of Israel*, 255 n. 7; for the opposite view that the passage is concerned with a present transgression see the comments made by Wolff, *Hosea*, 167.
222. For further discussion of the attitudes shown towards Gilgal in the material see below, pp. 138ff.
223. For the association of these terms with divorce see Dt. 22:13; 24:3; Lev. 21:7, 14.
224. In contrast, it is used of political activity in Ezek. 16:28f.; 23:30.
225. E.g. Ward, *Hosea*, 169, 182f., though the view was more popular among earlier commentators this century than it is today.
226. 1 Sam. 10:26.
227. So Gelston, 'Kingship in the Book of Hosea', *OTS* 19, 1974, 81; Wolff, *Hosea*, 158, 184; Mays, *Hosea*, 131, 143.
228. *Hosea*, 185.
229. 1 Kings 15:27ff.
230. 1 Kings 16:8ff.
231. 1 Kings 16:16ff.
232. 2 Kings 9:14ff.
233. P. 146.
234. Cf. A. Alt, *Essays on Old Testament History and Religion* (1966), 250f.
235. Cf. Mays, *Hosea*, 32. In contrast, Harper, *Amos and Hosea*, 247, interprets as 'a king, probably of the Davidic family', and consequently feels obliged to date the saying later than Hosea's period.
236. See 1 Sam. 15:17; Ps. 18:44.
237. Cf. J.R. Bartlett, 'The Use of the Word ראש as a title in the Old Testament', *VT* 19, 1969, 2f.
238. Against Mauchline, 'Hosea', 555, who holds that Hosea believed in the charismatic principle of leadership.
239. For ממלכות meaning 'royal office' rather than 'realm' see 1 Sam. 15:28; 2 Sam. 16:3; Jer. 26:1. Cf. Mays, *Hosea*, 27.
240. 1 Kings 21:1ff.
241. For the Israelite view that kings are subject to the law of God see, for example, Ps. 89:30ff.
242. 2 Kings 9-10.
243. Either Jeroboam II or possibly Zechariah, the last member of Jehu's dynasty.
244. *Biblical and Oriental Studies* I (1973), 112f. n. 21.
245. Cf. 9:13; 10:10; 11:6; 13:16 etc.
246. See 2 Kings 16:31ff.; 18:19.
247. E.g. 7:8, 9, 11; 8:10; 12:2.
248. *Hosea*, 18.
249. *Hosea*, 12f.
250. 2 Kings 9:3, 6ff.
251. For the political orientation of Hosea's message see 7:3-7; 13:9-11 etc.
252. 2 Kings 11:1.
253. 2 Kings 11:4ff.

254. On the question whether Jehu's actions had primarily a political motivation see Hayes and Miller, *Israelite and Judean History*, 412f.
255. Pp. 98ff.
256. Cf. Nicholson, *Deuteronomy and Tradition*, 100, 105; Clements, *Abraham and David* (1967), 66.
257. The ambiguity is reflected in the English translations. RV, RSV and JB understand the saying in a favourable sense; RVm and NEB in an unfavourable one, though with considerable variation. The dismissal of the words by Good, 'Hosea and the Jacob Tradition', *VT* 16, 1966, 139 n. 2, as 'smugly Judean' is unsatisfactory in view of the uncertain meaning.
258. P. 61.
259. *Hosea*, 210. Mays, *Hosea*, 160, in contrast comments: 'probably an editor has inserted 'but Judah' in the text which was originally a continuation of the reproach against Ephraim'. However, Wolff's comment seems apt, that the placing of עד immediately after the subject strongly suggests that an antithesis is intended.
260. Cf. Prov. 9:10; 30:3.
261. Cf. Ps. 89:8.
262. Cf. Ps. 34:10; Dan. 7:21. For a discussion of this latter passage see M. Noth, *The Laws in the Pentateuch and Other Studies* (1966), 215ff. Wolff, *Hosea*, 210, inclines to the view that קדושים refers to the pious among God's people, and takes the suffix of סבבני as applying to the prophet, not to Yahweh.
263. In Hosea, as elsewhere in the Old Testament, Baal, not El stands in opposition to Yahweh. Wherever El refers to a god other than Yahweh this is made clear by a qualifying adjective such as אחר (Ex. 34:14) and זר (Ps. 44:21) (*contra* Andersen and Freedman, *Hosea*, 603).
264. van Selms, 'The Southern Kingdom in Hosea', 109f., suggests that רד is a corruption of דר, and refers to the Ugaritic expression *dr ilm*, 'the assembly of the gods'. He inclines to the view that in the prophet's opinion Judah was equally guilty with Israel.
265. 'Early Hebrew Myths and Their Interpretation', *Myth, Ritual and Kingship* (ed. S.H. Hooke, 1958) 161 n. 1.
266. Widengren compares the Arabic *rāda*.
267. Pp. 93ff.
268. See above, pp. 110ff.
269. See above, pp. 65ff.
270. Cf. Jer. 2 *passim*; 3:6-9. See J.W. McKay, *Religion in Judah under the Assyrians*, pp. 20ff., for the rise of Canaanite cults in Judah in the 7th century.

NOTES TO CHAPTER III

1. E.g. 2:8; 4:4-5; 5:21-24.
2. 2:6-7; 3:9-11, 15; 4:1; 5:7, 10-12, 14-15; 6:4-7, 12; 8:4-6.
3. The connection between 7:9, with its reference to high places and sanctuaries, and 7:10-11 is editorial based on the purely external link made by their common reference to the fall of Jeroboam. This is clear on form critical grounds, the former belonging to an autobiographical vision report, the latter to a biographical narrative. So Mays, *Amos,* 123, who comments, 'This difference in style indicates that the block is not an original oral or literary unit. The biographical narrative has been set in its present place because of the connection between 7:9 and 11'.
4. E.g. 4:1-2; 7:1; 12:8-9.
5. Another prominent theme is, of course, criticism of the monarchy in Israel, but that question is not of relevance here. I am concerned simply to indicate the marked difference of emphasis between the messages of Hosea and Amos.
6. *When Prophecy Failed,* 49f.
7. E.g. 2:4-15; 4:12-15; 5:3-7; 9:1-9. This terminology is not found in Amos; cf. E. Jacob, 'L'Héritage cananéen dans le livre du prophète Osée', *RHPR* 43, 1963, 250-9.
8. E.g. 4:6; 5:4; 6:6. This terminology, too, is absent from Amos. For a fuller discussion of this question see B.J. van der Merwe, 'A Few Remarks on the Religious Terminology in Amos and Hosea', *Die O.T. Werkgemeenskap in Suid-Afrika: Studies on the Books of Hosea and Amos,* 143ff.
9. See above, pp. 8 and 60.
10. There are, in fact, many points at which the messages of Amos and Hosea differ. Among these may be mentioned briefly the absence of reference to visionary experiences in Hosea and also the lack of interest in the nations.
11. For the importance of the Deuteronomists in the editing of the prophetic books see Carroll, *When Prophecy Failed,* 49; Clements, *Prophecy and Tradition,* 46ff.; Wolff, *Hosea,* xxxi f.
12. 2 Kings 23:15-20.
13. This was especially so at the time of Ahaz in the attempt by Syria and Ephraim to depose him (Is. 7:5-6).
14. The MT has ושחטה שטים העמיקו. שטים is a word of uncertain meaning, possibly an orthographic variant of סטים, and in this case to be translated, 'revolters have gone deep in slaughter'. So *BDB*, 962. Unfortunately this is not the only difficulty. שחטה is a *hapax legomenon,* explained by G.R. Driver, 'Studies in the Vocabulary of the Old Testament VI', *JTS* 34, 1933, 40, as an Aramaism signifying 'lewdness'. However, the hunting metaphor of v. 1 suggests that שחת 'pit' is intended, giving a suitable parallel to פח and רשת.

In this case a parallel might be expected to Mizpah and
Tabor, suggesting that שטים should be read, as commonly
accepted. The LXX differs considerably from the MT in
v. 2, though it continues the hunting metaphor from v. 1
with its ὃ οἱ ἀγρεύοντες τὴν θήραν κατέπηξαν; but it can
scarcely be used as a guide for emendation purposes.

15. Reading שבי בית ישראל as a suitable parallel to the
priests and royal court, with Rudolph, Hosea, 116. The
omission of the word is to be explained as haplography.
16. It is unclear whether Mizpah in Benjamin or in Gilead is
intended.
17. So Wolff, Hosea, 94.
18. So Mays, Hosea, 79.
19. See in particular A. Alt, 'Hosea 5:8-6:6. Ein Krieg und
seine Folgen in prophetischen Beleuchtung', Kleine
Schriften II, 163ff. On this question see above, pp. 67ff.
20. 'Hosea 5:8-6:6: An Alternative to Alt', JBL 85, 1966,
281ff.
21. Die Samuelbücher. ATD (1960), 15.
22. So, for example, Wolff, Hosea, 158, who argues against
associating this with Saul's accession to the throne which
is connected, not with Gibeah, but with Gilgal and perhaps
Mizpah. See above, p. 109.
23. Hosea, 143, though on 131 in commenting on 9:9 he rules out
the reference to Saul's kingship.
24. Cf. Is. 31:2.
25. Cf. 1 Sam. 15:23 where און is parallel to תרפים and seems
to carry the specific connotation of idolatry.
26. 2 Kings 15:25.
27. Hosea, 122, though see my comments on pp. 147ff. below.
28. So Wolff, Hosea, 96 and 183.
29. Ibid., 112.
30. 1 Kings 16:32.
31. 2 Kings 10:27. The reference in Amos 8:14 to הנשבעים
באשמת שמרון is not evidence to the contrary. For several
possible meanings of this problematic text see J.L. Mays,
Amos, 149f., and his comment, 'Amos does not refer to any
shrine or public cult in Samaria nor is there any mention
in other sources of one after the destruction of the shrine
to Baal by Jehu'.
32. Cf. Wolff, Hosea, 140. H.-J. Kraus, Worship in Israel,
152, argues that such a cult object was located in a
sanctuary in Samaria, but Wolff's arguments are more
convincing.
33. 'Some Additional Arabic Etymologies in Old Testament
Lexicography', VT 11, 1961, 385. He argues that זמה often
refers to infamy of a sexual nature, comparing Lev. 18:17;
19:29; Jer. 13:27, and that שכמה may have this sense here.
34. Hosea, 122; E. Meyer, Geschichte des Altertums 3 (1954),
16f., argues similarly.
35. Shechem: A Traditio-historical Investigation (1959) 290.
Cf. also Nyberg, Studien zum Hoseabuche, 42f.; A. Weiser,
Das Buch der zwölf kleinen Propheten I (1949), ad loc. who

suggests that the background to Hos. 6:7-11 was a cultic pilgrimage from east Jordan to Shechem.
36. *Deuteronomy and Tradition,* 63.
37. 'The Prophets and the Problem of Continuity', *Israel's Prophetic Heritage,* 16, and 'Actualization and the Prophetic Criticism of the Cult', *Tradition und Situation,* 100.
38. 'Linguistic and Textual Problems', *JTS* 39, 1938, 156.
39. Josh. 20:7.
40. So the majority of commentators. See, for example, Harper, *Amos and Hosea,* 263; Wolff, *Hosea,* 90; Mays, *Hosea,* 77; W.L. Holladay, 'Chiasmus, the Key to Hosea XII 3-6', *VT* 16, 1966, 59. Ackroyd, 'Hosea', *Peake's Commentary,* 608, is somewhat more cautious about this identification in 4:15, and especially in 10:5 where he comments (611), 'Here a reference to Bethel is less appropriate and a more general reference to some religious building may be intended'.
41. Thus Nicholson, *Deuteronomy and Tradition,* 82, states this categorically in his discussion of the provenance of Deuteronomy.
42. און may also carry the meaning 'trouble' as in Is. 10:1; Ps. 7:15, for example.
43. So Mays, *Amos,* 89. See also n. 25 above.
44. Cf. E. Hammershaimb, *The Book of Amos* (1970), 79, who comments, ' און ..... is an expression for the powers of evil, but also for that which is empty and powerless, which has no existence in itself', and compares Is. 41:29. See also A. Neher, *Amos* (1950), 103. This is the interpretation adopted by JB in commenting on Bethaven in Hos. 4:15.
45. R. de Vaux, *Ancient Israel: Its Life and Institutions* (1973), 291f.
46. See above, pp. 77f.
47. *Hosea,* 89. The argument is not convincing since other second person verbs remain despite the consequent difficulty in meaning.
48. *Ibid.*
49. As Mays, *Hosea,* 77, comments: 'Hosea's prohibition would close the doors of the shrine where kingship began'.
50. I have noted already on   above the significant absence of a corresponding word of judgement pronounced on the Judean sanctuary at Beersheba.
51. The MT has the feminine plural עגלות. G.R. Driver, 'Linguistic and Textual Problems: Minor Prophets I', *JTS* 39, 1938, 163, understands this as a deliberately contemptuous form. In contrast, Nyberg, *Studien zum Hoseabuche,* 73, believes the original reading was the feminine singular עגלת, understood in a collective sense as 'herd of calves' referring to 'die Gemeinde der Kalbsverehrer'. F.F. Hvidberg, *Weeping and Laughter in the Old Testament* (1962), 99 n. 2, also holds that the original form was feminine singular, but understands it to refer to the goddess Anat, comparing the Ugaritic text I AB V 18, where

'glt is Anat, Baal's beloved one and sister. In contrast Pedersen, *Israel* 3/4, 713 n. 470, conjectures that the form עגלות has arisen by scribal error by dittography of ית in בית.

52. As noted above, the MT has עגלות, and it is therefore difficult to understand the suffixes as referring to this.
53. *Hosea,* 141. The translation offered in the NEB is, therefore, to be preferred to that of RSV.
54. For a full discussion of the meaning of this expression see P.H. Vaughan, *The Meaning of 'bāmâ' in the Old Testament. A Study of Etymological, Textual and Archaeological Evidence* (1974).
55. For a brief survey of some of the work on this subject see P.R. Ackroyd, 'Hosea and Jacob', *VT* 13, 1963, 254ff.
56. So Ackroyd, *art. cit.*, 256f. Cf. W.L. Holladay, 'Chiasmus, the Key to Hosea XII 3-6', *VT* 16, 1966, 59; J.R. Mauchline, 'Hosea', *IB* 6, 696; Wolff, *Hosea,* 213; Mays, *Hosea,* 164 and 170.
57. Cf. H.L. Ginsberg, 'Hosea's Ephraim, More Fool than Knave. A New Interpretation of Hosea 12:1-14', *JBL* 80, 1961, 344f.; E.M. Good, 'Hosea and the Jacob Tradition', *VT* 16, 1966, 146.
58. 'Genesis xxxii 23-33: Some Remarks on the Composition and Character of the Story', *NedThT* 1, 1947, 149ff.
59. See n. 56 above.
60. *Art. cit.*, 258.
61. *Ibid.*
62. For this view see Ginsberg, *art. cit.*, 339ff.; Good, *art cit.*, 146; and in strong disagreement Ackroyd, *art. cit.*, 251.
63. I am grateful to J.F.A. Sawyer for pointing this out.
64. Cf. G. von Rad, *Genesis* (1972), 338f.
65. *Ibid.*, 284.
66. There is no need to suppose that the Jacob traditions on which Hosea draws differ materially from those of the Pentateuch. Cf. Holladay, *art. cit.*, 55; U. Cassuto, *Biblical and Oriental Studies* (1933), 79ff.
67. Inherent in the Jacob tradition is the theme of commitment to God, as in Gen. 28:20ff., for example. Moreover, it is possible that Gen. 35:1-4 reflects a regular pilgrimage from Shechem to Bethel in which the worshippers committed themselves to renounce foreign gods. Cf. G. von Rad, *Genesis* (1972), 337, who places the origins of this as early as the period of the Judges.
68. This is not, of course, to deny that Bethel, like other sacred sites, was taken over by Israel's ancestors from the Canaanites, but that, as far as Israelite tradition is concerned, its origins were associated with Jacob and his encounter with God. See R. de Vaux, *Ancient Israel. Its Life and Institutions,* 291f.
69. At this point the RSV, from which the translation is with this exception taken, emends to 'house of Israel' and commits the reading Bethel to a footnote, correctly I believe.

70. E.g. by Wolff, *Hosea,* 181; Rudolph, *Hosea,* 205f. See also JB.
71. 'Hosea', *Peake's Commentary,* 611. Cf. Nyberg, *Studien zum Hoseabuche,* 83f.; NEB.
72. Thus Wolff, *Hosea,* 181, comments on the MT 'Bethel': 'Aside from the context, this is improbable *merely* because Hosea usually calls Bethel בית און' (the emphasis is mine).
73. See, for example, Nyberg, *Studien zum Hoseabuche,* 62; Rudolph, *Hosea,* 162; Wolff, *Hosea,* 176; Mays, *Hosea,* 127.
74. 'The Structure and Meaning of Hosea VIII 1-3', *VT* 25, 1975, 706ff.
75. E.g. Dt. 22:13; 24:3; Lev. 21:7, 14.
76. See my article cited above, n. 74, especially 707-709.
77. Cf. N.H. Tur-Sinai, *The Book of Job* (1967), 550; J. Barr, *Comparative Philology and the Text of the Old Testament* (1968), 26f. and 331, who argues for the form נָשֵׁר in preference to נֶשֶׁר.
78. Contrast RSV 'the fruit of our lips' with NEB 'cattle from our pens'. See below, pp. 151ff.
79. See above, pp. 128ff.
80. See above, pp. 67f.
81. *Hosea,* 90.
82. *Notes on the Hebrew Text and the Topography of the Books of Samuel* (1960), 99 and map facing 390. Cf. also *BDB,* 110. In contrast KB^2 regards the name Bethaven as a 'defacing substitute of Bethel' in Joshua and Samuel as well as in Hosea.
83. *Joshua* (1972), 93.
84. *Joshua, Judges and Ruth* (1967), 83.
85. For the variety of suggested nuances see above, p. 124.
86. 'Joshua', *IB* 2 (1953), 584; cf. *BDB,* 110.
87. Cf. the play of אלהים / אלילים in Psalm 96:5.
88. For a similar example see the play on קץ / קיץ in Amos 8:2.
89. J. Ziegler, *Septuaginta XIII, Duodecim Prophetae* (1943), 130, on the basis of the LXX τῷ οἴκῳ Ὢν regards און as the original reading here. It seems more likely, however, that the LXX has harmonised the form here with that of the previous passages rather than that the form Bethel should have been restored in the MT only in this instance. On this point see Wolff, *Hosea,* 206.
90. Since the LXX οἴκῳ Ὢν is neutral whereas the MT בית און is polemical it may well be that the MT form is later. Cf. Amos 5:26 where by ingenious vocalisation the Hebrew text is reinterpreted for polemical purposes.
91. Pp. 125ff.
92. See E. Jacob, 'Der Prophet Hosea und die Geschichte', *EvTh* 24, 1964, 283f.; Wolff, *Hosea,* 167; Mauchline, 'Hosea', 666f.
93. See Mays, *Hosea,* 136; Ackroyd, 'Hosea', 610.
94. The expression 'my house' is not to be taken here as a reference to a sanctuary but to the land of Israel. For a discussion of this passage, and of other related expressions, see my article, 'The Structure and Meaning of Hosea VIII 1-3', *VT* 25, 1975, 701ff.

NOTES TO CHAPTER III

95. This is the translation proposed by Wolff, *Hosea,* 207.
96. See, for example, JB 'their altars shall be reduced to heaps of stones'; RSV 'their altars also shall be like stone heaps'. Cf. Harper, *Amos and Hosea,* 390; Mays, *Hosea,* 168f.
97. E.g. 8:11; 10:1.
98. A glimpse of the importance of the שׁוֹר in agriculture is seen in Prov. 14:4.
99. *Comparative Philology and the Text of the Old Testament,* 176.
100. Cf. R.J. Williams, *Hebrew Syntax* (1967), 49.
101. So NEB 'common as heaps of stones'.
102. So Mays, *Hosea,* 169.
103. So Wolff, *Hosea,* 207, cited above, p. 139; JB, see n. 96 above. For a clear example of *kaph veritatis* see Neh. 7:2; cf. GK 118x.
104. E.g. 4:1-2, 12-13, 17-18; 5:1-2, 7; 6:4-6, 7-10; 7:1-7, 8-10, 11-16; 8:1-13 etc.
105. As, for example, in 9:15 discussed above, p. **138** and the reference to the 'days of Gibeah' in 9:9 and 10:9.
106. So also JB; cf. among the ancient versions the Vulgate (ed. R. Weber, 1969) which renders 'in Gilgal bubus immolantes'.
107. Ps. 106:20.
108. *CTCA* 3 V 8, 19, 44; 16 VI 42.
109. 8:5-6; 13:2; 10:5 עֲגָלוֹת on which see above, pp. 192f.,n.51.
110. Cf. Rudolph, *Hosea,* 232. Calf images are associated explicitly only with the sanctuaries at Bethel and Dan (1 Kings 12:28-29). The loose reference in Hosea to the 'calf of Samaria' (8:5-6) is, in view of 10:5, to be understood as the image at Bethel. On this point see Wolff, *Hosea,* 140.
111. On this see Harper, *Amos and Hosea,* 390; Rudolph, *Hosea,* 232; cf. the Peshiṭta, *The Old Testament in Syriac According to the Peshiṭta Version,* ed. on behalf of the International Organization for the Study of the Old Testament by the Peshitta Institute of the University of Leiden (1980), *lsryqwt' dbḥtwn twr'* The LXX, *Septuaginta* XIII (ed. J. Ziegler, 1943), differs widely, rendering εἰ μὴ Γαλααδ ἔστιν· ἄρα ψευδεῖς ἦσαν ἐν Γαλγαλ ἄρχοντες θυσιάζοντες, apparently understanding שָׂרִים where MT has שְׁוָרִים.
112. Dt. 32:17; Ps. 106:37.
113. Cf. G.R. Driver, 'Linguistic and Textual Problems: Minor Prophets I', *JTS* 39, 1938, 163.
114. *Hosea,* 169. Cf. D. Grimm, 'Erwägungen zu Hosea 12:12 "in Gilgal opfern sie Stiere" ', *ZAW* 85, 1973, 339ff.
115. E.g. 2:15; 4:12-14, 17-18; 13:2.
116. Cf. Ps. 69:32; Lev. 9:4, 18; Dt. 17:1; 18:3; 2 Sam. 6:13.
117. Cf. Harper, *Amos and Hosea,* 389, who comments despairingly: 'with אַךְ no sense can be made'.
118. See above, pp. 126f.
119. So, for example, Mays, *Hosea,* 98, who speaks of 'prophetic radicalism against the cult'; Wolff, *Hosea,* 62, 120.

Similarly, among older commentators, see J.A. Bewer, *'The Literature of the Old Testament in its Historical Development* (1933), 97.
120. Among scholars holding this opinion are Mauchline, 'Hosea', *IB,* 628; Ackroyd, 'Hosea', *Peake's Commentary,* 609, who comments that 6:6 is not 'a negation of all sacrificial observance'; W. Brueggemann, *Tradition for Crisis. A Study in Hosea* (1968), 95ff. Cf. also H. Kruse, 'Die "Dialektische Negation" als Semitisches Idiom', *VT* 4, 1954, 391.
121. Cf. with minor variations Wolff, *Hosea*, 207; Mays, *Hosea,* 166.
122. On the possible meaning of ושמן למצרים יובל see D.J. McCarthy, 'Hosea XII 2: Covenant by Oil', *VT*14, 1964, 215-221.
123. For אם meaning 'though' cf. Is. 1:18; Amos 9:2-4; and especially 1 Sam. 15:17.
124. Cf. Amos 5:22 for similar criticism.
125. For the meaning of the preposition כ in כגלים see above pp. 140f. I incline to the view that it is here an example of *kaph veritatis*. On this point see further my article, 'Widening Horizons: Some Complexities of Hebrew Grammar', *Horizons in Semitic Studies. Articles for the Student* (ed. J.H. Eaton, 1980), 87f.
126. 257 2.
127. *Hosea,* 219. See p. 122 above for Wolff's comment on 6:8.
128. *Hosea,* 225.
129. E.g. 4:12; 8:4-6; 10:5-6.
130. E.g. 4:10, 12-14, 18; 5:7; 7:4; 9:1.
131. Nor is there any reference to this practice in Amos. Contra Wolff, *Hosea,* 101 and 122, where he suggests that there may be allusions to child sacrifice in 5:7 and 6:8. It should be noted, however, that he describes 5:7b as one of the most obscure verses in the entire book, and both here and in commenting on 6:8 is very tentative on this point. Since on p. 101 he links 5:7 with 13:2, the highly ambiguous verse here under discussion, one feels that זבחי אדם of this saying may have influenced his interpretation elsewhere.
132. There has been some discussion about the precise meaning of this phrase העביר באש. That it does refer to a sacrificial ritual is convincingly argued by J.W. McKay, *Religion in Judah under the Assyrians.* SBT Second Series 26 (1973), 40.
133. 2 Kings 16:3.
134. 2 Kings 21:6.
135. See v. 20.
136. GK 128 1; A.B. Davidson, *Hebrew Syntax* (1901), 32.
137. Cf. also Is. 1:4; 9:5; Gen. 16:12 among many other examples.
138. *Amos and Hosea,* 392.
139. Against this emendation see the discussion on p. 142 above.
140. Cf. JB; Mays, *Hosea,* 171.

NOTES TO CHAPTER III   197

141. G.R. Driver, 'Linguistic and Textual Problems: Minor
     Prophets I', *JTS* 39, 1938, 164, proposes to emend
     כתבונם to כמבנית, giving the meaning 'according to the
     likeness of idols'. The corruption of כמבנית to the
     present form of the MT, however, is not easily accounted
     for and is purely speculative; and the meaning obtained is
     inferior to that of the MT.
142. Possibly a dialect form of תבונתם. See Rudolph,
     'Eigentümlichkeiten der Sprache Hoseas', *Studia Biblica
     et Semitica*, 314.
143. Kissing, either literally or metaphorically, as an
     expression of worship or homage is referred to in 1 Kings
     19:18; Job 31:27; Ps. 2:2.
144. 2 Kings 23:10; Jer. 32:35.
145. Ezek. 23:37.
146. The psalm cannot be dated with any certainty, but the
     evidence of vv. 27 and 47 suggests the exilic period, if not
     the early post-exilic period. See A.A. Anderson, *Psalms* II.
     NCB (1972), 736.
147. Cf. JB. So also LXX καρπὸν χειλέων.
148. Cf. the Vulgate (R. Weber, ed., 1969): et reddemus vitulos
     labiorum nostrorum.
149. See above, pp. 47f. where I have argued that the
     association of vv. 2-4 with vv. 5ff. is redactional.
150. In particular the words שוב and כשל בעון, and the
     forswearing of reliance on Assyria and on man-made idols.
151. P. 134.
152. Note must be taken of several instances where a noun which
     might have been expected to have the construct form appears
     in the MT as an absolute. Among these are Dt. 33:11
     מתנים קמיו, and Prov. 22:21 אמרים אמת. The latter, though
     not the former, could be understood, of course, as having
     the two nouns in apposition.
153. *Hosea*, 186.
154. The existence in Hebrew of enclitic *mem* is uncertain,
     despite the fact that Andersen and Freedman, *Hosea*, 645,
     describe the word in question as 'an unassailable example
     of the enclitic particle'. Although there are strong
     advocates for it, such as, for example, M. Dahood, *Psalms*.
     AB III (1970), 408f., and H.D. Hummel, 'Enclitic Mem in
     Early North-west Semitic, especially Hebrew', *JBL* 76, 1957,
     85ff., there are other scholars who remain sceptical. Thus
     G.R. Driver in a review in *JSS* 10, 1965, 116, expresses
     grave doubt whether any example of enclitic *mem* is to be
     found in the Hebrew text, and laments that through the
     ingenuity of some it is 'growing like a weed'! On this
     question see further my brief discussion in 'Widening
     Horizons: Some Complexities of Hebrew Grammar', in *Horizons
     in Semitic Studies* (ed. J.H. Eaton, 1980), 84ff.
155. Ps. 68:14.
156. Gen. 49:14; Jud. 5:16.
157. See particularly p. 143.
158. *Hosea,* 186.

159. Cf. Is. 1:11ff.; Amos 5:21f. etc.
160. P. 143.
161. מן here is to be understood not as privative but as expressing comparison.
162. The text here is difficult. On this see E.W. Nicholson, 'Problems in Hosea VIII 13', *VT* 16, 1966, 355ff.
163. On the exegesis of this verse see my article, 'The Structure and Meaning of Hosea VIII 1-3', *VT* 25, 1975, 707.
164. The NEB understands it differently, reading the negative בל in place of כל. On this see R. Gordis, 'The Text and Meaning of Hosea XIV 3', *VT* 5, 1955, 88-90.
165. For possible instances of this meaning see Neh. 6:19; Ps. 39:3.
166. *Hosea,* 231, though without offering any further explanation of the error, surprising though it is.
167. This is, of course, abundantly clear from the framework of the books of Kings, for example.
168. Cf. 2 Kings 22:17 (מעשה ידיהם); 23:4ff., and the political dimension of Josiah's reform in casting off allegiance to Assyria.
169. For a brief comment on this matter see p. 166 n. 9.
170. If this argument is correct it would, of course, imply that enclitic *mem* either did not exist or was not recognised at this time. Cf. H.D. Hummel, 'Enclitic Mem in Early North-west Semitic, especially Hebrew', *JBL* 76, 1957, 107, n. 110, who argues that after the archaic period (down to 10th C.) enclitic mem was chiefly a feature of Jerusalem poetic style. It persisted, he believes, in poetry in association with court and temple till the exilic period. Thus, after the archaic period, it is found most commonly in Isaiah, Jeremiah and the Psalms. My discussion of the problematic expression פרים שפתינו, concerned as it is with a purely consonantal text, is based on the premise that the Massoretic vocalisation is not arbitrary but faithfully reflects ancient traditions of pronunciation and meaning preserved in synagogue use over the centuries.
171. *Hosea,* 187.
172. *Ibid.*

NOTES TO CONCLUSION

1. The expression is Engnell's, and is applied by him to the process of oral transmission, in *The Call of Isaiah. An Exegetical and Comparative Study*. UUÅ (1949). It seems equally appropriate to the matter under discussion here.
2. Cf. E.W. Nicholson, *Deuteronomy and Tradition*, 83. Similarly Clements, *Isaiah and the Deliverance of Jerusalem*, 97, though his view of the origins and purpose of Deuteronomy differs widely from Nicholson's. I refer to this work of Clements' on the grounds that it is his latest reaffirmation of a view for which he has argued over a number of years.
3. For different views of the origin and purpose of Deuteronomy from that proposed by Nicholson see R.E. Clements, 'Deuteronomy and the Jerusalem Cult Tradition', *VT* 15, 1965, 300-312; G. von Rad, *Studies in Deuteronomy* (1953); O. Bächli, Israel und die Völker: eine Studie zum Deuteronomium (1962).
4. We may single out for mention Wolff, 'Hoseas geistige Heimat', *Gesammelte Studien* (1964), 244f. and 248-250, who argues that Hosea's concern with cultic worship and his familiarity with the sacral traditions of early Israel are drawn from Levitical circles. His emphasis, however, on the close links between Hosea and Deuteronomy is as strong as that of scholars such as Nicholson who hold a different view of the origins of Hosea's thought.
5. Cf. Nicholson, *Deuteronomy and Tradition*, 47ff. Nicholson himself accepts the amphictyony theory propounded by Noth, *Das System der zwölf Stämme Israels*. BWANT IV (1930). However, the view that this 'all Israel' orientation of the material has its roots in ancient tradition and is not associated with the institution of monarchy and the united kingdom does not depend on the acceptance of this theory which is now increasingly questioned. See, for example, A.D.H. Mayes, *Israel in the Period of the Judges* (1974), 106ff., who rejects Noth's theory but traces the unity of Israel as the people of Yahweh to an even earlier time at Kadesh.
6. Nicholson, *Deuteronomy and Tradition*, 94.
7. *Ibid.*, 100.
8. *Ibid.*, 83.
9. *Ibid.*, 100.
10. 'The Form and Structure of the Covenantal Formulations', *VT* 9, 1959, 357.
11. 31:31.
12. 36:16-32.

BIBLIOGRAPHY

P.R. Ackroyd	'Hosea', *Peake's Commentary on the Bible*, revised ed. London and Edinburgh, 1962.
	'Hosea and Jacob', *VT* 13, 1963, 245-259.
L.C. Allen	*The Books of Joel, Obadiah, Jonah and Micah*, NICOT, Michigan, 1976.
A. Alt	'Hosea 5:8-6:6. Ein Krieg und seine Folgen in prophetischen Beleuchtung', *Kleine Schriften* II, München, 1959, 163-187.
	Essays on Old Testament History and Religion, Oxford, 1966.
A.A. Anderson	*Psalms*, NCB, London, 1972.
F.I. Andersen and D.N. Freedman	*Hosea*, AB, New York, 1980.
A.A. Anderson	*Psalms*, NCB, London, 1972.
	Deuteronomium, Zürich, 1962.
J. Barr	*Comparative Philology and the Text of the Old Testament*, Oxford, 1968.
	Biblical Words for Time, SBT First Series 33, revised ed. London, 1969.
	'Trends and Prospects in Biblical Theology', *JTS* NS 25 (1974), 265-282.
J.R. Bartlett	'The Use of the Word ראש as a Title in the Old Testament', *VT* 19 (1969), 1-10.
J.A. Bewer	*The Literature of the Old Testament in its Historical Development*, revised ed. New York, 1933.
W. Beyerlin	*Origins and History of the Oldest Sinaitic Traditions*, Oxford, 1965.
P. de Boer	'Genesis xxxii 23-33: Some Remarks on the Composition and Character of the Story', *NedThT* I, 1947, 149-163.
D. Bonhoeffer	*The Cost of Discipleship*, London, 1959.
J. Bright	'Joshua', *IB* 2, New York, 1953.
	A History of Israel, revised ed. London, 1972.
W. Brueggemann	*Tradition for Crisis. A Study in Hosea*, Richmond, Virginia, 1968.
G.W. Buchanan	'Eschatology and the "End of Days" ', *JNES* 20 (1961), 188-193.

BIBLIOGRAPHY

M.J. Buss	*The Prophetic Word of Hosea. A Morphological Study,* BZAW 111, 1969.
R.P. Carroll	*When Prophecy Failed. Reactions and Responses to Failure in the Old Testament Prophetic Traditions,* London, 1979.
U. Cassuto	*Biblical and Oriental Studies* I, Jerusalem, 1973.
H. Cazelles	'The History of Israel in the Pre-exilic Period', *Tradition and Interpretation* (ed. G.W. Anderson), Oxford, 1979.
T.K. Cheyne	*The Book of Hosea,* CBSC, Cambridge, 1913.
R.E. Clements	*God and Temple. The Idea of the Divine Presence in Ancient Israel,* Oxford, 1965.
	'Deuteronomy and the Jerusalem Cult Tradition', *VT* 15 (1965), 300-312.
	Abraham and David, SBT Second Series 5, London, 1967.
	Prophecy and Tradition, Oxford, 1975.
	Isaiah and the Deliverance of Jerusalem. A Study of the Interpretation of Prophecy in the Old Testament, JSOT Supplements 13, Sheffield, 1980.
D.J.A. Clines and D.M. Gunn	' "You tried to persuade me" and "Violence! Outrage!" in Jeremiah XX 7-8', *VT* 28 (1978), 20-27.
D.J.A. Clines	'Hosea 2: Structure and Interpretation', *Studia Biblica 1978,* I, JSOT Supplements 11, Sheffield, 1979, 83-103.
A. Condamin	'Interpolations ou Transpositions?' *RB* 11 (1902), 389-391.
R.B. Coote	'Hosea 14:8: "They who are filled with grain shall live" ', *JBL* 93 (1974), 161-173.
M. Dahood	*Psalms,* AB, New York, 1970.
	'Hebrew-Ugaritic Lexicography I', *Biblica* 44 (1963), 289-303.
G.A. Danell	*Studies in the Name Israel in the Old Testament,* Uppsala, 1946.
A.B. Davidson	*Hebrew Syntax,* 3rd ed. Edinburgh, 1901.
E. Day	'Is the Book of Hosea Exilic?' *AJSL* 26 (1909-10), 105-132.

G.R. Driver	'Studies in the Vocabulary of the Old Testament VI', *JTS* 34 (1933), 375-385.
	'Studies in the Vocabulary of the Old Testament VIII', *JTS* 36 (1935), 293-301.
	'Linguistic and Textual Problems: Minor Prophets I', *JTS* 39 (1938), 154-166.
	'Abbreviations in the Massoretic Text', *Textus* 1, Jerusalem (1960), 112-131; 4, 1964, 76-94.
	Review of M. Dahood, *Proverbs and North-west Semitic Philology* [Rome, 1963], *JSS* 10 (1965), 112-117.
S.R. Driver	*Notes on the Hebrew Text and the Topography of the Books of Samuel*, 2nd ed. Oxford, 1913.
J.H. Eaton	*Psalms,* TC, London, 1967.
	Vision in Worship, London, 1981.
O. Eissfeldt	*The Old Testament: An Introduction,* Oxford, 1965.
G.I. Emmerson	'The Structure and Meaning of Hosea VIII 1-3', *VT* 25 (1975), 700-710.
	'Widening Horizons: Some Complexities of Hebrew Grammar', *Horizons in Semitic Studies. Articles for the Student* (ed. J.H. Eaton), Birmingham, 1980.
I. Engnell	'Profetia och Tradition. Nagra synpunkter pa ett gammaltestamentligt centralproblem', *SEÅ* 12 (1947), 94-123.
	'Hosea', *SBU* (eds. I. Engnell and A. Fridrichsen), Gavle, 1948-52.
	The Call of Isaiah. An Exegetical and Comparative Study, UUA, Uppsala, 1949.
	Critical Essays on the Old Testament, London, 1970.
G. Farr	'The Concept of Grace in the Book of Hosea', *ZAW* 70 (1958), 98-107.
F.C. Fensham	'The Covenant-idea in the Book of Hosea', *Die Ou Testamentiese Werkgemeenskap in Suid-Afrika: Studies on the Books of Hosea and Amos,* Potchefstroom, 1966, 35-49.
G. Fohrer	*Introduction to the Old Testament,* London, 1970.
D.N. Freedman	See F.I. Andersen.

A. Gelston	'Kingship in the Book of Hosea', *OTS* 19 (1974), 71-85.
M. Gertner	'The Masorah and the Levites. Appendix on Hosea XII', *VT* 10 (1960), 241-284.
H.L. Ginsberg	'Hosea's Ephraim, more fool than knave. A New Interpretation of Hosea 12:1-14', *JBL* 80 (1961), 339-347.
	'Lexicographical Notes', *Hebräische Wortforschung. Festschrift zum 80. Geburtstag von Walter Baumgartner*, VTS 16, 1967, 71-82.
	'Hosea, Book of', *EJ* (ed. C. Roth), New York, 1971.
E.M. Good	'Hosea 5:8-6:6: An Alternative to Alt', *JBL* 85 (1966), 273-286.
	'The Composition of Hosea', *SEÅ* 31 (1966), 21-63.
	'Hosea and the Jacob Tradition', *VT* 16 (1966), 137-151.
R. Gordis	'Hosea's Marriage and Message; A New Approach', *HUCA* 25 (1954), 9-35.
	'The Text and Meaning of Hosea XIV 3', *VT* 5 (1955), 88-90.
C.H. Gordon	'Hos. 2:4-5 in the Light of New Semitic Inscriptions', *ZAW* 54 (1936), 277-280.
J. Gray	*The Legacy of Canaan*, VTS 5, 1965.
	Joshua, Judges and Ruth, NCB, London and Edinburgh, 1967.
D. Grimm	'Erwägungen zu Hosea 12:12 "in Gilgal opfern sie Stiere" ', *ZAW* 85 (1973), 339-347.
A.H.J. Gunneweg	*Mündliche und schriftliche Tradition der vorexilischen Prophetenbücher als Problem der neueren Prophetenforschung*, FRLANT 73, Göttingen, 1959.
E. Hammershaimb	*Some Aspects of Old Testament Prophecy from Isaiah to Malachi*, Copenhagen, 1966.
	The Book of Amos, Oxford, 1970.
W.R. Harper	*Amos and Hosea*, ICC, Edinburgh, 1905.
J.H. Hayes and J.M. Miller (eds.)	*Israelite and Judean History*, OTL, London, 1977.
R. Hentschke	*Die Stellung der vorexilischen Schriftpropheten zum Kultus*, BZAW 75, Berlin, 1957.

H.-W. Hertzberg	*Die Samuelbücher*, ATD, 2nd ed. Göttingen, 1960.
H.H. Hirschberg	'Some Additional Arabic Etymologies in Old Testament Lexicography', *VT* 11 (1961), 373-385.
W.L. Holladay	'Chiasmus, the Key to Hosea XII 3-6', *VT* 16 (1966), 53-64.
H.D. Hummel	'Enclitic Mem in Early North-west Semitic, especially Hebrew', *JBL* 76 (1957), 85-107.
F.F. Hvidberg	*Weeping and Laughter in the Old Testament*, Leiden, 1962.
E. Jacob	'L'Héritage cananéen dans le Livre du Prophète Osée' *RHPR* 43 (1963), 250-259.
	'Der Prophet Hosea und die Geschichte', *Ev Th* 24, 1964, 281-290.
A.R. Johnson	*The Cultic Prophet and Israel's Psalmody* Cardiff, 1979.
O. Kaiser	*Introduction to the Old Testament. A Presentation of its Results and Problems*, Oxford, 1975.
A.S. Kapelrud	*God and His Friends in the·Old Testament*, Oslo, 1979.
D.A. Knight	*Rediscovering the Traditions of Israel*, SBL Dissertation Series 9, Montana, 1973.
H.-J. Kraus	*Worship in Israel*, Oxford, 1966.
H. Kruse	'Die "Dialektische Negation" als Semitisches Idiom', *VT* 4 (1954), 385-400.
G.M. Landes	'The Canonical Approach to Introducing the Old Testament: Prodigy and Problems', *JSOT* 16 (1980), 32-39.
H.G. Liddell and R. Scott	*A Greek-English Lexicon*, revised ed. Oxford, 1940.
J. Lindblom	*Hosea Literarisch Untersucht*, Abo, 1927.
	'Wisdom in the Old Testament Prophets', *Wisdom in Israel and in the Ancient Near East*, VTS 3 1955, 192-204.
	Prophecy in Ancient Israel, Oxford, 1962.
E. Lipínski	'באחרית הימים dans les textes préexiliques', *VT* 20 (1970), 445-450.
D.J. McCarthy	'Hosea XII 2: Covenant by Oil', *VT* 14 (1964), 215-221.

BIBLIOGRAPHY

J.W. McKay	*Religion in Judah under the Assyrians,* SBT Second Series 26, London, 1973.
J.L. McKenzie	'Knowledge of God in Hosea', *JBL* 74 (1955), 22-27.
E.H. Maly	'Messianism in Osée', *CBQ* 19 (1957), 213-225.
K. Marti	*Das Dodekapropheton,* KHC, Tübingen, 1903.
J.D. Martin	'The Forensic Background to Jeremiah III 1', *VT* 19 (1969), 82-92.
J. Mauchline	'Hosea', *IB* 6, New York, 1966.
A.D.H. Mayes	*Israel in the Period of the Judges,* SBT Second Series 29, London, 1974.
J.L. Mays	*Hosea,* OTL, London, 1969.
	Amos, OTL, London, 1969.
B.J. van der Merwe	'A Few Remarks on the Religious Terminology in Amos and Hosea', *Die Ou Testamentiese Werkgemeenskap in Suid-Afrika: Studies on the Books of Hosea and Amos,* Potchefstroom, 1966.
E. Meyer	*Geschichte des Altertums* 3, Stuttgart, 1954.
S. Mowinckel	*Prophecy and Tradition,* Oslo, 1946.
J. Muilenburg	'The Form and Structure of the Covenantal Formulations', *VT* 9 (1959), 347-365.
P.A. Munch	*The Expression Bajjôm Hāhû: Is it an Eschatological Terminus Technicus?,* Oslo, 1936.
A. Neher	*Amos,* Paris, 1950.
E.W. Nicholson	'Problems in Hosea VIII 13', *VT* 16 (1966), 355-358.
	Deuteronomy and Tradition, Oxford, 1967.
	Preaching to the Exiles, Oxford, 1970.
E. Nielsen	*Shechem. A Traditio-historical Investigation,* Copenhagen, 1959.
F.S. North	'Hosea's Introduction to his Book', *VT* 8 (1958), 429-432.
M. Noth	*Das System der zwölf Stämme Israels,* BWANT IV. 1, Stuttgart, 1930.
	The History of Israel, 2nd ed. London, 1960.
	The Laws in the Pentateuch and Other Studies, Edinburgh and London, 1966.
H.S. Nyberg	*Studien zum Hoseabuche,* UUÅ, Uppsala, 1935.

G. Östborn	*Yahweh and Baal: Studies in the Book of Hosea and Related Documents,* LUA 51, 6, Lund, 1956.
H. Oort	'Hosea', *ThT* 24 (1890) 345-365; 480-505.
R. Patai	'The Goddess Asherah', *JNES* 24 (1965), 37-52.
J.P.E. Pedersen	*Israel; its Life and Culture,* Copenhagen, 1926-40.
L. Perlitt	*Bundestheologie im Alten Testament,* WMANT 36, Neukirchen, 1969.
R.H. Pfeiffer	*Introduction to the Old Testament,* revised ed. London, 1948.
N.W. Porteous	'The Prophets and the Problem of Continuity', *Israel's Prophetic Heritage* (eds. B.W. Anderson and W. Harrelson), London, 1962.
	'Actualisation and the Prophetic Criticism of the Cult', *Tradition und Situation* (eds. E. Würthwein and O. Kaiser), Göttingen, 1963.
G. von Rad	*Studies in Deuteronomy,* SBT First Series 9, London, 1953.
	Der heilige Krieg im alten Israel, Zürich, 1958.
	Old Testament Theology, Edinburgh and London, 1965.
	Genesis, OTL, revised ed. London, 1972.
W.L. Reed	*The Asherah in the Old Testament,* Texas, 1949.
H.H. Rowley	'The Marriage of Hosea', *BJRL* 39 (1956), 200-233.
W. Rudolph	*Hosea,* KAT, Gütersloh, 1966.
	'Eigentümlichkeiten der Sprache Hoseas', *Studia Biblica et Semitica Theodoro Christiano Vriezen Dedicata* (eds. W.C. van Unnik and A.S. van der Woude), Wageningen, 1966, 313-317.
K. Rupprecht	'עלה מן הארץ (Ex. 1:10 Hos. 2:2) "sich des Landes bemächtigen"?' *ZAW* 82 (1970), 442-447.
J.F.A. Sawyer	'Notes and Studies. The Meaning of בצלם אלהים ('in the image of God') in Genesis i-xi, *JTS* NS 25 (1974), 418-426.

BIBLIOGRAPHY

J.F.A. Sawyer	'Hôšîaʻ', *TWAT* (eds. G.J. Botterweck and H. Ringgren), Stuttgart, 1982.
A. van Selms	'The Southern Kingdom in Hosea', *Die Ou Testamentiese Werkgemeenskap in Suid-Afrika: Studies on the Books of Hosea and Amos*. Potchefstroom, 1966.
N.H. Snaith	*Mercy and Sacrifice. A Study of the Book of Hosea*, London, 1953.
J.A. Soggin	*Joshua*, OTL, London, 1972.
A. Sperber (ed.)	*The Bible in Aramaic III. The Latter Prophets according to Targum Jonathan*, Leiden, 1962.
W.F. Stinespring	'A Problem of Theological Ethics in Hosea', *Essays in Old Testament Ethics. J. Philip Hyatt in Memoriam* (eds. J.L. Crenshaw and J.T. Willis), New York, 1974, 133-142.
N.H. Tur-Sinai	*Halashon Vehasefer* II, Jerusalem, 1950, 304-323.
	The Book of Job, revised ed. Jerusalem, 1967.
P.H. Vaughan	*The Meaning of 'bāmâ' in the Old Testament. A Study of Etymological, Textual and Archaeological Evidence*, SOTS Monograph Series 3, Cambridge, 1974.
R. de Vaux	*Ancient Israel. Its Life and Institutions*, 2nd ed. London, 1965.
	'Method in the Study of Early Hebrew History', *The Bible in Modern Scholarship* (ed. J.P. Hyatt), Nashville, 1965.
J.M. Ward	*Hosea: A Theological Commentary*, New York, 1966.
R. Weber (ed.)	*Biblia Sacra Iuxta Vulgatam Versionem*, Stuttgart, 1969.
A. Weiser	*Das Buch der zwölf kleinen Propheten* I, ATD 24, Göttingen, 1949.
A.C. Welch	*Kings and Prophets of Israel*, London, 1952.
C. Westermann	'The Way of the Promise through the Old Testament', *The Old Testament and Christian Faith* (ed. B.W. Anderson), London, 1964.
R.N. Whybray	*Readings in Biblical Hebrew* II (ed. J.H. Eaton), Birmingham, 1978.

G. Widengren	*Literary and Psychological Aspects of the Hebrew Prophets,* UUA, Uppsala, 1948.
	'Early Hebrew Myths and their Interpretation', *Myth, Ritual and Kingship* (ed. S.H. Hooke), Oxford, 1958.
R.J. Williams	*Hebrew Syntax. An Outline,* Toronto, 1967.
R.E. Wolfe	'The Editing of the Book of the Twelve', *ZAW* 53 (1935), 90-129.
H.W. Wolff	' 'Wissen um Gott' bei Hosea als Urform der Theologie', *EvTh* 12 (1952-3), 533-554.
	'Hoseas geistige Heimat', *Gesammelte Studien,* Munich, 1964 232-250.
	Hosea, BKAT, Neukirchen-Vluyn, 1965. [ET: *Hosea,* Philadelphia, 1974].
T. Worden	'The Literary Influence of the Ugaritic Fertility Myth in the Old Testament', *VT* 3 (1953), 273-297.
J. Ziegler (ed.)	*Septuaginta XIII. Duodecim Prophetae,* Göttingen, 1943.

BIBLICAL REFERENCES

In the section on Hosea, italic references indicate the main passages discussed.

GENESIS	PAGE
1-11	168
8	180
9:6	185
16:12	196
22.17	185
28	130
28:11	129
28:13-15	130
28:20ff.	193
32:13	185
32:23-33	193
34:3	173
35	130
35:1-4	193
35:11f.	130
35:13	129
35:14-15	130
35:15	129
49:1	187
49:14	197

EXODUS	
1:10	267
19:7f.	93
22:15	173
24:3	93
24:7	93
34:13	178
34:14	189

LEVITICUS	PAGE
9:4	195
9:18	195
18:17	191
19:29	191
21:7	188, 194
21:14	188, 194
26:6	30

NUMBERS	
14:4	97, 110
14:9	177
36:2	185

DEUTERONOMY	
4:29	187
4:30	187
12:3	178
16:21	178
17:1	195
17:15ff.	162
18:3	195
19:14	181
20:4	185
22:13	188, 194
22:29	175
24:3	188, 194
27:17	181
29:33	176

DEUT. (Cont'd.)	PAGE	1 SAM. (Cont'd.)	PAGE
30:2-3	163	14:39	81, 185
30:6	163	15:17	97, 188, 196
31:29	187	15:23	191
32:10	186	15:28	188
32:17	195	15:29	66
33:7	67	16:4	187
33:11	197		

JOSHUA		2 SAMUEL	
3:10	186	3:14	175
7:2	136	3:17	103
18:12	136	3:25	173
20:7	192	6:13	195
22:22	185	11:26	26
24:20	40	16:3	188
		19:41ff.	105
		19:42ff.	187

JUDGES			
3:9	185		
5:16	197	1 KINGS	
6:36f.	185	8:30	53
8:19	81	12:25	182
11:8	97, 110	12:26-33	167
14:15	173	12:28-29	195
19-21	109, 121	15:13	107
19:3	173	15:27ff.	188
		16:8ff.	188
1 SAMUEL		16:16ff.	188
4:21-22	127	16:18	182
7:17	121	16:32	191
8	107	18:21	174
8:5	110	19:18	197
8:6	107	21:1	182
10:26	188	21:1ff.	188
13:5	136		
14:23	136, 185		

INDEX

2 KINGS	PAGE
8:18	182
9	171
9-10	188
9:3	188
9:6ff.	188
9:14ff.	188
9:16ff.	186
9:27	186
10:27	191
10:28ff.	112
10:30	112
11:1	188
11:4ff.	188
11:17	175
14:27	185
15:25	191
16:3	182, 196
16:5	181
16:31ff.	188
17:16-17	147
18:19	188
19:32-37	184
21:6	196
22:17	198
23	135, 147, 150
23:4ff.	198
23:10	197
23:15ff.	183
23:15-20	190
23:19	150
23:20	150, 196

ISAIAH	
1:4	196

ISAIAH (Cont'd.)	PAGE
1:11ff.	198
1:18	196
2:3	44, 180
2:20	176
3:7	176
3:18	176
4:1	176
4:2	176
5:30	176
7:1-6	181
7:3	172
7:5-6	190
7:18	176
7:20	176
7:21	176
7:23	176
8:3	172
9:3	186
9:5	196
10:1	192
10:20	176
11:6ff.	30, 32
11:14	177
12:6	176
13:19	66
24:14	177
24:15	177
26:21	53
29:19	148
30:2	177
31:1	176
31:2	191
40:27	173
41:8	173

ISAIAH (Cont'd.)	PAGE	JER. (Cont'd.)	PAGE
41:14	176	31:27	29, 171
41:29	192	31:31	199
48:17	176	31:31-34	32
49:7	176	32:35	197
54:5	26	34:16	176
54:7	26	41:5	187
54:8	26	51:20	185
		51:33	184
JEREMIAH			
2	189	EZEKIEL	
2:3	173, 180	16:28f.	188
2:4	173, 180	23:13	182
2:14	173, 180	23:30	188
3:1	171	23:37	197
3:6-9	189	34:25	30
3:8ff.	184	36:16-32	199
3:20	180	37:15-23	85
3:22	177	37:22	97
4:1	180		
4:2	81, 183	HOSEA	
4:7	181	1	5, 10, 15
5:2	81, 183		17-20, 25
5:12ff.	87		28, 36, 37,
7	134		97, 158, 167,
7:1-15	184		169, 170, 172
7:12ff.	100		5, 9, 36, 89,
13:27	191	1-3	108, 165, 169,
21:4	185		172
22:11	104		2, 179
22:18f.	104	1:1	18, 90, 185
25:30	43, 44	1:2	89, 95
26:1	188	1:2-9	28-30, 58, 90,
30:9	104	*1:4*	97, 101, 106
31:11	180		

INDEX

HOSEA (Cont'd.)	PAGE	HOSEA (Cont'd.)	PAGE
1:4 (Cont'd.)	*110-112*, 175,	2:11-14	24
1:5	31, 36, 37,	2:13	19, 173
	158, 175, 184	2:13f.	38
1:6	17, 37, 90, 92	2:14	32, 35, 174, 175
1:7	9, 20, 31, 62, 87, *88-95*, 116, 179, 184	2:15	19, 22-24, 75, 173, 195
1:8	17, 172	2:16	14, 22-24, 27, 39, 54, 185
1:9	37, 90, 95, 171, 172	*2:16-17*	9, 12, *14-15*, 19, 20, *21-24*, 35, 37, 39, 43, 157, 171
2	39, 173		
2:1	95, 96		
2:1f.	95		
2:1-2	95, 96, 98	2:17	21, 22, 43, 170, 173, 183
2:1-3	9, 20, 62, 171		
2:2	88, *95-98*, *100-101*, 102, 110, 179, 186	2:18	24, *25-27*, 35, 38, 39, 173
2:3	95	2:18-19	25
2:4	15, 174	*2:18-25*	9, *24-40*, 47, 158, 171, 173, 175, 178
2:4-5	171		
2:4-15	21, 190		
2:4-17	14, 22, 24, 25, 38, 40	2:19	25, 38, 39, 173
2:5	47		
2:6	35, 175	*2:20*	24, 25, *30-32*, 35, 37, 92
2:7	19, 23	2:20-22	25
2:7-8	24	2:21	24, 98
2:8	14, 23, 24, 38, 176	*2:21-22*	25, *27,* 35
		2:22	24, 27, 37, 185
2:8-9	23		
2:9	23, 103, 174	2:23	25, 37
2:10	19, 23, 35, 175	*2:23-24*	25, 30, *33-34*, 35
2:10-11	173		
2:11	14, 19, 23	2:23-25	25

HOSEA (Cont'd.)	PAGE	HOSEA (Cont'd.)	PAGE
2:24	25, 28	4:6-10	143
2:24-25	25	4:8	152, 171
2:25	24, 25, *28-30*, 33, 35, 96, 98, 171, 175	4:10	185, 196
		4:12	82, 171, 178, 185, 196
3	3, 12, 17-20, 170, 172	4:12-13	195
		4:12-14	78, 195, 196
3:1	14, 18, 19, 47, 54, 104, 185	4:12-15	190
		4:13	81, 126
3:1-5	12-14	4:14	79, 126, 182
3:3	13, 153	*4:15*	62, 74, *77-83*, 108, 124, *125-127*, 136, 138, 179, 180, 192
3:3-4	12, 13, 102		
3:4	13, 102, 104, 153, 187		
3:4-5	103		
3:5	9, 12, 13-14, 20, 62, 88, 98, *101-105*, 112, *113*, 116, 157, 170, 179	4:16	183
		4:16-19	126
		4:17-18	195
		4:18	196
		5:1	174, 181, 190, 191
4	94		
4-11	5, 9, 40	5:1-2	120, 122, 195
4-14	3, 89, 165, 169, 172	5:2	191
		5:3-7	190
4:1	126	5:4	24, 52, 53, 185, 190
4:1-2	167, 174, 190, 195		
		5:5	62, *65-67*, 69, 134, 135, 179
4:1-3	185		
4:3	31, 98	5:6	52, 53, 65-67, 103, 135, 152
4:4	79		
4:4-5	126	5:7	122, 195, 196
4:5	180, 184	5:8	120, 121, 124, 136, 137, 165
4:6	75, 93, 152, 171, 185, 190		
		5:8f.	181

INDEX

HOSEA (Cont'd.)	PAGE	HOSEA (Cont'd.)	PAGE
5:8-14	71-73, 76	6:10-7:2	86
5:8-6:6	*67-74*, 178-180, 191	6:11	62, 74, *86-88*, 171, 179, 183, 184
5:8-7:16	122		
5:9	99, 183	7:1	47, 86, 183, 190
5:10	62, 68, 69, 70, 99, 179	7:1-7	195
5:10-14	*68-70*, 71, 182	7:2	147
5:11	69, 181	7:3	105, 187
5:12	62, 69, 70, 99, 179, 182	7:3-7	165, 188
		7:4	196
5:13	63, 69, 70, 99, 179, 182	7:5	187
		7:5f.	105
5:13f.	92	7:7	105
5:13-14	69	7:8	188
5:14	53, 54, 62, 70, 72, 99, 177, 179, 181	7:8-9	181
		7:8-10	195
		7:9	188
5:15	53, 54, 71, 72, 181	7:10	134, 135, 180
		7:11	22, 42, 188
6:1	181	7:11f.	92
6:1-3	48, 71, 73, 174, 177	7:11-12	42
		7:11-16	195
6:1-6	48, 73	7:13	182
6:4	62, *70-74*, 175, 179, 181, 182	7:14	34, 35
		7:15	182
6:4-6	48, 73, 178	7:16	32, 187
6:5	45, 185	8:1	58, 133, 135, 183
6:6	48, 143, 153, 190, 195	8:1-3	133, 174, 182, 183, 194, 198
6:8-10	73, 195		
6:7-11	192	8:1-13	182, 195
6:8	122, 144, 196	8:2	26, 176
6:9	79, 123, 185	8:4	105-107, 109

HOSEA (Cont'd.)	PAGE	HOSEA (Cont'd.)	PAGE
8:4-6	196	10:1	75, 153, 195
8:5	47, 106, 122	10:1-2	143
8:5-6	133, 195	10:2	153
8:6	79	10:3	79, 105
8:8	186	10:4	31
8:9	28	10:5	124, 127, 133, 136, 192, 195
8:10	187, 188		
8:11	75, 195	10:5-6	127, 196
8:11-13	143	10:6	176
8:12	94	10:7	105
8:12-13	178	10:8	98, 128
8:13	153, 198	10:9	109, 121, 195
8:14	62, *74-77*, 99, 179	10:9-10	85
		10:10	179, 188
9:1	34, 35, 79, 196	*10:11*	62, *83-86*, 179
		10:11-13	84, 85
9:1-9	190	10:12	84, 85, 174, 177
9:3	21, 98, 176, 186		
		10:13	76, 84, 86
9:4	82, 133, 153	10:13-15	84, 85, 122, 131
9:5	153		
9:6	186	10:14	32, 76
9:8	133	10:15	105, 124, 131
9:9	109, 121, 191, 195	11:1	40, 99, 183
		11:1f.	43
9:10	22, 99, 170	11:1-7	40, 41
9:12	79, 96	11:1-9	41
9:13	188	11:3	40, 47
9:14	11	11:4	40
9:15	10, 108, 133, 138, 171, 174, 187, 195	11:5	176
		11:5-6	132
		11:6	32, 76, 188
9:16	11, 28, 96	11:7	171
9:17	186	11:8	43, 49

INDEX

HOSEA (Cont'd.)	PAGE
11:8-9	*40-42*, 171, 176
11:8-11	9, *40-45*
11:9	40, 42, 43, 47, 114, 176
11:10	41, 43-45, 157
11:11	41, 42, 176, 186
12	130
12-14	5, 9, 40
12:1	42, 61, 62, 89, *113-116*, 179, 180
12:1-14	193
12:2	31, 129, 144, 176, 181, 188, 196
12:3	62, *63-65*, 67, 69, 85, 131, 179
12:3-5	63
12:3-6	192, 193
12:4	28, 63, 65, 144
12:4f.	96
12:4-5	128, 129, 144
12:5	124, 128, 130, 134, 135, 137
12:7	177, 185
12:8-9	190
12:8-10	144
12:8-14	129
12:9	21, 79, 82, 144
12:12	79, 108, 122, *139-145*, 195

HOSEA (Cont'd.)	PAGE
12:13	96, 99, 128
12:14	185
13:2	*146-151*, 195, 196
13:3	146
13:4	21
13:5	21
13:6	22, 75
13:7	177
13:9-11	188
13:10	105, 107, 187
13:10f.	108, 187
13:10-11	165, 166
13:11	105-107, 109
13:12-13	178
13:14	10
13:15	47
13:16	188
14:1	32, 94, 96, 178
14:2	47
14:2-4	48, 51, 92, 151, 197
14:2-9	171
14:3	134, 135, 146, *151-155*, 198
14:4	51, 92, 155, 185
14:5	48, 49
14:5ff.	197
14:5-8	*46-49*, 51, 177
14:5-9	9, *46-52*
14:8	28, 46, 177
14:9	46, *49-52*

HOSEA (Cont'd.)	PAGE	AMOS (Cont'd.)	PAGE
14:10	177	6:4-7	190
		6:8	66
JOEL		6:12	190
4:13	184	7:2	183
4:16	43, 44	7:5	183
		7:9	117, 190
AMOS		7:10-11	190
1 & 2	75	7:10ff.	187
1:1	179	7:11	104, 117, 190
1:2	43, 44	7:12	179
2:4	179	8:2	180, 194
2:5	75, 179	8:4	63
2:6-7	190	8:4-6	190
2:8	190	8:7	66
3:1	180	8:14	100, 191
3:4	44	9:2-4	196
3:8	44	9:11	179
3:9-11	190		
3:15	190	MICAH	
4:1	190	1:3	53
4:4	124	1:5	183
4:4-5	190	3:9-10	180
5:5	78, 82, 83,	4:2	44
	100, 124, 126,	5:4	148
	136, 137, 139		
5:7	190	ZECHARIAH	
5:10-12	190	9:6	66
5:14-15	190	10:9	171
5:18	187		
5:21f.	198	MALACHI	
5:21-24	190	1:10	126
5:22	196		
5:26	194	PSALMS	
6:1	100	2:2	197

INDEX

PSALMS (Cont'd.)	PAGE
7:15	192
14:7	180
18:44	110, 188
20:2	180
24:6	187
27:8	187
34:10	189
39:3	198
42:2	186
44:21	189
47:5	67
50	185, 186
51:10	177
68:14	197
69:32	195
81	185, 186
84:2	186
89:8	189
89:30ff.	188
91:14-16	175
96:5	194
104:21	63
106:20	195
106:27	197
106:37	195
106:37-38	150
106:47	197
126:5f.	177

JOB	
5:23	30
24:2	181
31:27	197
37:3f.	44

PROVERBS	PAGE
9:10	189
14:4	195
15:20	148
22:21	197
22:28	181
23:10	181
30:3	189
31:11	26

RUTH	
2:13	173
3:13	81

CANTICLES	
5:6	187

LAMENTATIONS	
5:3	155

DANIEL	
7:21	189
12:13	187

NEHEMIAH	
6:19	198
7:2	195

2 CHRONICLES	
6:21	53

ROMANS	
5:10	34

INDEX OF AUTHORS

Ackroyd, P.R.,	128f., 131, 165, 171, 178, 192ff., 196
Allen, L.C.,	177
Alt, A.,	67, 179, 181, 188, 191
Andersen, F.I.,	166, 171, 176, 184, 186f., 189, 197
Anderson, A.A.,	185, 197
Anderson, B.W.,	173, 185
Anderson, G.W.,	187
Bächli, O.,	199
Barr, J.,	140, 168, 174, 183, 194
Bartlett, J.R.,	186, 188
Bewer, J.A.,	172, 196
Beyerlin, W.,	93
de Boer, P.,	128
Bonhoeffer, D.,	173
Bright, J.,	136, 165, 186, 188
Brueggemann, W.,	196
Buchanan, G.W.,	187
Buss, M.J.,	54, 177
Carroll,	
Cassuto, U.,	111, 193
Cazelles, H.,	187
Cheyne, T.K.,	180
Clements, R.E.,	3, 12f., 67, 102, 166ff., 172, 184, 187, 189f., 199
Clines, D.J.A.,	23f.
Condamin, A.,	173
Coote, R.B.,	177
Crenshaw, J.L.,	167
Dahood, M.,	182, 197
Danell, G.A.,	56, 66, 89, 94, 186

INDEX

Davidson, A.B.,	196
Day, E.,	165
Driver, G.R.,	123, 165, 177, 179, 190, 192, 195, 197
Driver, S.R.,	136
Eaton, J.H.,	47, 174, 177f., 184, 196
Eissfeldt, O.,	28f., 165, 167, 169, 172, 175
Emmerson, G.I.,	174, 182f., 194, 196ff.
Engnell, I.,	56f., 101, 165, 168, 199
Farr, G.,	55
Fensham, F.C.,	167
Fohrer, G.,	54, 165ff., 169, 172, 179
Freedman, D.N.,	166, 171, 176, 184, 186f., 189, 197
Gelston, A.,	63, 106f., 179, 187f.
Gertner, M.,	64
Ginsberg, H.L.,	57f., 64, 165, 170, 179, 181, 193
Good, E.M.,	3, 120f., 166, 168f., 178, 180, 189, 193
Gordis, R.,	105, 173, 187, 198
Gordon, C.H.,	171
Gray, J.,	136, 177
Grimm, D.,	195
Gunneweg, A.H.J.,	166
Hammershaimb, E.,	168, 192
Harper, W.R.,	3, 56, 61, 65, 70, 78, 100, 148, 165, 169, 178, 180f., 186, 188, 192, 195
Harrelson, W.,	185
Hayes, J.H.,	165, 181, 186, 189
Hentschke, R.,	182
Hertzberg, H.-W.,	121
Hirschberg, H.H.,	123
Holladay, W.L.,	192f.
Hooke, S.H.,	189
Hummel, H.D.,	197f.

Hvidberg, F.F.,	182, 192
Hyatt, J.P.,	186
Jacob, E.,	174, 178, 190, 194
Johnson, A.R.,	184
Kaiser, O.,	8, 174
Kapelrud, A.S.,	169
Knight, D.A.,	165
Kraus, H.-J.,	191
Kruse, H.,	196
Landes, G.M.,	7, 168
Liddell, H.G.,	183
Lindblom, J.,	17ff., 165, 169ff., 175
Lipínski, E.,	187
McCarthy, D.J.,	196
McKay, J.W.,	189, 196
McKenzie, J.L.,	174
Maly, E.H.,	184
Marti, K.,	56
Martin, J.D.,	171
Mauchline, J.,	47, 54, 167, 173, 175, 177, 180, 184, 186, 188, 193f., 196
Mayes, A.D.H.,	99, 179, 186, 199
Mays, J.L.,	2f., 36, 54, 66, 71ff., 75, 78, 81, 84, 121, 127, 142, 152f., 155, 165, 169f., 172ff., 186ff.
van der Merwe, B.J.,	190
Meyer, E.,	191
Miller, J.M.,	165, 181, 186, 189
Mowinckel, S.,	84f., 165, 168

INDEX

Muilenburg, J.,	163
Munch, P.A.,	176
Neher, A.,	192
Nicholson, E.W.,	123, 162, 187, 189, 192, 198f.
Nielsen, E.,	123
North, F.S.,	167
Noth, M.,	99, 179, 186, 189
Nyberg, H.S.,	170, 176, 183, 187, 191f., 194
Östborn, G.,	186f.
Oort, H.,	173
Patai, R.,	178
Pedersen, J.P.E.,	193
Perlitt, L.,	167
Pfeiffer, R.H.,	2, 170f.
Porteous, N.W.,	123, 174, 185
Procksch, O.,	173
von Rad, G.,	168, 179, 185, 193, 199
Reed, W.L.,	178
Roth, C.,	179
Rowley, H.H.,	172
Rudolph, W.,	106, 165, 167, 170, 173, 175f., 178ff., 186, 191, 194f., 197
Rupprecht, K.,	186
Sawyer, J.F.A.,	168, 177, 185, 193
Scott, R.,	183
van Selms, A.,	78, 104, 180, 187, 189
Snaith, N.H.,	3, 165, 173, 184
Soggin, J.A.,	136
Sperber, A.,	183
Stinespring, W.F.,	3, 169f.

Tur-Sinai, N.H.,	165, 179, 194
Vaughan, P.H.,	193
de Vaux, R.,	99, 171, 185, 192f.
Ward, J.M.,	122, 166, 169, 173, 175, 179, 184, 188
Weber, R.,	195, 197
Weiser, A.,	191
Welch, A.C.,	185
Westermann, C.,	173
Whybray, R.N.,	174
Widengren, G.,	115, 166f., 189
Williams, R.J.,	185, 195
Willis, J.T.,	167
Wolfe, R.E.,	167, 179f.
Wolff, H.W.,	3, 5, 16, 26, 36, 41, 60, 63, 72f., 75, 84f., 89, 92, 94f., 103f., 106, 109, 111, 114, 122f., 125f., 136, 139, 146f., 154, 165ff., 169ff., 173ff., 179ff., 199
Worden, T.,	183
Würthwein, E.,	174
Ziegler, J.,	194f.
van Zyl, A.H.,	180

HOSEA
An Israelite Prophet in Judean Perspective

Grace I. Emmerson

Three kinds of material in the book of Hosea are commonly thought to be insertions into the northern prophet's work by Judean editors: expressions of hope for the future; references to the southern kingdom; and polemical statements against the cultic practices of the northern sanctuaries.

Grace Emmerson presents a lucid study of the relevant passages, asking in each case: Is the Judean shaping a natural development of the prophet's message, by which the prophetic word has been newly addressed to a different audience at a different moment in history, or have its new emphases overlaid or even radically altered the Israelite prophet's meaning?

The conclusions of this redaction-critical investigation are these: most expressions of hope are authentically Hosean, but, as against Hosea, Judean editors have emphasized the need for repentance as a prerequisite for salvation; that only a few of the references to Judah and the Davidic dynasty are Judean supplementation, Hosea himself taking a positive attitude toward the Davidic monarchy; and that polemic against the northern cult is not Hosean at all, but wholly Judean in line with prevailing Deuteronomistic theology in the southern kingdom of Judah.

Dr Grace Emmerson is Lecturer in Theology in the University of Birmingham.